Exploring Bangkok

Exploring **Bangkok**

An Architectural and Historical Guidebook

Robin Ward

Foreword by ***Nithi Sthapitanonda***

Photographs by ***Robin Ward***

Li-Zenn

Li-Zenn Publishing Limited
Bangkok

First published in 2014 by Li-Zenn Publishing Limited

Li-Zenn Publishing Limited
81 Sukhumvit 26, Klongton, Klongtoey, Bangkok 10110 Thailand
T: +66 (0) 2259 2096, F: +66 (0) 2661 2017; li-zenn@li-zenn.com, www.li-zenn.com

Publisher: Nithi Sthapitanonda
Managing Director: Suluck Visavapattamawon
Executive Directors: Pisut Lertdumrikarn, Prabhakorn Vadanyakul, Kiattisak Veteewootacharn

National Library of Thailand Cataloging in Publication Data
Ward, Robin.
Exploring Bangkok -- Bangkok: Li-Zenn, 2014.
304 p.
1. Architecture -- Bangkok. I. Title.
720.9593
ISBN 978-616-7800-33-2

Managing Editor: Suluck Visavapattamawon
Project Manager: Natvadee Nattharoj
Editorial Assistant: Porta Euarchukiatti
Map illustrator: Atistan Hema
Book design: Robin Ward
Typeset in Myriad Pro by Robin Ward
Printed and bound in China by Tiger Printing (Hong Kong)

Contents

Foreword

Bangkok came into existence over 200 years ago. The population grew from a few hundred thousand then to over 10 million today. The people took advantage of being at a geographical and cultural crossroads, the centre of trading in this region. Many of them were from different cultures and ethnic groups which settled in Bangkok and formed diverse communities. The city's buildings display the influences of those cultures—from the West and the East—which have created an extraordinary fusion of architectural forms. Some buildings and urban landscapes reflect traditional Thai architecture but many of the decorative features originated from other sources. My foreign friends have said that every corner of the city is different, that Bangkok has character. The influences of cross-cultural trading, patterns of settlement, politics and cultural exchanges created the architectural diversity seen today.

Historians, researchers and writers were amazed upon seeing the palaces, temples and houses when they came to Thailand, especially in Bangkok. One of them was Robin Ward who has been visiting Thailand for over 30 years. He was struck by the variety of architecture, the blend of old and new, and saw the need for an architectural guidebook to Bangkok. He took notes and photographed the buildings he saw and researched their history. I met him two years ago when he told me about his project, *Exploring Bangkok*. It offers a well informed view of more than 300 buildings and his comments are welcome and valuable. He has experience working and travelling in other parts of the world and looked at Thai architecture from that perspective, as well as being sensitive to the local point of view. Such a book about the city has not been done before.

Exploring Bangkok will appeal to architecture and design professionals, Thai and international students, residents and visitors. It will become a standard reference to historic and contemporary architecture in Bangkok and how the city looks in the early 21st century. I thank Robin for putting it together and fully support its publication, because I would like to see Thai architecture made known to the wider world. The team at Li-Zenn Publishing has been working closely with Robin for two years, leading to the successful completion of the project. I would like to express my thanks to Li-Zenn's staff for their efforts, and especially to those architects who gave their full support to this publication.

Nithi Sthapitanonda, National Artist

Bangkok 2014

Rama V Monument on Royal Plaza

Introduction

Exploring Bangkok uncovers the history of the City of Angels (Krung Thep) and describes its evolution by looking at its architecture—from the royal capital founded at Thonburi by King Taksin following the destruction of Ayutthaya, looted and torched by the Burmese in 1767, to the ocean of modernity around the historic centre.

The historic centre recognised today is not Thonburi on the west bank of the Chao Phraya River but its successor on the east bank, Rattanakosin Island, established by King Rama I in 1782. He founded the Chakri dynasty and created Bangkok's enduring architectural identity—and the illusion that the city is an ancient settlement—when he built the Grand Palace and Wat Phra Kaew (Temple of the Emerald Buddha). Those buildings established the Rattanakosin style, inspired by and intended to recall the glories of Ayutthaya. Founded officially in 1350 after the disintegration of the Sukhothai kingdom, Ayutthaya was sited on an island in the Chao Phraya River, the River of Kings, 80 kilometres north of Bangkok. It was defensible (until the Burmese onslaught) and accessible to foreign trade, for which it was an entrepôt and from which it flourished. Its gilded palaces and temples dazzled foreign visitors in its 18th-century heyday, as Bangkok's Grand Palace complex does now.

Bangkok has more development and diversity compressed in its two centuries than many older cities—Venice for example, to which it was likened, as Ayutthaya was, by European visitors. The riverbank panorama of chedis and glittering roofs on Rattanakosin Island seemed as romantic as St. Mark's Cathedral, the Doge's Palace and the Grand Canal. Bangkok had canals (klongs) and boatmen who paddled standing up like gondoliers which resulted in the nickname 'the Venice of the East', as seen from the decks of ships on which most foreigners arrived. A closer examination of the site would have exposed life in Bangkok's Grand Palace to have been more like that lived by and under the rule of Ottoman sultans in the Topkapi Palace in Istanbul.

By the end of the reign of Rama III in 1851 Bangkok was the capital of a Siamese empire whose sway reached the sultanates of Malaya and extended into the kingdoms of Laos and Cambodia, and Bangkok's population grew to reflect it with ethnic minorities from far-flung places. It was threatened by colonisation from French Indochina and the British Empire. Some territory was lost but Siam was not colonised. That was due to the wisdom and adaptability of kings Mongkut (Rama IV) and Chulalongkorn (Rama V). M. R. Kukrit Pramoj writing in 1984 declared: 'King Mongkut and King Chulalongkorn preempted western colonisation by, as it were, colonising Siam themselves. That is to say, they built in the country, especially in Bangkok, a western architectural façade, behind which the old and original Siam hid itself.'

Chinese traders and communities were long-established without territorial ambitions. Europeans were more acquisitive. Rama IV and Rama V chose modernisation, diplomacy and concessions to maintain sovereignty. The Bowring Treaty of 1855 between Siam and Britain, and subsequent accords with other European powers and the United States, opened Bangkok to foreign shipping, trade and influence. The city grew during the reign of Rama V (1868-1910). He reformed the kingdom's administration and modernised its infrastructure with Western technology while preserving its essential culture, religion and his dynastic power (government departments were headed by princes). He travelled, notably to Singapore, British India and Europe which he first visited in 1897. When he returned from the West he built a new palace at Dusit and a European-style grand avenue, Ratchadamnoen, to reach it. Many of Bangkok's historic buildings are of his time, some of the most prominent designed by Italian architects who were among the Western experts he employed.

Global politics and economic depressions after the First World War strained the status quo. In 1932 a coup d'état replaced the absolute monarchy with a constitutional one. The People's Party leaders of the coup imposed modernist architecture and the Democracy Monument on Rama V's avenue. The Second World War, during which Thailand was occupied by the Japanese, prevented further development. Things changed in the 1950s and 1960s with the start of jet-age tourism and the influx of Americans during the Vietnam War. Klongs were filled in for roads; traffic and pollution became as notorious as the city's reputation was as a sexy rest and recreation zone for the US military.

In the 1980s expressways were built but they attracted more cars. Rail transit was seen as a big fix, with the elevated skytrain and a metro line constructed. Consumer culture boomed unaffected by spasmodic military coups (the most recent in 2014) and political unrest. A spectacular economic crash in 1997 was a temporary blip in the high-rise and shopping mall urbanism which has altered Rama V's city radically. The population in his day was 500,000 people, one million in the 1950s. Official figures now have the metro area as 10.5 million (an estimate which does not include many maids, construction and other itinerant workers who are registered in the provinces).

The devastating flood of 2011 reminded Bangkokians of the vulnerability of the low-lying metropolis to environmental calamity, rising sea levels and climate change. The city, built on a flood plain at an elevation of 1.5 metres above sea level, is sinking like Venice gradually each year. High rainfall and tides in 2011, the paving of the flood plain for suburbs and industrial sites, and klongs for roads, led to the disaster. Natural drainage was prevented, a problem that provoked future-thinking architects to sketch eco-sensitive floating communities living with water rather than constraining it, and the authorities to plan concrete barriers, floodways and other engineering stopgaps.

Beyond the klongs dug to protect Rattanakosin Island from the fate of Ayutthaya, Bangkok is in a constant state of reinvention. New buildings imitate the latest global design trends which are adapted by some architects to express Thai style and to be eco-friendly. Young architects who have studied abroad bring back creative ideas, challenging the status quo and protectionism. On paper, foreign architects are not employed, or are described as 'consultants'. Bangkok has no buildings by international 'starchitects' (two are under construction but legal issues and local sensitivities prevent their architects being acknowledged in this book). Regulations have been relaxed recently to allow ASEAN member architects to work in Thailand, where they will encounter the juxtaposition of old and new in Bangkok unrestrained by urban planning. The city is fragmented and visually stimulating. Its story is told not only in royal palaces and temples but also in its bewildering townscape where the futuristic skytrain runs above boulevards, expressways leap across rows of shophouses and skyscrapers rise out of slums.

In the last 30 years more buildings have arisen than in any period in the city's history. Their distribution, the demand for densification downtown, gentrification of historic areas and the development of suburban centres are changing its appearance and ambience. The suburbs, a sprawl of housing estates, malls and expressways, will soon get rail transit. Many government departments and university campuses have been relocated to these edge cities. The Chao Phraya River is being rediscovered. Historic Rattanakosin Island is besieged by tourism, and its narrative contested by those who live there and officialdom which prefers set-piece preservation. Bangkokians seem unfazed by frenetic modernity, although some now question its environmental costs. The Venice of the East has more elevated expressways than canals but there are numerous neighbourhoods with distinct identities in the layers of chaotic modern development, and Buddhist temples still outnumber shopping malls.

Bangkok's complexity, sprawl, and climate make any guide to it a challenge to organise. This book's eight tours are focussed on the accessibility of city's central districts and the Chao Phraya River. The tours are organised for walking, cycling and public transit—the Bangkok Mass Transit System (BTS) skytrain, Metropolitan Rapid Transit (MRT) metro and the Chao Phraya Express Boat services. Many entries are a short walk or tuk-tuk or taxi ride from stations or piers, which are marked on maps. Entries are numbered and keyed to the maps; the area covered by each tour is shown on a map of metro Bangkok.

More than 300 buildings and structures are featured, selected for their design excellence, innovation, environmental sustainability, heritage conservation or cultural interest; or because they indicate urban trends, or are significant for their social, political, economic or ethnic histories. All have been visited and photographed. The selection is restricted to those which are public, i.e., those which can be entered, or viewed and photographed from the street. Interiors are generally not noted unless open to the public.

Each entry is illustrated with one or more photographs. Each entry features the building's name, the street it is on, the date of completion and architect where known. Periodic renovations and restorations of early palaces and temples made them works in progress; their architects remain anonymous and dates can be are vague, e.g., 'Ayutthaya era'. Where a building's name has changed, the most recent is cited. The kingdom's name, Siam, was changed to Thailand in 1939. The text reflects this: buildings, people and events before that date are referred to as Siamese, Thai thereafter. Kings are referred to as Rama I, II and so on; their time on the throne as 'first reign, second reign' etc.

Rendering Thai into English spelling is troublesome; the BMA's Lumpini Park for example is spelled Lumphini by the MRT. Names of buildings or locations in this book are spelled as they appear at transit stations and piers; on the Bangkok Metropolitan Administration (BMA) signs outside its chosen heritage sites; in publications by the Association of Siamese Architects (ASA), and on websites posted by organisations, institutions, architects and their clients.

Entries are indexed according to their numbers. A glossary of architectural terms is provided.

This book would not have been possible without my wife Porta—my local fixer, translator, proof reader, map checker and indexer—and the help and hospitality of her family in Bangkok. I thank my excellent publisher Khun Nithi Sthapitanonda and his enthusiastic team at Li-Zenn. I am grateful to Khun Sathien Tejapaibul for arranging introductions to Khun Nithi and Khun Sumet Jumsai, who provided information about heritage conservation; and to other people in the city who responded to my research enquiries.

Robin Ward

Bangkok 2014

The Reclining Buddha at Wat Pho

1

Rattanakosin Island

In April 1782 King Rama I crossed the Chao Phraya River to establish 'The great city of angels, supreme, royal, divine'—to paraphrase the long, ceremonial name of Bangkok. It is shortened in Thai as Krung Thep Maha Nakhon (City of Angels). The etymology of the English 'Bangkok' is thought to be a village or land by a river (bang), where olives (mahkok) grow, or on an island (koh).

The site, on the shipping route from the sea to Ayutthaya, was inhabited by a Chinese community. There was a customs post at the mouth of the river and a royal palace and fort at Thonburi from where Rama I crossed. He directed the Chinese to move downstream when he planned the new capital. At its centre he created a royal compound based on the template at Ayutthaya. He built the Grand Palace and Wat Phra Kaew and laid out an adjacent ceremonial park, Sanam Luang.

Rama I's predecessor, King Taksin, had surveyed the site of Bangkok and dug a defensive moat, Klong Khu Muang Derm (Old City Canal), in 1771 to protect it. Taksin, a warrior, the saviour of the kingdom after the fall of Ayutthaya, realised that Thonburi was vulnerable to assault, but if Bangkok was to have been a backup bastion it was never tested. Thonburi was not attacked. The king's reign imploded after he was reported delusional, was overthrown and eventually executed. One of his generals, Chaophraya Chakri, was crowned Rama I.

Rattanakosin Island was created by King Taksin's canal. Rama I completed the waterway, adding defensive walls and forts—fragments of the walls and two forts survive, one in the Banglamphu part of the island, the other on Ratchadamnoen Avenue. He enlarged the site and built a second canal, Klong Rob Krung (Canal Surrounding the City), begun in 1782; a third, Klong Phadung Krung Kasem (Canal of City Contentment), was dug in 1857. The klongs form a semi-circular ring like the old canals of Amsterdam. All three were spared the modern mania for filling in Bangkok's waterways for roads. Pollution has contaminated them but they preserve something of the pre-automobile urbanism which has vanished elsewhere in the city centre.

The canals are crossed by some handsome bridges built by Rama V to enhance his processional route to Dusit Palace. Part of the improvement, inspired by public spaces he saw on his first visit to Europe in 1897, formalised the layout of Sanam Luang, or Royal Field, the city's oldest park and the location for royal ceremonies and cremations. It was a popular site for military tattoos, circuses, kite-flying, political rallies and a weekend market. The market was moved to Chatuchak in 1982 to clear the ground for the city's bicentennial. In 2001 the BMA proposed an underground development with car and tourist bus parking and a shopping mall but it was never realised. Political rallies and intrusion by street vendors and homeless people were stopped by a fence and gates fitted as part of a renovation in 2010.

The kingdom's administration was located at the Grand Palace until the late 19th century, when modern ministries were established and buildings commissioned for them by Rama V. The administrative reforms were inspired by British colonial governance which the king had observed on his travels. Because there were no Siamese precedents the new buildings reproduced Western designs and because their styles were favoured by the king. At first they were located in the palace compound, later outside it.

Western architecture was given ostentatious royal approval with the construction of Chakri Maha Prasat Throne Hall for Rama V at the Grand Palace, where several other European-style buildings can be seen. None eclipse the Siamese splendours begun by Rama I. Over subsequent reigns the palace acquired an accretion of fabulous structures. The ruins of Ayutthaya were never rebuilt but their original grandeur lives on in the architecture of the

Rattanakosin era (1782-1932). Its style remains popular, especially for temples.

Bangkok does not have a mature heritage conservation programme. Preservationists liken the city to Singapore before the authorities there realised that modernisation was destroying the heritage which attracts visitors. Rattanakosin Island is an exception. The Fine Arts Commission, founded within the Association of Siamese Architects in 1968, and the Siam Society's Arts Committee campaigned to protect it. Scholarly conservation is now applied to its palaces, temples and significant public buildings.

Restoration of the Grand Palace for the Bangkok bicentennial in 1982 raised the profile of heritage preservation. Plans were proclaimed along with land use and height guidelines to beautify and preserve the area's historic character. These coalesced in the 1990s as The Master Plan for Conservation and Development of Krung Rattanakosin and Old Towns. Its heritage sites are familiar from any tourist guide. To enhance them, urban design schemes are rolled out periodically by a committee. But its desire to preserve Rattanakosin as a cultural resource to support the national narrative and tourism raises community concerns.

There are several distinct neighbourhoods in the old city which prevent the island being fossilised in an idealised past. For communities preservation needs to be pragmatic, not ideological—the approach should be inclusive, not only sympathetic to historic streetscapes but also to the needs of residents. This is a challenge to the Master Plan, and for the Crown Property Bureau which has much of the city's heritage architecture in its care. The plan would create a linear park along the river from the Grand Palace to Wat Pho, with views opened up for tourists. Nagaraphirom Park developed by Crown Properties and the BMA in 2010 at Tha Tien was part of it. A reassessment now recognises shophouses are as much a part of the historic fabric as palaces and temples. Community life is more difficult to sustain.

The Grand Palace and Wat Phra Kaew could fill a book. Space here prevents a description of all their buildings and decorative delights, but the most significant and accessible are described.

1

The Grand Palace

Na Phra Lan Road

This was the home of the Chakri dynasty and the centre of its monarchs' power and administration. It had a population of several thousand from low to high rank, a density now equalled daily by tourists. Kings no longer live in the palace but it is still used for royal, religious and state ceremonies. Its architectural pageantry has beguiled all who have seen it, as King Rama I intended in 1782 when he began to recreate the style and splendour of the lost city of Ayutthaya.

Tiered roofs, prangs and chedis glitter in a dazzling display behind gates and crenellated walls of brick and white stucco. The first buildings were wooden, the walls a log palisade, until bricks were salvaged from the ruins of Ayutthaya and barged down the Chao Phraya River. Rama II extended the walls to Wat Pho creating the compound seen today. The walk around it is almost two kilometres.

It is divided, as Ayutthaya's royal zone was, into outer, middle and inner courts. The outer court housed ministries of state, army barracks and elephant stables; the middle court royal apartments and ceremonial halls. The inner court, furthest from the public entrance, was the harem, a community crowded with royal consorts and children, ladies-in-waiting and maids, protected by a battalion of female guards.

The architecture is a mix of Rattanakosin and European styles, notably around the middle court's plaza. On its east side is the Phra Maha Monthian group of interconnected apartments, audience and throne halls dating from 1785 where kings resided, coronations were held and foreign ambassadors received.

To the west is the Phra Maha Prasat ensemble. Rama I was enthroned here in a building which was struck by lightning and burned in 1790. Its replacement, the Dusit Maha Prasat Throne Hall, has a cruciform plan which springs to a tiered roof and golden spire which symbolises ascent to Mount Meru, the centre of the Buddhist cosmos. The building is used for the lying-in-state which precedes any royal cremation. Nearby is a perfect pavilion, Phra Thinang Aphorn Phimok Prasat. It is a classic of Siamese arts and crafts, built for Rama IV to board his palanquin or put on ceremonial regalia.

The south side of the plaza is dominated by Rama V's Chakri Maha Prasat Throne Hall (1876–1882), designed for ceremonies and banquets. Pundits pontificated about its Renaissance-style façade and trio of golden spires, likened to 'a farang wearing a Siamese hat'. The westerner was architect John Clunis, a Scottish engineer from Singapore (the façade recalls Government House where Rama V stayed during his visit there in 1871). The central spire completed the project in time for the centenary of the Chakri dynasty and Bangkok. An Italian mosaic portrait of the king can be seen above the entrance. The interior is opulent. There are paintings of Siamese envoys with Louis XIV and Queen Victoria, and Rama IV receiving British and French diplomats. There is a grandiose annex, Borom Ratchasathit Mahoran Hall, added recently in Rama V revival style.

Rama I's facsimile of Ayutthaya was enlarged by successive rulers. Phra Thinang Suthaisawan Prasat, with a balcony where kings appeared to their subjects and watched military parades passing outside the compound's east wall, was rebuilt by Rama III. Rama V commissioned a potpourri of European-style buildings, among them Borom Phiman Mansion (C. Sandrezcki, c. 1900) built for Prince Vajiravudh (Rama VI), designed in French Second Empire style like the Louvre in Paris. To the north is the Ministry of Finance (Joachim Grassi, 1870), an Italianate palazzo with an entrance rotunda. It was rehabilitated as the Queen Sirikit Museum of Textiles in 2012.

The palace was restored for the bicentennial of the Rattanakosin era and for the 60th anniversary of the reign of HM King Bhumibol Adulyadej (Rama IX).

2

Wat Phra Kaew

Na Phra Lan Road

Separate from the Grand Palace but within its walls is Wat Phra Kaew, the Temple of the Emerald Buddha. Its forms and counter-shapes are a medley of overlapping dimensions, like a temple mural scaled up and given volume.

The primary building is the ubosot, or ordination hall, begun in 1782 by Rama I as the Chapel Royal which established the Rattanakosin style. It houses the

holiest Buddha image in the kingdom, a jade sculpture of unknown origin found after bolt of lightning fractured a chedi in Chiang Rai in the 15th century. It changed hands and locations several times. It was repatriated from Vientiane which had been captured in 1778 by King Taksin's general in the north, Chao Phraya Chakri, the future Rama I.

The icon, set high on a gilded wood throne, is surprisingly small. All around are murals of the Buddhist cosmos, the Buddha's life, enlightenment and tales from the Jataka, typical subjects of temple art. Outside, bronze Khmer-style lions guard the perimeter and eight prangs symbolising Buddhist themes stand in line. Rama III increased the height of the throne when he restored the wat in 1832. On the exterior of the hall he added a fringe of 112 gilded bronze garudas grasping nagas to chase evil spirits away, and inlays of coloured glass. The walls rise to a triple-tiered, tiled roof leaping with gold cho fas at every extremity.

The adjacent Upper Terrace is a sparkling skyline of classical Siamese architecture: the bell-shaped Phra Siratana Chedi, built by Rama IV to house a Buddha relic from Sri Lanka where the chedi's style originates (the golden mosaic tiles were added by Rama V); Phra Mondop, built in 1788 on a square plan with a tiered roof supported on columns replaced the original scripture library destroyed accidentally by fireworks; Prasat Phra Dhepbidorn (1856-1882) with four gables and a tiered roof topped with a Khmer-style prang was intended as a new home for the Emerald Buddha. Rama IV thought the icon should be placed higher than anything else in the compound but the building proved too small for ceremonies and was repurposed as the Royal Pantheon. Two gilded stupas, one ringed with monkeys and demons, stand beside it. The terrace has a model of Angkor Wat, commissioned by Rama IV when the Khmer temple was part of his territory.

Statues of giants guard the gates of the wat's cloisters which are decorated with murals of the Ramakien, the Siamese version of the Ramayana, the Hindu epic. Rama I commissioned not only a complete translation of the saga but also the 178 sequential panels which illustrate it on the cloister walls. Much decayed by the humid climate they were repainted periodically, and restored in 1982.

3

City Pillar Shrine

Ratchadamnoen Nai, south-east corner of Sanam Luang

Guardian spirits of the city inhabit this shrine built to house the foundation pillar raised by Rama I in 1782. It houses two gilded pillars, the taller being the original which the king moved from Thonburi. Rama IV replaced it with his own to strengthen his status. Both stand side by side, the older one having been reinstated from outside the shrine in 1986 after over a century of neglect. They contain the city's horoscopes. As at other auspicious sites, visitors can have their fortunes told in the compound. The pillars, which mark the point from where distances to all points in the city and beyond are measured, were the logical starting point for the city's first tram line in 1888, and last in 1968 when the network closed. A section of track can be seen outside. The shrine's Rattanakosin-style pavilion dates from 1853. It was restored in 1986 and again in 2006.

4

Supreme Court

Ratchadamnoen Nai

Sarot Sukkayang, 1939

After the coup in 1932 the break from the past was expressed in architecture. The style chosen by the People's Party which seized power was modern, in the

reductive classicism-meets-Art Deco favoured by national socialist dictators at the time. The Supreme Court's entrance is a four-storey recess faced with six giant columns with Art Deco capitals under a horizontal canopy linked to a cornice which extends across long wings.

The building was part of a justice centre constructed to celebrate the recovery in 1938 of judicial sovereignty, ending the rights of foreign states to hold extraterritorial powers in Siam. The Second World War and political instability delayed its completion for two decades. There were three buildings. The Appeals Court (1943) was torn down in 2013 for a renewal plan first proposed in 1986. The Court of Justice (1940) and the Supreme Court (finished in the 1950s) were spared. Their association with the People's Party renders them suspect by some; others see them as heritage resource that should be preserved.

A new Ministry of Justice building revealed in a computer rendering in 2012 is also controversial, not only for its Rattanakosin revival style but also because its projected height violated the Rattanakosin conservation regulations intended to preserve the supremacy of Chakri architecture. Opponents sought legal advice to stop it, to no avail.

5

National Museum

4 Na Phra That Road

Objets d'art collected by Rama IV at the Grand Palace were displayed there in a museum established by Rama V in 1874. It evolved to become the National Museum, the oldest public museum in Thailand and the largest in South-East Asia. It is located at Wang Na (the Front Palace, begun in 1782), the residence of Rama I's brother and subsequent 'deputy kings'. Rama V reduced their status to Crown Prince in 1875. He rehabilitated Wang Na in 1887 to display the royal collection. The museum was renovated in 1926 and has been upgraded periodically since then.

Wang Na's architecture is venerable, decorated beautifully in Ayutthaya style. Buddhaisawan Chapel (1787) was built

to house a 15th-century, gilded bronze Buddha image, Phra Buddha Sihing. The chapel murals, typical of the art with scenes from the life of the Buddha, are the city's oldest. A sculpture from the fifth reign on the podium's former platform for boarding elephants represents the deity Rama with a bow and arrow.

The inner residential complex was built around two courtyards. In the grounds around it are several delicate pavilions of which Sala Samran Mukhamat, originally at Dusit Palace, is the most elaborate. Nearby is Tamnak Daeng (Red House), a teakwood relic from the old palace at Thonburi which Rama II moved to the Grand Palace. Rama IV gave it to his deputy. It was restored in 1967. By that time the collections—from Bencharong ceramics to a life-size model of a battle elephant—had grown. Two halls were built in Modern Thai style to add space for exhibits.

There are three main collections: Thai History; Archaeological and Art History; Decorative Arts and Ethnology. The Gallery of Thai History (Siwamokkhaphiman Hall) displays the Sukhothai-era King Ramkhamhaeng stone inscribed with the earliest example of the Thai alphabet.

6
National Theatre
2 Rachini Road
Samaichalerm Kridakorn, 1965

The theatre commands its site like a leading actor the stage. It was designed for classical performing arts which are symbolised here with a sculpture of Ganesh, Hindu god the arts, in the gable above the main entrance and Khon masks on the side walls. The style is Modern Thai with dramatic massing and an energetic elevation above a wide porte cochère. There is a statue (Sanan Silakorn, 1965) of King Pinklao, Rama IV's brother and deputy who lived at the Front Palace, now the National Museum. The theatre was built in the former palace grounds.

7
Monument to the Expeditionary Force
Na Phra That Road
Prince Narisara Nuvativongse, 1921

In 1918 Rama VI sent a military detachment to France to demonstrate his support for the Allies during the First World War and to assist future diplomacy. This chedi-like structure was designed by artist and architect Prince Naris. It has the names inscribed and contains the ashes of 19 of the force's soldiers who died. It is disputed that any of them saw action (the casualties might have been a caused by accidents or sickness) because the war ended before the force could be fully acclimatised, trained

and deployed. Its soldiers, nurses and airmen joined the Allies' victory parade at the Arc de Triomphe in Paris in 1919. Rama VI presided at a wreath-laying ceremony when the memorial was unveiled.

8

Dome Building, Thammasat University

Tha Pra Chan Campus, 12 Pra Chan Road

Jittasen Aphaiwong, 1938

On the left bank of the Chao Phraya River this is the iconic visual symbol of the university founded in 1934 by Pridi Banomyong, a statue of whom was erected outside in 1984. Originally the Administration Hall, it was designed as a centrepiece to link two colonial-style structures. It was renovated in 1985 to create the Pridi Banomyong Memorial Hall. There is a waterfront park.

The 'dome' (actually a spire) was replicated at Thammasat's Rangsit campus which was master planned (Sumet Jumsai Associates, 1986) to produce graduates for the booming economy of the 1980s. Tha Pra Chan Campus had a reputation for volatile politics, which boiled over in pro-democracy demonstrations brutally repressed in 1976.

9

Memorial Sculpture Garden Thammasat University

Tha Pra Chan Campus, Na Phra That Road

Surapol Panyawachira sculptor, Anek Charoenpiriyaves landscape designer

In the shadow of the university's Modern

Thai-style Auditorium Building (1961) is the most provocative public art in Bangkok. It commemorates the 1976 student uprising and other pro-democracy events. It took 20 years for the subject to be aired in this way. The mass murder of students on 6 October 1976 when armed government forces invaded the campus was too controversial to touch.

The garden was begun in 1996. The primary memorial, unveiled in 2000, spells out '6 October' in expressionist typography. There are bronze details in the letters' counter shapes: a student lynched on Sanam Luang, a student's head under a military boot . . . Words of Dr. Puey Ungphakorn, the university rector, are inscribed around the base of the memorial. He resigned to protest the bloodshed and was forced into exile in Britain. He had been a member of the Seri Thai (Free Thai) resistance movement during the Japanese occupation in the Second World War. Free Thai members are portrayed on one of several other sculptures in the garden. The works are explained in texts engraved on steel plaques.

10

Wat Mahathat

3 Maha Rat Road

There are royal temples and people's temples. Only a few are of the highest order of which this is one: royal, first class. It is a patchwork of buildings from different periods, post-Ayutthaya although the wat was established earlier. It was renovated in 1783 and enlarged with patronage from the Front Palace. The ubosot and viharn are set in a cloistered courtyard lined with Buddha images in colonnades where beams rest on curiously slanted posts. Much of the wat is crammed with kuti, a school, offices and a meditation centre. The kingdom's oldest Buddhist university and library originated here, where Supreme Patriarchs were resident.

The wat is hidden from Sanam Luang by the Khmer-style Thawon Watthu Building (Prince Narisara Nuvativongse, 1916). Begun in 1895 it was intended as a royal funerary hall but was converted for the royal library, later the National Library. In 1997 it was retrofitted as a museum, the King Chulalongkorn Memorial Hall.

11

Silpa Bhirasri Memorial Museum
Silpakorn University

Wang Tha Phra Campus, Na Phra Lan Road

1987

The university founded in 1943 began as an art school set up by Corrado Feroci in 1932. Florence-born Feroci had been invited to Siam in 1923 by the government to teach at the Fine Arts Department. He was appointed Sculptor to the King of Siam in 1924. He took a Thai name, Silpa Bhirasri, and citizenship in 1944. Among his works are statues of monarchs and the Democracy and Victory monuments.

The museum and sculpture hall, respectively his studio and foundry, display maquettes and casts of statues he designed and made, including a bust of Prince Narisara Nuvativongse, a friend and occasional collaborator. Prince Naris was the last royal resident at Wang Tha Phra, the western of three palaces now the campus site. The crenellated wall and gate on Na Phra Lan Road are relics of it, rebuilt by the prince. Its remaining buildings are now Silpakorn University Art Centre where there is a sculpture garden, Siamese and Italianate heritage architecture and a gingerbread pavilion.

Feroci's studio has two big windows facing north for the indirect sunlight artists like. The sculpture hall is an industrial space with the original travelling crane preserved above the artworks. His work remains popular—copies of his statues of Chakri kings can be bought at Chatuchak. There is a statue of him (by Sanan Silakorn, 1972) behind the Fine Arts Department building (Ercole Manfredi, 1919) which faces Sanam Luang. The frieze on the Fine Arts façade is Stile Liberty as are gateposts on Na Phra That Road. Residents of the palaces included the masters of the royal elephants. The department's charming spirit house traditionally contains a coil of rope in memory of them.

12

Na Phra Lan Shophouses

Na Phra Lan Road

1909

With retail on the ground floor and living space upstairs this row of shophouses conforms to type, but with an opulent overlay. The façade is Italianate in an extended Palladian manner. The central bay is enriched with Tuscan and Ionic columns and flanked by two wings terminating in smaller bays, each identical.

The Crown Property Bureau undertook a comprehensive upgrade in 2009, funding 75 percent of the cost, the tenants the balance. The transformation showed how other historic shophouses can be revitalised with community involvement. Unfortunately, some original tenants found the new rents unaffordable and moved away. The building is in prime tourist territory and its renovation inevitably led to gentrification. The project's high standards of conservation were rewarded with a Unesco Asia-Pacific Heritage Award in 2011.

13

Thanachart Bank, Tha Phra Chan Branch

Maha Rat at Na Phra Lan Road

1909

Rented to the bank by Crown Properties since 1969 this is another architecturally ambitious shophouse design, like the Na Phra Lan example. The style is Italianate with variations. The bays have Dutch gables with curved pediments, Art Nouveau plaster bas-reliefs, and festoons along the entablature. There are classical columns and round-arched windows with fanlights and fretwork. The façade is angled neatly to turn the street corner into Maha Rat Road. The building was renovated in the 1990s and in 2014, along with an adjoining row which leads to Tha Chang.

14

Tha Chang

Na Phra Lan Road

Tha Chang means 'Elephant Pier' because it is where the royal elephants at the Grand Palace were brought to the river by their mahouts to be washed and bathed. It is also known as Buddha Image Pier, for the bronze image now at Wat Suthat. The Buddha was brought

from Sukhothai by river raft on the orders of Rama I in the early 1800s and landed at this spot. Elephant bathing had preceded that event, so the name Tha Chang stuck.

15
Wat Pho
2 Sanam Chai Road

There are few moments more serene than to gaze upon the ethereal smile on the face of the Reclining Buddha at Wat Pho. The image is brick, stuccoed and covered with gold, and the ebony soles of its feet are inlaid with mother-of-pearl illustrating the 108 auspicious signs. It is the largest and most graceful reclining Buddha in the kingdom.

Wat Pho was founded in the Ayutthaya era. It is the city's oldest and largest temple, with more Buddha images than any other and the most chedis. There are two sections bisected by Soi Chetuphon: the south side of the soi is the working and residential part; the north is the historic compound. King Taksin declared the wat a royal monastery but it was a small one and dilapidated when Rama I was crowned.

In 1788 the new king began to improve the site. Some 20,000 labourers cleared and filled the swampy ground for the grand buildings the king planned. He changed the name from Wat Potharam (already shortened by people as Wat Pho) to Wat Phra Chetuphon in 1801 and declared it a royal temple, first class. The new name came from a forest retreat in India visited by the Buddha. Most of the 800 or so Buddha images around the wat were from the estimated 1,250 collected by Rama I from the provinces and brought to Bangkok where they were distributed to temples.

The four largest of the 95 chedis were erected by Rama I and the three successive Chakri rulers. He built an ubosot set in a cloistered quadrangle with a viharn at each of the four compass points. Rama III replaced it with the present structure, a classic of Rattanakosin style. The roof is high, triple-tiered, pitched steeply and supported on columns in line on aisles outside. A balustrade displays a sequence of marble bas-reliefs of the Ramakien, which also is featured on the mother-of-pearl doors. These open to an interior where the principal image, Phra Buddha Theva Patimakorn, originally from Ayutthaya, sits on a high altar which contains a casket with bones of Rama I, placed there by Rama IV.

Stone figures around the wat arrived from China as ships' ballast in the 19th century; the ballast was discarded when rice was loaded; millers and merchants presented the statues to temples. There are rock gardens, topiary and a carp pond with a waterfall on a Khao Mor, or model hill, built in the third reign.

There have been periodic restorations at Wat Pho. The most recent was completed in 2007. The most radical was by Rama III who renovated the temple as a centre of learning. The scripture library (Phra Mondop), with a roofscape and pinnacle of Chinese ceramics, was built as a place where all people could study. He commissioned pictorial lessons and texts carved and engraved on stone slabs. A renowned school of traditional medicine and massage evolved, its activities illustrated on its walls. He built a viharn decorated with murals to house his famous work, the Reclining Buddha.

16
Tha Tien
Maha Rat Road

The community began in King Taksin's time, at the pier from where goods traded were shipped to the provinces or landed to supply the city. There was a royal residence, lodgings for foreigners and Tha Tien market. The wooden buildings at the pier convey something of that history although they are not particularly old. Rama V rolled out an urban renewal scheme, the first planned shophouse community in Bangkok. The shophouse rows are punctuated with classical pediments that announced the three entrances to the market. They are the only reminders of it because a rehabilitation

by Crown Properties has cleaned up the area and preserved the shophouses but erased much that was authentic of community life here.

The name 'Tha Tien', or 'flat ground', refers to a legend, that two giants, one at Wat Pho and the other at Wat Arun, fought over a debt one had not paid; the land was laid waste; Indra heard the rumpus and descended, separated the fighters, sent them back to their wats and turned them to stone, as temple guardians.

17

Charoen Rat 31 Bridge

Klong Ku Muang Derm, between Chakphet and Maha Rat roads

Public Works Department, 1911

Six 'charoen' (prosperity) bridges were built by Rama VI, for his 31st birthday in this case. The 'birthday bridges' were concrete, each decorated differently. The balustrades here were cast with tigers, a symbol of strength in the Chinese zodiac. The year 1911 was not the Chinese Year of the Tiger but it was when the king formed a Siamese arm of the Boy Scouts, called Tiger Cubs, and the paramilitary the Wild Tiger Corps.

On the north side of the canal, at the intersection of Maha Rat and Sanam Chai roads, is Phra Ratchawang Police Station (1914), constructed on the site of an old palace. The style is neoclassical with a pediment above each window and a parapet and four Ionic columns marking the entrance. A station for the MRT extension is on Sanam Chai Road. The stylish modern building at Rachini and Maha Rat roads is Rajini School.

18

Asadang Shophouses

Asadang Road

c. 1900

Klong Ku Muang Derm, the Old City Canal, is a tree-lined image of Bangkok as it was. The illusion is magnified by these rows of brick and stucco shophouses parallel to the klong. The rows are long, two-storeys with decorative Dutch gables crowning bays which break the monotony. The buildings were part of a development remarkable for its cohesive urbanism and architectural quality. Two identical rows survive on Ban Mo Road. Siam Commercial Bank was conceived in one of its shophouses in 1904, as start-up bank called the Book Club.

19

Museum Siam

4 Sanam Chai Road

Mario Tamagno, 1922

A contemporary bronze sculpture symbolising rainbows under which the Thai people evolved stands in front of this museum in the old Ministry of Commerce Building. The ministry was established by Rama VI in 1920 and based here until 1989 when it moved to Nonthaburi. The abandoned edifice had been the first purpose-built modern office block in Siam. It is now the first interactive museum in Thailand.

The National Discovery Museum Institute rehabilitated the building. The museum opened in 2008. A national narrative is presented with visual flair and new technology. The exhibition design, a departure from the static display of objects in glass cases, was designed to attract the mall and iPhone generation, and Thai people and tourists of all

ages. The building's heritage features were conserved along with the circulation plan, starting in the lobby where the original and impressive cantilevered staircase serves all three floors and the frontal corridors. The latter are open like Tuscan loggias on a façade composed in Renaissance style. It is one of many designs by Italian architects who changed the look of Bangkok around the turn of the 19th century.

20

Drum Tower and Clock Tower

Sanam Chai Road

Sumet Jumsai, Sawan Im-Arrom, 1982

This Siamese-style drum tower rebuilt several times since 1782 housed three drums, one on each level: to mark dawn and dusk; a fire alarm; a warning of enemy attack. Rama III remodelled it as a Chinese pagoda; Rama IV returned it to Ayutthaya style. Rama V tore it down for Saranrom Park. The nearby clock tower, a fusion of Asian and Western elements piled up like a pagoda, was first constructed inside the Grand Palace for Rama IV. Both towers were reconstructed for the Bangkok bicentennial.

21

Territorial Defence Command

2 Charoen Krung Road

Public Works Department, 1924

This theatrical pile of neoclassicism with an arched entrance, Ionic columns and pediments angled dramatically at the corner of Sanam Chai and Charoen Krung roads shows the influence of Italian architects at the Public Works Department. Strictly speaking the style is Beaux-Arts, the predominant form of classicism at the time. Called the Rajavallop Building it was built by Rama VI as barracks for 1st Battalion, King Rama V Royal Guards. The Territorial Defence Command (the Army Reserve Command) has occupied it since 1955. The passage at the entrance leads to an inner courtyard. Two floors of the building were refurbished for the King Vajiravudh Museum, opened in 1999 to celebrate the life of Rama VI and his military interests. The Territorial

Army evolved from the Wild Tiger Corps founded by the king. He was the first Siamese monarch to be educated abroad, at Britain's Royal Military College, Sandhurst, and at Oxford University.

22
Saranrom Park
Charoen Krung Road, between Sanam Chai and Rachini roads
1875

Rama IV's garden at Saranrom Palace was redesigned for Rama V as a royal park and zoo, inaugurated at a garden party attended by the king. It was planned by Henry Alabaster, a deputy British consul who understood botany and surveying and was an advisor to Rama V. The informal layout of paths lends it an English air. The main entrance on Charoen Krung Road has a regal swagger with rusticated and banded gateposts with twin Ionic columns and elaborate iron gates cast in London. The king allowed the public to pass through these to view the gardens on Saturday afternoons.

There are many features typical of Western 19th-century landscape design: indigenous and imported flora, ornamental ponds, a French-style cast-iron fountain, a bandstand, an orangery, Chinese pagoda and a royal monument, in Khmer-style, to Queen Sunandha. Many of the architectural features followed Rama V's visit to Europe in 1897. The garden's animals were later moved to Dusit Zoo. The government transferred the park to the Bangkok Metropolitan Authority (BMA) in 1960 and it has been open to the public since then.

23

Dutch Draw Bridge

Klong Ku Muang Derm, Rachini Road at Saranrom Park

Sumet Jumsai, Sawan Im-Arrom, 1985

The east gate of Saranrom Park leads to this 'Saphan Hok Baeb Vilanda', or Dutch Draw Bridge. Several Dutch-style canal bridges were built across klongs in Bangkok in the 19th century. One such bridge had been built in Ayutthaya where there was a Dutch East India Company settlement. They were wooden with a deck which could be raised to allow boats to pass. This example is a reconstruction of a bridge built here in the fourth reign.

24

The Asadang

94 Asadang Road

Direk Senghluang and Chitlada Senghluang, 2011

A blueprint for heritage preservation in the neighbourhood, the Asadang is a follow-up to the Bhuthorn bed and breakfast inn, opened in 2010 in a rehabilitated shophouse (96-98 Phraeng Phuthon Road). This second venture is a bigger property with nine guest rooms decorated in antique style. The façade is Italianate with baroque gables, continued in a row of shophouses on Phraya Si Road and echoed in a twin across the street. These were built during the fifth reign, part of a uniform development bounded by Asadang, Charoen Krung, Fuang Nakhon and Phraya Si roads.

25

Wat Ratchabophit

Ratchabophit Road

1870

This was the last temple to be built in the tradition that kings build one specific to their reigns. Rama V accepted the obligation and saw it through with originality and panache. It is one of three maha sema wats (the others are Wat Boromniwat and Wat Ratchapradit) where all areas within the boundary wall are

for monastic rites, not just the ubosot marked with bai sema, of which there are none here. There is a unique circular cloister shaped like a doughnut from whose central void a giant Sri Lankan-style chedi rises from a drum-shaped base. The chedi is covered in Benjarong ceramics as are other surfaces in the compound. The cloister intersects with four halls that branch from its edge in cruciform plan oriented to the four points of the compass, or representing a mandala.

The ubosot directly north of the chedi looks Siamese but has a surprise inside—a gilded Gothic Revival interior created around 1900. Western styles were a legacy of Rama IV. Rama V continued to import them, influenced during visits to Singapore and British India between 1870 and 1872, and to Europe in 1897. Guardian figures carved in the doors to the compound were modelled on soldiers of the Corps of Royal Pages and wear Western uniforms.

26

Royal Cemetery, Wat Ratchabophit

Asadang Road

c. 1900

Inside Wat Ratchabophit's Asadang Road entrance is a fascinating cemetery created by Rama V for his clan. It is crammed with Siamese chedis and Western classical, baroque and Gothic monuments. The largest structure is a mausoleum with three prangs decorated elaborately in Khmer style, like a miniature Angkor Wat but modelled directly from Prang Sam Yot, a ruin in Lopburi. Nagas slide down the sides of the stair at the entrance and writhe on the gable above it. Interpretative panels around the grounds identify the tombs (34 in all) and for whom they were erected. The aura of reverence is relieved by the landscaping and enjoyable architectural diversity.

27

Wat Ratchapradit

Rachini Road

It is a short walk from Wat Ratchabophit to Wat Ratchapradit across Pi Kun Bridge on the Old City Canal (the bridge was named for a memorial beside it to a queen born in the Year of the Pig). The temples, both royal, first class, are separated by a wider span. Wat Ratchabophit is ostentatious, unconventional. Wat Ratchapradit is intimate, packed tightly on a small compound.

The king's builders in 1864 found the ground unstable, so a foundation of broken ceramic jars was laid to support the various structures which, as if in miniature on the constrained site, represent the variety of architectural forms found at Thai temples. The ubosot has gilded gables with hang hong and cho fas; doors are hand-carved, floral patterned, gilded; a Buddha image glows under a tiered baldachin in the dim interior where murals illustrate twelve rituals of the kingdom; Songkran, Loy Krathong . . . The ceiling is coffered; the roof is supported outside on columns with lotus-like capitals and shafts clad in diamond-patterned marble. Window surrounds are tiered in mondop manner; the walls are clad in marble as is the wat's austere chedi.

A life-size statue of Rama IV is housed in a Khmer-style pavilion on the west side of the ubosot (a similar structure for scriptures is on the east side). This was the first temple of the Thammayut sect

which was founded by Rama IV when he was abbot at Wat Bowonniwet. The king's interests included astronomy, which led to his death after he contracted malaria on an expedition to Prachuap Khiri Khan province to observe the solar eclipse of 1868. His ashes were placed by Rama V under the principal Buddha image in the ubosot. An evocative mural inside the entrance shows him observing the eclipse. The wat was restored in 2012.

28

Privy Council Chambers

Saranrom Road

Sumet Jumsai, SJA+3D, 2004

The challenge here was to provide the Privy Council with a building that would reflect its royal status and fit the historic Rattanakosin context. The site, formerly part of Saranrom Palace, is in the heart of the old quarter. The intervention required an identity that would be neither presumptuous nor too playful (by the architect of the Robot Building). A reflecting pool complements its postmodern façade which recalls temples and Rama V's Italianate palazzi. The façade is a screen on which steel I-beams imitate gables, or classical pediments. The plan is U-shaped to preserve a grove of trees. The elevation overlooking Saranrom Park blossoms into stylised foliage (hence the nickname, the 'Tree Building'). A Romanesque-style brick structure thought to have been a water tower for Saranrom Palace was rehabilitated as a guardhouse.

29

Saranrom Palace

Sanam Chai Road

Egon Müller, 1868

Rama IV built this for his retirement but died before he could pass the crown to his successor who inherited the building in 1868. It was the residence of royals until assigned to the Ministry of Foreign Affairs in 1885. The ministry moved to another site in 1887 but returned in 1926. During that interval the palace was the official residence of the crown prince, and was also used to accommodate foreign royal and other guests.

The original building on Sanam Chai Road and an east wing were threatened by a multi-storey replacement proposed

in 1968. The wing was torn down for a four-storey office building; this in turn was replaced by a replica of the wing in 2007. The original building was refurbished (Christiani and Nielsen 2010). Its style is Palladian with baroque pretension. There are two storeys, the ground floor obscured somewhat by the plaza's recent reconstruction and a plinth with a statue of Rama IV, and its extravagant canopy added in 2013.

30

Ministry of Defence

Sanam Chai Road

Joachim Grassi, 1884

The Ministry of Defence was the result of the Rama V's reforms which centralised military command at this headquarters, arsenal and barracks. He presided at the opening ceremony. The building was the biggest in Bangkok. The plan is square with two inner courtyards. There are four Renaissance-style elevations, consistent and spectacularly long. The main entrance facing the Grand Palace is dignified with a classical pediment, the emblem of the Royal Guard and a porte cochère with 12 gigantic classical columns. This powerful presence is amplified by a collection of antique artillery on the front lawn where a tall flagpole is mounted on a fluted pedestal. The cannons face sideways, a tactical retreat after it was pointed out in 2002 that they were aimed at the Grand Palace.

31

Royal Thai Survey Department

Kalayana Maitri Road

Stefano Cardu, 1892

Exuberant Renaissance in style, this was the Royal Military Academy established by Rama V in 1887. It moved in 1909 to Ratchadamnoen Nok and the building was occupied by the Army Chief of Staff until 1931 when the Survey Department moved in. The department was founded by Rama V in 1885. Its first director, James

McCarthy, a surveyor with experience in British India, mapped the kingdom and was honoured with a royal title for his services. The building houses a museum of the department's cartography. The façade extends left and right of a central bay which has a pediment above a porch supported by four classical columns with rusticated banding. Rama V's coat of arms with a crown, parasols, and Erawan is rendered at the top of the central bay as a cartouche, like European heraldry.

32

Chang Rong Si Bridge

Klong Ku Muang Derm, between Kalayana Maitri and Bamrung Muang roads

Public Works Department, 1910

Several of the 17 birthday bridges built by Rama V survive. The name of this one refers to a nearby royal rice mill and elephants which crossed the original timber bridge to it. Prince Damrong Rajanupab donated funds to rebuild it in concrete with classical balustrades. The name of the bridge appears on posts at each end along with the number '129' marking the 129th year of the Chakri dynasty. The dog heads are for the Year of the Dog when the bridge was constructed.

33

Ministry of Interior

Asadang Road

Public Works Department, c. 1894

Palladian composition—a central bay with entrance and pediment, flanking loggias and wings—and details all in stucco imitating stone are balanced elegantly across this elevation. The statue out front represents Prince Damrong Rajanupab, one of Rama V's closest advisors, who played a leading role implementing the king's administrative reforms. The prince headed the Ministry of Interior when it was established in 1894. The statue (by Sanan Silakorn, 1968) is a conventional likeness in the tradition of Silpa Bhirasri whose figurative style is still favoured by officialdom.

34

Charoen Sri 34 Bridge

Klong Ku Muang Derm at Bunsiri Road

Public Works Department, 1914

One of Rama VI's six birthday bridges, this has elaborate balustrades, lion heads as keystones on the arch and plaques halfway across inscribed with the name of the bridge and its date (2457 in the Thai calendar). Four pillars, each with a wide urn, were crafted in Renaissance style. The Thai figure '4' appears at the base of each pillar to mark the bridge as the fourth of the six, and its completion during the king's fourth year on the throne.

35

Wat Buranasiri

5 Asadang Road

You can be alone shaded by holy trees in this quiet wat off the tourist trail and admire its architecture without disturbance. Begun during the third reign by a prince, it was completed for Boonsri Buranasiri, a government official after whom it was named. It has a classic diversity of structures and details, all delicate. The ubosot has gilded doors and windows and a porch at both ends. The roof is tiered modestly. There is Chinese decoration on the gables where bai raka and cho fas perch on the bargeboards

like birds. The chedi has tiers rising to a slender spire. There is a small Chinese bell tower and dwellings in Western chalet style.

36

Chao Poh Suea Shrine

468 Tanao Road

Built during the second reign near what is now Bamrung Muang Road, this Taoist shrine was the Chinese community's only shrine in the old city. It was relocated during the fifth reign to the present site which was provided by Rama V when Bamrung Muang was widened as part of his modernisation plans. Known as the Tiger Temple, it recalls a local legend of a repentant tiger which cared for a mother whose only son it had killed. Couples seeking fertility make offerings to gain the tiger's virility; others seek good luck and protection from the shrine's warrior god, Xuan Tian Shang Ti. The post and beam interior is typical of this building type, as are the roof ridge animated with dragons, the red and gold decor and clouds of incense smoke at busy times.

37

Phraeng Sanphasat Palace Gate

Tanao Road at Phraeng Sanphasat Road

c. 1900

This isolated curiosity buttressed with bricks by the BMA and Fine Arts Department in 1973 is evidence that the area was once royal and residential. The Renaissance-style arch was the entrance to a palace, the home of Prince Sanphasat Suphakij, destroyed by a fire in the neighbourhood in 1967. Another aristocrat's mansion, Issarasena Palace (1887), is hidden behind a row of restored shophouses on Asadang Road, just south of Charoen Sri 34 Bridge.

Three parallel streets, Phraeng Sanphasat, Phraeng Nara and Phraeng Phuthon—collectively Sam Phraeng, or the three phraengs community—were named after three princes who lived in the area. The pattern of settlement changed when Rama V built Dusit Palace. Royals moved away, roads were widened and rows of two-storey shophouses appeared. A market square was laid out on Phraeng Phuthon. The square is now a pocket park, part of a 1990s makeover led by a community conservation group. Canal-side walkways were repaved and landscaped, and rows of fifth- and sixth-reign shophouses repainted. The shophouses, which contain some old-style retail and food outlets, preserve the character of the low-rise city which spread out from the Grand Palace in the 19th century.

38

Talaphat Suksa School

63 Phraeng Nara Road

This teak, brick and stucco structure was once a palace built for Prince Narathip Prapanpong, a son of Rama IV. Its teakwood loggia bracketed above the sidewalk is an unusual feature with delicate fretwork. On the building's east side, a curved gable with a plaster motif gives a clue to its former status. The prince was a patron of performing arts and had a theatre in the courtyard. His heirs sold the property which became a school after 1932 and is now a lawyer's office.

39

City Hall

Bangkok Metropolitan Administration Plaza

Samaichalerm Kridakorn, 1962

Bamrung Muang Road, originally a track to Wat Suthat, bursts into this plaza, a vast public space above underground parking. The plaza is dominated by the BMA Building (City Hall). The architecture is Modern Thai at its most forbidding. The front elevation is 15 bays wide, 11 of them in a projecting row with pointed arches, all grafted onto city hall's 1955 structure. The 1960s addition was to have been taller until it was observed that it would be higher than and disrespectful to Wat Suthat. Inscribed in traditional lettering on a plaque on the south side of the plaza is Bangkok's ceremonial name, claimed to be the longest of any city in the world.

40

Giant Swing

Bangkok Metropolitan Administration Plaza

This was the site of Saochingcha Market, named after the Giant Swing (Sao

Ching Cha). The present swing is half the height of the original which was built c. 1784 for the annual Brahmin ceremony of thanks for fertile fields and good crops. Men, four at a time in a boat-like mount, swung to high arcs to reach a bag of gold tied to a pole. This ceased in the 1930s after fatal accidents. The swing was rebuilt with century-old teak in 2007. There is a Brahmin compound on the plaza's west side dating from 1784, restored recently. Its priests attend royal

ceremonies, a tradition established by Rama I. There are images of Hindu gods in three Siamese-style brick and stucco shrines.

Shops on nearby Bamrung Muang Road and in its sois sell Buddha statues and religious paraphernalia. A century ago the road was one of the busiest shopping streets in the city, with more variety than now. Vintage shophouses survive between City Hall Plaza and Asadang Road. They were built in the Singapore style imported by Rama V after his visit there in 1871, with an arcaded sidewalk within the structures since filled in by shopkeepers.

41
Wat Suthat
146 Bamrung Muang Road
1852

Sublime architecture elevates Wat Suthat above even its royal, first class status. The viharn, or Royal Chapel, is reputedly the tallest and is certainly the most elegant in Bangkok, and the ubosot the longest in the kingdom. The chapel is raised in a quadrangle lined with cloisters containing over 150 Buddha images in uniform seated pose. Construction was started by Rama I in 1782. The ubosot, which sprawls on a rectangular podium next door, was added by Rama III. It has a multi-tiered roof protecting a huge image, Phra Buddha Trilokachet, cast at the time for this site; below it are 80 statues of attentive disciples commissioned by Rama IV.

The chapel houses Phra Sri Sakyamuni Buddha, in bronze eight metres high, found in the ruins of Sukhothai. Rama I had it barged down the Chao Phraya River to Tha Chang from where it was hauled to the wat. Its base contains the ashes of King Ananda Mahidol (Rama VIII) who died of gunshot, still unexplained, at Borom Phiman Mansion in the Grand Palace in 1946. He entered customary monkhood here. A statue (Silpa Bhirasri, Paitum Muangsombron, 1959) commissioned by his brother, Rama IX, stands in the north-west corner of the cloisters.

The chapel's teakwood structure is engineered in the traditional way to support a multi-tiered roof: there are internal, longitudinal and cross beams on columns; the roof extends over the exterior walls where it rests on columns with gilded lotus capitals. Murals inside are wall-to-wall, illustrating lives of the Buddha and of people in early Bangkok. All date from the fourth reign. There are model Chinese pagodas around the chapel and many stone statues from China similar to those at Wat Pho.

42

Romaneenart Park

Maha Chai and Siri Phong roads

1999

Five watchtowers in the park were part of Bangkok Central Prison, subsequently the Department of Corrections which closed the jail for an out-of-town location in the 1990s. The site was remade imaginatively by the BMA as a public park and museum. A section of wall, the Italianate main gate and colonial-style administration and cell block buildings (all by Joachim Grassi, c. 1890) were preserved along with the watch towers.

43

Sala Chalermkrung Royal Theatre

66 Charoen Krung Road

Samaichalerm Kridakorn, Narot Pothiprasart engineer, 1933

Rama VII commissioned this Art Deco movie theatre to celebrate the 150th anniversary in 1932 of the Chakri dynasty and Bangkok. Architect Samaichalerm, an aristocrat who had studied at the ultra-conservative école des Beaux-Arts in Paris drafted a contemporary design. The structure is ferroconcrete with a column-free auditorium and Euro-modernist massing and smooth surfaces on the façades..

The 1,250-seat theatre was a magical piece of neon-lit modernity, the first air-conditioned theatre in South-East Asia and the first in the kingdom to show talking pictures. During the Second World War foreign films were unavailable so the management staged live shows and allowed the building to be used as an air-raid shelter. It was renovated with a new screen and seating in 1968. It closed in 1991 for a rehabilitation by Crown Properties, as a performance centre for Khon. Art Deco features, some in Thai style, were retained in an adaptive reuse which set a high standard for heritage conservation in Bangkok. The venue reopened on 2 July 1993, the 60th anniversary of its inauguration.

44

Old Siam Plaza

Phahurat Road, between Tri Phet and Burapha roads

Design 103 International, 1993

This retro-style shopping centre was built on the site of Talat Ming Muang

covered market. Neo-colonial façades responded to the historic neighbourhood but the development was controversial. Residents were displaced and historic buildings replaced with a fake.

The entrance on Phahurat Road is a pastiche that suggests a royal mansion, not inaccurately because there was one nearby on Chakphet Road. It was called Wang Burapha (the Palace of the East) and gave its name to the neighbourhood. It was torn down for redevelopment in 1954 and replaced with movie theatres and stores including Central's first which appealed to the affluent classes. Old Siam never lured them despite its underground parkade. It did attract Sikh traders from adjacent Little India, whose religious focus is an enormous temple, Gurduara Sri Guru Singh Sabha (565 Chakphet Road), built in 1981 but with roots planted in the area since 1912.

45

Nightingale-Olympic Department Store

70 Tri Phet Road

Wang Burapha's fashionable retail shifted to Siam Centre and Chit Lom in the 1970s. A post on CNN's website lifted the lid off this relic caught in a time warp, with a 1960s inventory of foreign brands. The business sold imported cosmetics, musical instruments and sports gear to affluent shoppers. Construction of its seven-storey building, said to have been the tallest in the city, coincided with the Olympic Games held in Tokyo in 1964. All that is left are the ground floor, a mezzanine reached by a sweeping staircase and a façade of concrete brise-soleil shielding the upper, now abandoned floors—and a circular logo with the Olympic torch and a medal.

46

Poh Chang College of Arts and Crafts

86 Tri Phet Road

Prakit Buabutr, c. 1950

Now part of Rajamangala University of Technology, Poh Chang School as it was called was opened by Rama VI in 1913. The inspiration for it came from Rama V who was concerned about the loss of traditional arts and crafts skills as the kingdom was modernised. Among its staff during the sixth reign was architect Edward Healey whose work for Rama VI at Vajiravudh College established the Modern Thai style, of which this is an example. It replaced the original build-

ing which was hit by bombs during the Second World War. Two wings flank the centre block; roofs are traditional, columns have lotus capitals; bas-reliefs are in Art Deco style. Poh Chang's architecture department formed in 1929 was the precursor of the Faculty of Architecture, Chulalongkorn University.

47
Suankularb Wittayalai School
88 Tri Phet Road
Public Works Department, 1910
Rama V founded this school, originally military, for royal pages at the Grand Palace in 1882. The curriculum and enrolment grew requiring relocation in 1893 and later to this site, formerly part of Wat Ratchaburana. The heritage building, Tuek Yao (long building), stretches for 200 metres along Tri Phet Road, but not monotonously. Its Italianate elevations are airy with loggias and there is a slight curve in the perspective. The entrance with iron gates and a pediment breaks the rhythm with just the right note. The street elevation is repeated on the compound side where there is a sports field, a gymnasium and multi-purpose structure (1984) and an auditorium (1995). Rama V believed education would develop the country. There is a statue of him where students assemble to pay respect on Foundation Day. Part of the old build-

ing's ground floor houses the Museum of Thai Education. Classrooms remain on the second level. It is the country's oldest public secondary school. Its name recalls the original location near the rose garden (suan kularb) at the Grand Palace.

48
Wat Ratchaburana
Tri Phet and Chakphet roads
Also called Wat Liab after the Chinese merchant who built it in the late Ayutthaya era, the temple has been restored several times since the first reign. Its buildings, and Suankularb Wittayalai School, were sandwiched between two targets of Allied air raids during the Second World War, the Metropolitan Power Station (Wat Liab Power Plant) and Memorial Bridge. The power plant was wrecked in a raid in April 1945. Bombs destroyed a second plant at Samsen. By the end of the war, it was estimated that 60 percent of Bangkok's population had left the city for safety elsewhere. The school and the temple were damaged in the raids and rebuilt after the war. The wat's ubosot was rebuilt in 1962. Its Khmer-style prang was restored in 1962 and by the Metropolitan Electricity Authority in 2007.

49
Pak Klong Talat
Chakphet Road
This market is packed into a dense neighbourhood bounded by Memorial Bridge Plaza, Chakphet Road, Klong

Ku Muang Derm and the Chao Phraya River. Its name refers to the original site where the klong meets the river. During the first reign it was a floating market; in the fifth reign, a fish market, and later specialised in farmers' produce and flowers. Produce from the provinces was delivered by boat until trucks took over, arriving by dawn. The narrow streets are usually gridlocked with traffic as are the sidewalks with vendors' stalls. The architecture is a mishmash of mundane modern shophouses and fifth- and sixth-reign survivors.

The market's biggest and most ambitious enterprise is Yodpiman Flower City whose 1960s concrete and steel-trussed, wholesale sheds are the nucleus of a heritage-themed expansion. The sheds have been renovated and allow access to a boat pier and promenade, creating public spaces which emulate Asiatique the Riverfront. A bas-relief artwork at the south end of the site recalls the past.

50

Rama I Monument

Memorial Bridge Plaza, Tri Phet Road

Corrado Feroci, Prince Narisara Nuvativongse, 1932

Tri Phet Road leads to Memorial Bridge, but before it gets there it forks to pass a plaza ruled by this monument to Rama I and the pylons of Memorial Bridge which close the perspective with a theatrical flourish. The monument portrays the king seated on a throne surveying the city he established in 1782.

Prince Naris and Corrado Feroci worked on the design; the statue of the king was cast in Florence under Feroci's supervision. The backdrop, a triptych with its centre panel inscribed that the monument was 'a gift from the grateful nation', blends Siamese tradition with Art Deco, which is also the decorative style applied to the bridge. The grandiose piece of urban design was conceived by Rama VII to mark the 150th anniversary of Chakri rule and of Bangkok. It was a symbolic attempt to assert the monarchy at a time of political uncertainty. Less than three months after the plaza was crowded for a ceremony to unveil the monument and to declare the bridge open a coup d'état overthrew the absolute monarchy.

Phra Sumen Fort on the old city wall

2

Banglamphu & Samsen

Banglamphu has changed since cows, chickens and cats roamed the dusty compound at Wat Chana Songkram. The compound has been cleaned up and the wat is evidently wealthy. But it is still a handy shortcut between Phra Athit pier and Khao San Road, as it was when Banglamphu was a hippy hangout in the 1970s and Lonely Planet branded it as the foreign budget travellers' best bet for cheap digs. The temple was originally called Wat Klang Na, meaning 'in the middle of rice fields' and 'khao san' translates as 'milled rice', clues to the agriculture and trade once pursued here. The community grew around the wat which was established before the founding of Bangkok. The area's other big temple, Wat Bowonniwet, is one of the city's most historic and picturesque religious sites.

Banglamphu is part of Rattanakosin Island, but with a separate identity and less formal character than the core around the Grand Palace. Its name is derived from the land by the water and its lamphu trees. The neighbourhood today is bounded by the Chao Phraya River, Ratchadamnoen Klang and Klong Rob Krung. The north section of Rama I's defensive wall was parallel to the klong and reached the river at Phra Sumen Fort, which is preserved with part of the wall on Phra Athit Road. The road, built during the fifth reign, was named for another fort, long demolished. The fort is enhanced by a recent public park which allows access to the riverfront.

In the 19th century princes, aristocrats and mandarins built mansions with large gardens, some on the most desirable land on Phra Athit Road by the river where they benefitted from cool breezes and views. Some survive, partly obscured by more recent buildings none of which are high-rise because of height limits set by conservation rules. In the 1990s these were tested by a lawsuit brought by the BMA against New World department store after several floors were added illegally. Eventually they were dismantled. The only unusual aspect of that case was that demolition actually went ahead, 10 years later. The building was declared a public safety hazard and abandoned, a ruinous eyesore.

The area has many two-storey shophouses dating from the fifth and sixth reigns. Some of their rows have been interrupted by modern infill, little of it sympathetic to their scale. They tend to be overlooked as 'architecture' but being a vernacular building-type they have the virtue of utility, with the store at the sidewalk and living space upstairs. This low-rise but high-density housing now seems a perfect example of sustainability: the neighbourhood is traditionally walkable or was served by samlors; owners do not have to commute, nor do shoppers who live in nearby. Several rows have been restored, some chic with trendy eateries and funky shops. There is a street market on Chakrabongse Road and in sois off it. Food carts line the sidewalks. Older wooden dwellings can be found in the sois and troks.

The architectural variety—the fort, temples, a mosque, princely mansions, shophouses and boutique hotels—reflects the area's history and social mix. The mansions were designed in Western styles, as was the National Gallery, a Palladian pile on the edge of Banglamphu, facing Sanam Luang. It was built as the Royal Mint, one of several government departments which Rama V moved out of the Grand Palace to ease overcrowding. The building's Italian style is beguiling but the gallery is an under-exploited resource. It gets few visitors despite its proximity to the tourist sites around Sanam Luang and to Khao San Road, and has been starved of investment. A much-needed upgrade is planned.

Growth in the 1960s caused most of the mansions to be sold, and their owners to move to areas which offered the tranquility Banglamphu was losing. But it retains its community spirit—a local history museum, long campaigned for, opened in a rehabilitated heritage building in 2014. Khao San Road, once a curiosity where Western travellers congregated, is now established firmly in Bangkok's tourist economy. The legacy of the hippy trail is a new breed of boutique hotels and guesthouses in Banglamphu, overflowing along Samsen Road.

Samsen Road runs north to cross Klong Phadung Krung Kasem into Dusit district, whose royal landmarks are featured in the next chapter. The road is more commercial than Dusit generally but it has sites of cultural and historical interest, and the district, like Dusit, is attractive with an absence of high-rise architecture. Samsen was crown land and much is still. There were two palaces by the river (Thewawet and Bangkhunphrom) with truly palatial buildings, unlike many other royal villas or mansions also called 'palaces'. They became a cause célèbre when the Bank of Thailand took over their land for a new head office in 1970 and planned to demolish them. Heritage fans protested. Eventually both interests were served when the buildings were rehabilitated for the bank's museum, an early example of adaptive reuse and conservation.

Samsen was inland until the 16th century, when the river changed course into a canal dug as a shortcut to Ayutthaya. The community was recorded by foreigners on passing vessels as a prosperous riverine village with a wat, the delightful, relatively unknown Wat Bot Samsen. The village attracted missionaries—the area is home to the city's oldest Catholic community, with roots going back to the 17th century. It is also the location of the National Library and Wat Rachathiwat, one of the most beautiful and idiosyncratic of the 450 or so temples in Bangkok. The soi the wat is on leads to the river, an unspoiled spot as is much of the neighbourhood, for now. A controversial 1992 plan by the Ministry of Transport to build roads on both banks of the river from Rattanakosin to Nonthaburi resurfaced in 2014, for further feasibility study 'to ease traffic congestion'. Bangkok needs more roads? Has nothing been learned?

51

National Gallery

4 Chao Fa Road

Carlo Allegri, Mario Tamagno, 1902

The passage into the gallery's courtyard could be in a palazzo in Italy from where the architects came. It has a double door and a wide corridor leading to a sculpture garden with contemporary art. The biggest exhibit is the oldest—a water tank raised on a structure modelled on the Eiffel Tower.

The gallery was originally designed for the Royal Mint which was moved here from the Grand Palace. The mint moved again around 1970 and the property was transferred to the Fine Arts Department which rehabilitated the heritage building as the National Gallery in 1977. The main salon is a grand, neoclassical room with polished wood floors, Tuscan columns and wall and ceiling mouldings well preserved. The Palladian exterior is as it was in 1902, with round-arched windows alternating with pilasters, stucco patterned like stonework and kite-shaped tiles on the roofs. Rama V's coat of arms of Siam is centred on the pediment above the old entrance to the two-storey centre block, which is flanked by single-storey wings with fretwork on the eaves and roof ridges. The building was reflected on the surface of the Old City Canal, an idyllic image, almost Venetian, lost when that section of the canal disappeared under the approach road constructed for Phra Pinklao Bridge in 1973.

52

Maliwan Palace

39 Phra Athit Road

Ercole Manfredi, 1917

European-style mansions were built for royals and senior officials in Banglamphu around the turn of the 20th century. Some survive, having been rehabilitated as offices for government and other agencies. The UN International Children's Emergency Fund (Unicef) occupies a former royal villa (19 Phra Athit Road). The Far Eastern Regional Office of the UN Food and Agriculture Organisation (FAO) has been at Maliwan Palace since 1949.

The big, two-storey house has a whiff of Italian Art Nouveau on the front elevation which faces the river. The entrance is on Phra Athit Road but the house was designed to be accessible by boat, like others nearby with private piers. It was the home of Prince Vorarit, ambassador to Britain and the United States and a minister of public works. Crown Properties took over the property in 1937. During the Second World War, Free Thai agents met their leader, Pridi Banomyong, here and at what is now the Unicef office. The piers were convenient for the Thai Customs launches which secretly ferried the agents around.

53

Baan Phra Athit

102 Phra Athit Road

Mario Tamagno, c. 1925

The property was inherited by a minister of the Royal Household. He built this mansion following the fashion in palace circles for eclectic Western designs. The elevations are Italianate with a loggia connecting two separate structures, both with wide eaves and gabled bays, one with a tower and witch's hat turret. The tower anchors the composition which looks asymmetric but has a formal ground plan. There is a large and well preserved front garden and a courtyard behind the loggia. The effect is of a miniature Phaya Thai Palace.

The Goethe Institute cultural centre was here from 1962 until 1989, when Baan Phra Athit was acquired by Manager Media Group for which it was refurbished and enlarged in similar style (Habita Architects, 1990). An annex at the gate, which has its original posts and fence, is now a restaurant allowing partial access to the site.

55

Santi Chai Prakan Park

Phra Athit at Phra Sumen Road

1999

Restoration of Phra Sumen Fort was part of this project, a blend of landscape design and heritage preservation. The park was developed by Crown Properties and the BMA to create a public amenity and beautify the waterfront. The site

was occupied previously by a sugar mill and Sri Maharacha Timber Company. There is a sala dedicated to Rama IX and a bas-relief artwork showing traditional life. The landscape design has trees and lawns on artificially undulating ground which opens to a plaza with a panoramic view of Rama VIII Bridge. A waterfront walkway connects the park to Phra Athit pier and Phra Pinklao Bridge. The walkway and the park are exceptional in a city where most of the prime riverfront has, as the *Bangkok Post* put it, 'been hijacked by five-star hotels, temples and restaurants.'

54

Phra Sumen Fort

Phra Athit at Phra Sumen Road

1783

Fourteen forts were built along the old city wall parallel to Klong Rob Krung (also known as Klong Banglamphu at this point). This is one of only two that remain. They were designed in uniform style, octagonal at the base with a hexagonal, timber-framed watchtower above tiers of battlements. Each had storage for ammunition and weapons, and quarters for soldiers. All were built with brick covered with stucco. Part of the wall here was left exposed by the Fine Arts Department during restorations in 1981 and 1997, to show its construction. The watchtower was reconstructed. The klong was dug in 1782 by Lao prisoners of war taken during Rama I's campaigns. The fort was intended to resist attack from the river. Cannons poke out from the ramparts but were never fired in anger.

56

Phra Athit Shophouses

Phra Athit at Phra Sumen Road

c. 1920

A century ago rows of two-storey shophouses were the most popular urban building type in South-East Asia. Overseas Chinese communities had row after row of them, especially

in Singapore. Shophouses in Singapore are narrow and interior spaces deep-set, with a courtyard or light well halfway back. Their most obvious feature is an arcaded ground floor. The arcade provides a sidewalk five-feet wide (a 'five-foot way') the length of the row for shelter from the sun and rain. That model spread north into southern Siam during the fifth reign. Phuket Town retains complete streetscapes of the Singapore shophouse form. They were built with load-bearing brick party walls and timber beams supporting the upper floor. Roofing was kite-shaped tiles. In Bangkok the arcade and deep interior are less common. This row is typical, but rounded slightly to fit the curve where Phra Athit meets Phra Sumen Road. It is one of many owned by Crown Properties, which restored it recently along with a more conventional straight row around the corner (82-98 Phra Athit Road).

57
Kuru Sapha Printing House
Phra Sumen Road
1925

This is one of the earliest modernist buildings in Bangkok. The emphasis is horizontal. There is no decoration. The structure is concrete, walls are brick and stucco and the floors teak. Wat Sangwet Printing School, the first such school in the kingdom, was based in here until 1946. Texts for Wat Sangwet Wisayaram, also known as Wat Banglamphu, were printed in a teakwood building (1932) in the courtyard. The temple is across Klong Banglamphu from the Printing House, accessible by Hong U-thit Bridge on Lamphu Road.

In 1950 the school site became the headquarters of Kuru Sapha, a Ministry of Education department which printed and published student textbooks.
It moved out in 1958. The buildings were used for storage until 1995 when the Rattanakosin Committee and the Treasury Department planned to demolish them for a park. The community's

Bang Lamphu Civic Group preferred adaptive reuse and campaigned for it. The Fine Arts Department listed the buildings as a historic site. Eventually they were rehabilitated in 2014 as a community museum and the courtyard landscaped. On the sidewalk is a heritage panel about the Printing House, part of a public information programme by the BMA for historic sites; also of note is the road sign, a piece of old-style street furniture of a type still common, but no longer on every street corner across the city.

58
Siam Commercial Bank
Phra Sumen and Samsen roads
c. 1960

SCB's Banglamphu branch turns the street corner with vertical emphasis as if it wants to be taller. The eaves keep it in check. The building has presence but is not overbearing. The styling recalls Art Deco—the movie theatre modernism of the 1930s rather than the more austere government buildings on Ratchadamnoen. The curving corner feature was a graceful way to ease it into the historic townscape which was then almost entirely low-rise.

Across the intersection was New World department store (1982), not graceful and worse when it became a ruin after the BMA, in a rare reading of regulations, forced the owners, after a 10-year dispute, to demolish the upper floors which breached the Rattanakosin conservation area's height limit. Demolition was incompetent, caused a collapse and the remains were abandoned. Banglamphu's oldest department store, Tang Hua Seng (172-182 Chakrabongse Road), built in 1962 is still in business, unconsciously retro which is its charm.

59
Chakrabongse Mosque
Chakrabongse Road, Trok Surao
1960

The mosque is reached from an alley hidden behind shophouses and street

vendors across from Tang Hua Seng Department Store. It stands in a compound surrounded by tumbledown houses, some wooden like those found in the provinces. It dates from 1779. The original building was wood, as early mosques in Siam were. They were rebuilt in brick and stucco, or concrete like this building which is styled in the now ubiquitous Indo-Islamic manner. There is a columned porch, arabesque window screens and a tower with an onion-domed octagonal cupola for the call to prayer. There are no minarets for the muezzin; Islamic architecture in South-East Asia generally did without them. The prayer hall is on the second level where a niche in the wall at the point nearest Mecca is expressed externally in a semi-circular, onion-domed bay.

Banglamphu's Muslim enclave was known for its craftsmen and goldsmiths from the south who served the court following Rama I's conquest of Pattani. The king allowed this mosque for them, the only one within the old city walls.

60

Nittaya Curry Shop

136–40 Chakrabongse Road

Bangkokians trek across the city (or send maids or drivers) to niche-market shops, usually long-established. This curry store, opened in 1964, occupies a shophouse row typical of inner-city development in the early 20th century. It is still owned and operated by the founding family. Its curry pastes and recipes were spread by word-of-mouth and the company now exports its products. The global spread of Thai cuisine since the 1980s and its appreciation at home have added an unexpected ingredient to the food scene in Bangkok and the provinces. Heritage buildings which otherwise might be demolished are sought for their character and space, to be rehabilitated as cafés or restaurants.

61
Wat Chana Songkram
Chakrabongse Road

This pre-Rattanakosin temple once called Wat Klang Na was renamed 'War Victory Wat', a reference to battles with the Burmese in the 1780s when Rama I was assisted by Mon allies. The Mons were allowed to settle in the area and worship at this temple which the king donated to them as a reward. It was rebuilt and enlarged. The ubosot is of classical simplicity with a lofty central space and flanking aisles, or loggias, roofed with wood beams supported on massive columns. A golden Buddha image glows on the altar below a mural of angels; doors are carved intricately; the loggias are decorated with neo-traditional murals, their meanings explained helpfully on captions in Thai and English.

Outside, the peaks of the window surrounds lean forward, an artful effect animated with chofas and nagas. On the roof gables Narai rides Garuda, a typical temple image. The large compound has pagodas, shrines, a temple school in Modern Thai style, a bell tower, and

monks' quarters (some in wood, antique) in a leafy backyard where there is a 200-year-old bodhi tree.

62
Khaosan Garden
201 Khao San Road
c. 1910

More luxury than Lonely Planet, this Italianate villa stands at the end of a passage off Rambuttri Road beside Molly

Bar whose owners, Buddy Group, rehabilitated it. There is a French restaurant on the ground floor and a three-room museum about Banglamphu upstairs. The property extends through another passage to Khao San Road, the backpackers' haven, being gentrified as this makeover shows. Previously an art gallery, it was originally a family home called Baan Kraijitti, built by a director of the Fine Arts Department, Chaophraya Athornturasilp, as a wedding gift for his daughter Khunying Choey Kraijitti.

The villa's original features are a belle époque fantasy. Fretwork and heraldic plasterwork decorate the exterior gable; the walls have classical pilasters with Corinthian-style capitals; the hall has carved wood fittings, a frieze and plasterwork in Chinese style. There is a stained glass window in a private dining area and an Egyptian room with a frieze painted by Carlo Rigoli. The decor shows how European design favoured by Rama V was adopted enthusiastically by high society and those who aspired to join it.

63

Wat Bowonniwet

248 Phra Sumen Road

This royal temple, first class, formerly known as Wat Mai was built between 1824 and 1832. There are many varied structures in its courtyards, on pathways or reflected in klongs. To turn every corner reveals an intriguing picture—a golden mosaic-clad chedi, Chinese pavilions, gilded nagas below the powerful columns of the ubosot . . .

The compound is large because an adjacent temple, Wat Rangsi Sutthawat, was absorbed into Wat Bowon in 1923. The ubosot boasts a Sukhothai-era Buddha image, Phra Buddha Jinasiha, which was barged from Phitsanulok by Rama III. There are murals from the fourth reign attributed to Khrua In Khong, a monk and court painter who was the first Siamese artist to adopt and adapt Western techniques of perspective. His composite style proved popular, but few imitators equal his skill and artistry.

Prince Mongkut was abbot for 14 years before his coronation as Rama IV in 1851, and subsequent monarchs were ordained here. On the terrace of the golden chedi there is a statue of him made by sculptor Luang Theprojana in 1868. The king is shown holding a book and a sword, symbols of his learning and defence of the kingdom. It was the first such representation of a living king of Siam and the first to introduce a Western sculptural form. The chedi was built in 1831 and clad in stucco. Gold mosaic tiles were applied in 1964. It contains a chamber with small chedis housing holy relics. Four Chinese-style pavilions have bas-relief panels of the travels of Fa-hsien, a Chinese monk in the 5th century. Also on the terrace are six celestial beings, four Khmer-style prangs housing buddhas, and symbolic creatures at the four compass points. Lodged in a niche is an image, Phra Pairee Pinas, meaning 'enemies vanquished', so called because those of its donor were. People wishing the same come here to make offerings.

Reflected in a klong is a throne hall in Italianate style laced with Indo-Saracenic arches and floral fretwork built in 1914 for the Supreme Patriarch. The klong has a Chaipattana Aerator, a floating paddle-wheel device which oxygenates water, invented by Rama IX and tested here. Adding to the variety is the wat's library and a new museum in an incongruous Gothic-style seminary (Chua Patthamachinda, 1924) near the temple school. A four-year restoration of the wat was completed in 2010.

64

Mahamakut Buddhist University

Phra Sumen Road

c. 1912

Mahamakut University was founded

as Maha Makut Royal College by Rama V in 1893 in memory of his father King Mongkut. It was a temple school for monks and novices at Wat Bowonniwet. It was enlarged as a state university for religious and lay students in 1997 and an out-of-town campus was built in Nakhon Pathom province. The original building, across the street from the wat, became a library. The architecture is Dutch colonial style with a central bay and decorative gable; there is a Palladian window above the porch which has a flat arch with an Art Nouveau twist. Behind it in Trok Ban Phanthom is an annex, a bungalow in similar style.

65

Old City Wall

Phra Sumen Road

The historic streetscape opposite Wat Bowonniwet features a long row of old

shophouses, property of the temple which, like Wat Chana Songkram, owns land in Banglamphu and many tenanted buildings on it. The shophouses follow the alignment of the old city wall from Phra Sumen Fort. A short stretch of the wall has been preserved with a gateway and spire similar to those at the Grand Palace. It is the only one of 16 gates in the wall to survive. Originally its doors would have been teak, painted red. The old city wall was not destroyed by enemy attack but incrementally and thoughtlessly since the fifth reign, by modernisation and roads being built.

66

Wat Tritosathep

165 Prachathipatai Road

A son of Rama IV chose to make merit by building a temple next to his palace outside the city walls. He marked the overgrown site for clearing by scattering coins, to lure people to clear the land to find them. He died in 1863 before construction started. Another son stepped in, ordered klongs dug on all fours sides of the site and walls built around it, then died. Rama IV completed the work in 1868 and named it Wat Tritosathep, meaning 'the wat built by three noblemen'. He too died, that year. Not a good omen some might have said, or that the spirits of the land were unhappy.

The spirits should be content now. Since 2006 the wat has been completely reconstructed. The traces of the past have gone but the quality of the new work cannot be faulted. All the familiar elements are here: a cloistered compound with golden chedis (five on a marble podium) clad with Italian glass mosaics; an ubosot with mother-of-pearl doors and a tiered roof with eave brackets carved as hongsa; there are bai raka and hang hong on the gables and cho fas on the ridge-ends; roof tiles

are Chinese pattern. The interior of the ubosot is decorated with neo-traditional murals, a work in progress of exceptional artistry and clarity by National Artist Chakrabhand Posayakrit.

67
Hotel De Moc
78 Prachathipatai Road
1962
Two years after it opened as the Thai Hotel, the building and local streets stood in for Saigon during a location shoot for a Hollywood movie, *Operation CIA*. The film could be remade easily at the hotel—its period style is mostly unaltered. It is one of the earliest from the 1960s construction boom when Bangkok buzzed with US military personnel during the Vietnam War. The decor is not original but the hotel offers a very American range of facilities which evoke its era: coffee shop and restaurant, beer garden, business centre, travel agency and outdoor pool. Aside from the new name on the marquee, the exterior of the concrete structure is unaltered. There is a modular elevation and zigzag roof line, which is repeated on the canopy at the poolside bar. The hotel was rehabilitated and is marketed by owners Buddy Group as 'retro 1960s'. Mature shade trees contribute to the sense of time and place. Also out of the past is the nearby Hia Tai Ki (Corner Coffee Shop) at Wisut Kasat and Prachathipatai roads since 1952, a family-run survivor in a Starbucks world.

68
Wat Intharawihan
Wisut Kasat Road
This dates from the Ayutthaya period but, as with most others as venerable, there are no structures from that time. Originally called Wat Bang Khun Phrom Nok, it was rebuilt by Rama I to serve a community of Lao people allowed to settle here. The temple is famed for its 32-metre-high standing Buddha commis-

sioned by Rama IV to house a relic from Sri Lanka. The giant figure was finished in 1927 having taken 60 years to complete. It was clad in golden mosaic tiles for the Bangkok bicentennial (the face is gold leaf, applied later). The image is not free-standing but supported with a backing structure which has stairs leading to a viewing platform. An annual temple fair celebrates its completion.

69
Bank of Thailand
273 Samsen Road

The nation's central bank was founded in 1940. Since 1945 it has occupied this compound where there are two former royal palaces, Thewawet Palace and Bangkhunphrom Palace. The latter was threatened with demolition by a redevelopment plan in 1970, which provoked preservationist and architect Sumet Jumsai to organise a protest march with students from Chulalongkorn University to besiege the bank. The campaign was unprecedented and successful. Bangkhunphrom Palace was eventually rehabilitated as the Bank of Thailand Museum, opened in 1992. Restoration of Thewawet Palace, a three-storey Renaissance-style palazzo (Edward Healey, 1918), won a Unesco heritage award in 2005. A riverfront pavilion and a three-storey Italianate block with chalet-style gables (both by Emilio Giovanni Gollo, 1918), were also restored.

The protest not only saved the palace but also resulted in a fine modernist building (Design 103 International, c. 1980) which is sensitive to the site. Its nine-storey bulk is reduced by abutting lower layers. The emphasis is horizontal, solar shading is prominent. A postmodern block (Tandem Architects, 2001) also responded to the context, with a river-facing elevation in step with Bangkhunphrom Palace.

The compound's old perimeter fence and ornate entrance pillars were kept, notably at Bang Khun Phrom intersection from where a driveway led to Bangkhunphrom Palace. The extent of the site can be seen from Rama VIII Bridge. Directly south of the bridge is the bank's printing plant, an uncompromising industrial building (Santhaya and Associates, 1969) with an impressive concrete roof in corrugated form.

70

Bangkhunphrom Palace

273 Samsen Road

Mario Tamagno, 1906; Karl Siegfried Döring, 1913

There are two distinct parts to this palace: the older east block, a mélange of French Second Empire and rococo with a mansard roof and frothy stucco façades begun in 1901; and the west addition, a separate structure and style, like a tropical schloss flavored with Art Nouveau by its German designer who arrived in 1906 to work as an engineer for Royal Railway Department.

The east block was designed originally for one of Rama V's sons, Prince of Nakhon Sawan, who studied in Germany, returned, married and lived here until the 1932 coup, when he was exiled and never returned. The schloss was built for his mother following the death of the king in 1910. The buildings were connected and the east block's south wing overlaid with an extra floor and a roof terrace. The palace passed to the government 1932 and became the head office of the Bank of Thailand in 1945. It is now the bank's museum. The interiors are well preserved. Tamagno's salons are bright, neo-Renaissance; Döring's Art Nouveau decor, with a pre-Raphaelite fresco by Carlo Rigoli, is a delight.

71

Phranakorn-Nornlen Boutique Hotel

46 Thewet, Soi 1

2005

The hotel is hidden in an alley off the soi. It has a sustainability motto, 'slow life'. The feel is folksy. The entrance sets a quirky tone, with junk store finds and recycled doors. The main building is concrete, 1960s, disguised with bric-a-brac and hand-painted decor. A loggia opens to a leafy courtyard where there are wood decks, pebble and brick paving, water features, trees and plants. There is a crafts workshop. A vintage samlor is displayed like public art (pedal-powered samlors were banned from Bangkok's roads around 1960). An organic garden was planted on the roof to supply the kitchen with herbs and vegetables. Artist Chumpol Akkapantanon worked on the renovation. He is better known for Baan Silapin (Artists' House), Klong Bang Luang (Klong Bangkok Yai), an antique property rehabilitated as a creative centre in 2009.

72
National Library
Samsen Road
Fine Arts Department, 1966

The kingdom's primary public reference library was established as Vajiranana National Library of Siam when Rama V amalgamated three royal libraries at the Grand Palace in 1905. In 1916 Rama VI relocated it to the Thawon Watthu Building next to Wat Mahathat. The National Archives was formed that year and shared the building, as it does the present site at Samsen. Prince Damrong Rajanupab chaired the library and worked with its French director, Georges Coedès. The alliance led to the kingdom's first heritage preservation policy, defined initially by royal decree in 1923 and later by government acts, to protect ancient sites and structures. In 1932 the library was reconstituted under the Fine Arts Department as the National Library. Financing for a new building at Samsen was approved by the government in 1962. It was designed with a monumental Modern Thai-style façade and roofscape and five floors of open-plan modernism inside. Other buildings here include the King Vajiravudh Memorial Hall (1981), the King Bhumibol Adulyadej Commemorative Library (1990).

73
Arts and Cultural Centre, Suan Sunandha Rajabhat University
1 Uthong Nok Road

Among the modern buildings in this educational zone is a ghost palace, a dream of Rama V. Fans of urban archaeology will note the traces of its gardens, lakes and looping canals on the ground plan of the modern campuses of Suan Sunandha Rajabhat and Suan Dusit Rajabhat universities.

Suan Sunandha Palace was intended to house the king's numerous dependents when his successor moved into Dusit Palace next door. He named it in memory of Queen Sunandha. Architect

Alfredo Rigazzi drew the plans for gardens and houses. There were four types, mostly modular which was a novel idea for the time. Between 1911 and 1919, 32 dwellings were built and occupied. One became a finishing school for ladies-in-waiting to learn court etiquette. Only six survive because the site was subdivided after 1932 by the new régime, to expand national education. The most ambitious of Rigazzi's four house types were teak and concrete mansions like this one built in 1912. The composition has picturesque variations with gables, wide eaves, porches and a porte cochère. It was rehabilitated as an art centre for Suan Sunandha Rajabhat University in 1989.

74
Wat Rachathiwat
3 Samsen Road, Soi 9
Prince Narisara Nuvativongse, c. 1910

The soi seems a typical jumble of Bangkok urbanism with weather-stained shophouses and a modernist temple school. A Khmer-style arch is the only clue that anything worth a detour lies beyond, where the soi dead-ends in Venetian solitude at the Chao Phraya River. There is a pier where people make merit by feeding catfish, and there is the wonderful Wat Rachathiwat.

It is a royal, second class temple, a forest monastery in the 13th century reconsecrated in 1767. It faces the river and

is bisected by the soi. On the north side is Salakarnparian, a teakwood assembly hall inspired by the Ayutthaya-era Wat Suwannaram at Phetchaburi. It is raised above the ground for ventilation. The upper level is an immense post and beam structure lit from clerestory and side windows. The space has two rows of columns and side aisles. Sunlight filters in, as if in a forest glade. The roof is tiered, tipped with cho fas, eaves are supported by naga brackets, windows have fretwork.

On the south side is a leafy compound with a bodhi tree planted by Rama II at the gate. Rama IV, who gave the wat its present name, was a monk here, living in a modest dwelling which has been preserved among an eclectic group of structures which include a Khmer-style chedi guarded by sixteen sculpted singha, or mythical lions.

The most fascinating building is the chapel, the former ubosot, a brick ruin before Rama V began a reconstruction overlaid with a fusion of East and West. The exterior walls and columns are stuccoed, the lower roof tier is tiled and curved in French Second Empire style, the gables swirl with sumptuous Khmer-style decoration. The altar and Buddha image are framed with a baroque flourish of five successive royal seals, from Rama I to Rama V. Murals illustrate the Vessantara Jataka on the side walls below a coffered ceiling.

The project was a collaboration between Prince Naris and artist Carlo Rigoli, who arrived in Siam in 1910 to work on the Ananta Samakhom Throne Hall at Dusit Palace. The prince's knowledge of Siamese history and fine arts helped foreign architects and artists in royal service adapt their work to Rattanakosin-era sensibilities. He made preparatory sketches to guide Rigoli through the fables if not to the style of the murals which is European, unexpected at the end of the soi.

75
Saint Gabriel's College
565 Samsen Road

This Catholic school for boys was established in 1920 by the Brothers of Saint Gabriel, a charitable sect founded in 18th-century France. The site for the school was given by the priest at Saint Francis Xavier Church. Brother Martin de Tours of Assumption College in Bang Rak supervised the project. The original structure is the Martin de Castro building (Charles Beguelin, 1922), a handsome Italianate composition which stands at the right of the entrance. To the left is De Montfort Hall, (Sawai Mongkolkasem, 1969), one of the best examples of 1960s architecture in Bangkok. It recalls the Mediterranean modernism of Le Corbusier. Elements are well balanced with fenestration recessed and angled, elevations articulated with horizontal and vertical fins, and the complete building raised on pilotis.

76

Saint Francis Xavier Church

94 Samsen, Soi 11 (Soi Mittakam)

Named after a Jesuit who travelled in Asia to spread the gospel, this church dates from the third reign when Vietnamese and Cambodian Christian refugees were allowed to settle in Samsen. Rama III gave land and money for their first church, a bamboo structure built in 1834. It was destroyed by a storm and rebuilt. The congregation funded the present Renaissance-style building which opened in 1867. A plaque at the entrance recalls Maurice Gibarta, the priest who built it.

The west front has a porch with a trio of arches, a balustrade, and a gable with stucco decor and a rosette, all topped with a statue of Saint Francis Xavier. The interior has fanlight windows with newly etched glass panels showing missionaries and traders; round windows have stained glass saints. The courtyard has a statue of Christ healing the blind, thought to have been cast in Florence for Rama V.

The church was restored in 2010. It is part of Catholic enclave founded in the 17th century when King Narai of Ayutthaya gave land here for a Portuguese mission. The Church of the Immaculate Conception nearby (167 Soi Mittakam), founded in 1674, is the oldest Catholic church in Bangkok. The present building was begun by French bishop Monsignor Pallegoix in 1836. It was embellished during the fifth reign in Romanesque style by Joachim Grassi, based on his design of St. Joseph's Church at Ayutthaya.

77

Siam Hotel

Khao Road at Sangkhalok Road

Bill Bensley Design Studio, 2012

Rama V's blend of Siamese and European architecture was the inspiration for this resort, the initiative of Krissada Sukosol. The ambience seems personal, not formulaic as many resorts are. The linear spatial sequence through the property, from the street entrance and through the main block's atrium to a pier on the Chao Phraya River, is arranged elegantly as if in one of Rama V's palaces. The landscaping flows seamlessly with every step.

The design (lead architect Khemvadee Paopanlerd) is eclectic. There is an infusion of Art Deco; the atrium is steel and glass, with foliage and a pond like a 19th-century European plant house; there is an Islamic-style courtyard. Retro details, artisanal materials (some recycled), and the owner's collection of antiques and curios form much of the decor and furnishings. There are traditional Thai teak dwellings from Ayutthaya, salvaged originally by Jim Thompson. They lend the Siam a sense of the past, as does the

location in Dusit with its luxurious royal palaces. One of them is nearby, an estate built in 1905 for an aide of Rama V at the corner of Khao Road and Ratchawithi. The compound is now the Army Internal Audit Office. Its belle-époque villa with Venetian Gothic windows on a tower inspired by a Bavarian castle is visible. Several other heritage houses survive in the sois off Samsen Road.

78

Wat Bot Samsen

Samsen Road, Soi 16

Obscured behind concrete shophouses across Samsen Road from the ornamental gate of Sukhothai Palace is this small treasure from the Ayutthaya era. Wat Bot Samsen is a picture of how the temples of Bangkok in pre-Rattanakosin times looked, when they were the focus of village life. After 1782 most were renovated or rebuilt, enriched by the conspicuous merit-making of royalty.

This temple was renovated by Rama I after he founded Bangkok, but not radically. The architecture is early Rattanakosin style, restrained in comparison with later work. The chapel is small with a simple tiered roof and a porch below the gable at both ends. The golden Buddha image inside is four centuries old. It is set at a slight angle, said by the monks so it can look out the door to see the chedi which is tiered like a pagoda. It leans slightly due to subsidence. The builders of the chapel tried to avoid this problem with a raft foundation of teak logs for the brick and stucco structure. Even so, cracks appeared over the centuries. The Fine Arts Department stabilised the structure recently and conserved the interior's Ayutthaya-style painted doors, shutters and murals. A glorious vision of the Buddha's victory over the demon Mara is intact and covers the east wall. Some parts of the paintings, lost with no record, have been left as peeling stucco with no attempt to fill in the gaps by guesswork. The effect of time and light-touch conservation have preserved a pleasing patina—the chapel and chedi look their age unlike over-restored specimens.

Government House; Venetian Gothic style

3

Ratchadamnoen & Dusit

Ratchadamnoen, or King's Walk, is the premier avenue in the royal and government district of Dusit. Rama V developed it as the route from the Grand Palace to Dusit Palace, where he relocated in 1901. Other roads are perpendicular and parallel to it, forming a grid of vistas framed by showy government buildings and royal mansions. In the urban collage that is Bangkok, Dusit is a rare piece of rational planning. The avenue was inspired by those Rama V saw on his first visit to Europe in 1897. It is wide and ceremonial, the Champs Élysées of Bangkok. It terminates at Royal Plaza where there is an equestrian statue of the king in front of Ananta Samakhom Throne Hall, a neoclassical extravaganza completed in 1915 designed by a team of Italian architects he employed at the Public Works Department.

Dusit Palace was planned as an alternative to the Grand Palace, which was overcrowded and sweltering in summer, densely packed with buildings, some of which Rama V had built and others too historic to be altered. At Dusit, which was undeveloped, he had carte blanche. The area was rural, with orchards and paddy fields which he bought. The name refers to not to a single royal palace but several buildings and the grounds in which they are set: Suan Dusit or Celestial Garden as he called them. The architecture ranges from the modest to the monumental in a mélange of styles. The ensemble is the most enjoyably eccentric built by a king since Frederick the Great commissioned Sanssouci summer palace at Potsdam outside Berlin and adorned its grounds with water features, Chinoiserie and neoclassical follies. 'Sans souci' is French for 'carefree' which was Rama V's desire, not only for relief from the old city palace but also that the various villas he built at Dusit for male and female family members, consorts and courtiers be congenial.

After the coup d'état in 1932 the military occupied many of the buildings at Dusit Palace. They have since been returned to the Bureau of the Royal Household and restored. Much of the palace is concealed behind walls and neoclassical gateways but a considerable area can be visited. Some of the heritage buildings are open to the public; access to their interiors requires a ticket for Vimanmek Mansion, Rama V's residence. The most significant are described here (the full entrance fee to the Grand Palace normally includes Vimanmek).

Ratchadamnoen Nai (the inner part) along the edge of Sanam Luang which was landscaped for it runs between the Grand Palace and what is now the Royal Hotel; Ratchadamnoen Klang (the central strip) continues from the hotel to Phan Fa Bridge; Ratchadamnoen Nok (the outer section) leads from the bridge to Ananta Samakhom Throne Hall, by far the grandest of the royal and administrative buildings completed along the outer avenue during Rama V's reign. There are some royal mansions one of which, Parutsakawan Palace, is splendid in Art Nouveau style. Nearby is the extraordinary Venetian Gothic architecture of Government House.

The 1932 edition of *The Royal State Railway Guide to Bangkok* noted 'the broad and stately avenue called Ratchadamnoen, or royal promenade, flanked with rows of stately tamarind trees' was similar to the Champs Élysées, '. . . only, it lacks the fine buildings . . . but these will undoubtedly appear in time.' They did, a few years later. The guide was referring to Ratchadamnoen Klang which Rama V landscaped but did not develop. It became a commercial area with shophouses and residents and traders who were mostly ethnic Chinese. After the 1932 coup d'état they were evicted by the People's Party whose leaders unrolled an urban design to symbolise their dream of a democratic, progressive society. The new society excluded local Chinese who were discriminated against. Like all dictatorial urban designs, this one had a human cost.

The focal point was and still is the Democracy Monument (1939), set in a grand traffic circle with a backdrop of 15 public buildings which extend to both ends of the avenue's central strip. This cohesive townscape was built between 1937 and 1948. Construction was reinforced concrete with brick walls stuccoed; corners are rounded, with vertical concrete articulation; fins act as brise-soleil and define entrances. The style of the buildings conflated Art Deco with the horizontal emphasis of Frank Lloyd Wright and the melodrama of Mussolini. It is not known if the People's Party leaders knew of Wright, but their Prime Minister, Field Marshal Plaek Phibun Songkram, admired the Italian fascist dictator. The architecture has a totalitarian feel—the uniformity is relentless—but is softened with the curves at ends of each block. The party was big on nationalism and showed it on the monumental symmetry of the avenue's Beaux-Arts plan, which was perfect for military parades. But the public space was not just for watching them. The party's democracy of the public realm included a cinema and a department store on the same sidewalks as the Government Savings Bank and other agencies including the most popular, the state lottery.

Phibun wanted to move the capital up country. The buildings here show what it would have looked like. They are now ageing. Official plans to upgrade the avenue cite the Champs Élysées and imply French flair. The architecture is adaptable: two recent projects—the Ratchadamnoen Contemporary Art Centre and the Rattanakosin Exhibition Hall—transformed down-at-heels government buildings into attractions of international quality. The art centre is a contemporary space. The Rattanakosin Exhibition Hall tells the story of the Chakri monarchs. It is a significant intervention on an avenue haunted by history. There is no route in Bangkok that represents more potently the setbacks and successes in Thailand's long road to democracy. For more than a century Ratchadamnoen has witnessed the ebb and flow of power—from Rama V's vision to equal the grand boulevards of Europe, to the parade of the Free Thai soldiers at the end of the Second World War, and postwar protests at the Democracy Monument against military and more recent elected governments. It is a contested public space, its history and the memories it holds interpreted by competing narratives which its buildings represent and continue to be adapted to serve.

79

Royal Hotel

2 Ratchadamnoen Klang

Jittasen Aphaiwong, Pum Malakoul, 1940

Originally called the Rattanakosin Hotel this was 'one of the best East of Suez' according to a 1954 guidebook. It was popular with the beau monde, business travellers, army chiefs, diplomats and spies. It had a ritzy restaurant, banquet room, cocktail lounge, patisserie and a 'luxuriant tropical garden'. It maintained its status until the 1970s when it was sidelined by fashionable new hotels, but the architecture retains the vigour of youth with an entrance bay and canopy like an Art Deco cinema. The elevation curves to create a smooth transition from Sanam Luang to Ratchadamnoen Klang.

Outside the hotel the Old City Canal vanishes below a vast intersection created when Phra Pinklao Bridge was built across the Chao Phraya River in 1973. The klong was bridged in 1906 by Phan Phiphop (King's Crossing), an iron structure which was rebuilt in concrete when the road was widened. It was the first of three ornate bridges—one for each of Rattanakosin Island's three canals—on Rama V's route on Ratchadamnoen from the Grand Palace to Dusit. The route is punctuated with monuments. The Earth Goddess Fountain (Khmer style, by Prince Naris, c. 1910), a royal gift of drinking water to the people, can be seen across the bridge from the hotel.

80

14 October 1973 Memorial

Kok Wua intersection, Ratchadamnoen Klang

Terdkiat Sakdicumduang, 2001

Arrests of pro-democracy students from Thammasat University provoked a mass protest at the Democracy Monument in 1973. The army deployed tanks, soldiers and police fired on unarmed civilians, and the king intervened. A short-lived democratic government arranged a fund to compensate victims' families and approved a competition for a memorial. The winning design was announced in 1974 but took years to materialise because of red tape. The previous building on the site was the government's Thai TV News Agency which was torched during the protests.

The memorial is circular in plan, like the Democracy Monument but set back from the avenue where the events it recalls took place. The style is postmodern, avant garde at the time. There is an amphitheatre, a colonnade with historic photographs, and facilities below grade for the 14 October Foundation. The centrepiece is a ceramic chedi tipped with symbolic crystal torch, raised on a plinth inscribed with martyrs' names and a dove of peace. The space was conceived as a pocket park and invites contemplation. The rage against the tyranny of the time is not expressed. To feel that, a visit to the Memorial Sculpture Garden at Thammasat University is required.

81

Democracy Monument

Ratchadamnoen Klang

Jittasen Aphaiwong, Pum Malakoul architects, Christiani and Nielsen engineers, Corrado Feroci sculptor, 1939

This spectacular Art Deco set piece of People's Party propaganda was designed to dominate the royal processional route from the Grand Palace to Dusit. It stands on circular site in the middle of a 10-lane avenue, like the Arc de Triomphe on the Champs Élysées in Paris where some of the leaders of the coup d'état which unseated the absolute monarchy in 1932 had studied.

Four wing-shaped concrete pylons on

plinths symbolise the nation state and its constitution, the king and religion. The wings rise and protect a six-sided pavilion decorated with swords and topped with a symbol of the constitution. The pavilion has six openings alluding to the Party's principles: sovereignty, safety, prosperity, equality, freedom and public education.

The monument's height and radius, both 24 metres, mark the date of the coup (24 June); the pavilion's height is 3 metres (June being the third month in the Siamese calendar). Nagas animate the plinths which display bas-relief panels in European social realist style by Corrado Feroci. The panels show the revolutionaries planning the coup, the good life that would result from it and soldiers

as guardians of democracy. Subsequent events exposed the régime's delusions and dictatorship, an irony which heightens the monument's power to agitate and inspire. It is the city's prime site for political protest.

82
Ratchadamnoen Contemporary Art Centre
84 Ratchadamnoen Klang
Jittasen Aphaiwong, Pum Malakoul, 1937

The art centre (2013) is an adaptive reuse, by the Office of Contemporary Art and Culture, Ministry of Culture, of one of the avenue's identical buildings from the era of the People's Party. The exterior was repaired and repainted to accentuate its

1930s elevations. Inside, partitions from previous occupations were removed and the space stripped back to the original structure, revealing muted colours and textures on concrete posts, beams and brick walls. There are four storeys. The ground floor is almost twice the height of the others. Vertical circulation is by a staircase and an elevator. The interior spaces flow through exhibition areas which are flexible, to accommodate different types and sizes of art. Natural light penetrates from the street. Floors are concrete. Conservation preserved original features and made the interventions reversible.

The project fits a 2001 master plan to revitalise Ratchadamnoen with art galleries, cultural centres and museums—to be 'the Champs Élysées of South-East Asia'. Another intervention in a similar building, the Rattanakosin Exhibition Hall (100 Ratchadamnoen Klang) by the Crown Property Bureau, was completed in 2010. Its multimedia exhibit over four floors takes virtual journeys around the old city's royal, religious, artistic and social heritage.

83

Maha Chesdabodin Pavilion and Plaza

Ratchadamnoen Klang at Maha Chai Road

1990

This royal plaza was built on the site of the Chalerm Thai Theatre, demolished in 1989 to make way for it. Film fans once queued around the block for first-run movies at the theatre which was a component in the remaking of Ratchadamnoen by the People's Party after the coup of 1932. The plaza's plan, by Sumet Jumsai, is based on the octagonal form of Mahakan Fort. There is a memorial to Rama III (Prince Chesdabodin before ascending the throne) seated in front of a triptych, and a royal reception pavilion in Siamese style. Public space flows inclusively from the sidewalk on Ratchadamnoen to the plaza.

The most welcome benefit this project brought was the revelation of the fantastic roofline of Loha Prasat and Wat Ratchanadda which the movie theatre had obscured.

84

Loha Prasat, Wat Ratchanadda

Maha Chai Road at Ratchadamnoen Klang

Wat Ratchanadda's unique and extraordinary feature appears as if out of some ancient mist. It is called Loha Prasat, or metal castle. Only two metal prasats had been constructed before, one in Sri Lanka in the third century, the other in India 2,500 years ago. There is no trace of the Indian structure. Bangkok's metal castle is said to have been based on accounts of the ruins of the Sri Lankan one. Rama III laid the foundation stone. Rama V completed construction.

The building rises from a square plan in three tiers to a pagoda top, a structural illusion because there are seven levels. A spiral stair gives access to an upper terrace. The roofline is a forest of mondops tipped with 37 spires symbolising virtues in the quest for enlightenment. The interior, a labyrinth of corridors and tiny rooms designed for monks to meditate in, was never occupied. Restoration by the Public Works Department began in 1963 and the structure was strengthened with concrete. The project was eventually completed by the Fine Arts Department in 2007. The mondops were remade with blackened copper plates. Gilding is in progress. Original laterite bricks were exposed inside, where there is a museum with signage and interpretative panels installed in 2010.

85

Wat Thepthidaram

Maha Chai Road

c. 1840

Rama III founded this temple, easily missed in the shadow of Loha Prasat's spiky rooflines, and named it after a favourite daughter. The ubosot is flanked north and south by two chapels in a square compound with Chinese stone statues dotted around. The space is defined at each corner by a prang rising out of an arcaded neoclassical screen. The architecture of the ubosot and viharns is Sino-Siamese. Aside from coloured tiles the roofs have no elaboration, no chofas or bai raka. The gables, however, are awash with Chinese porcelain applied like mosaics to create flowers, garlands and peacocks. Window shutters and doors are decorated beautifully with

gold lacquer and plasterwork of almost rococo playfulness and delicacy. The ubosot houses a white stone Buddha image (Luang Por Khao); the south viharn contains dozens of brass figures of bhikkhunis (female monks).

Parts of the temple crumble in poetic decay which would resonate with its most famous inhabitant, early Rattanakosin-era poet Sunthorn Phu. His abode in a courtyard in the hutong-like monks' residential quarter was restored recently, as was the temple's ho trai, also in the monks' area. Conservation of the ho trai, based on scrupulous research and using traditional materials and craftsmanship, was rewarded with a Unesco heritage award in 2011.

86

Mahakan Fort

Ratchadamnoen Klang at Maha Chai Road

There were 16 gates along the old city wall and 14 forts of which this is one of two which have been preserved. The three-level structure was built with brick rendered with stucco and features a central turret with a wood-framed roof. The octagonal elevations are pierced with crenellations from where cannons could be fired and their gunners protected. The name derives from Phra Kan, the Hindu god of death (wished upon enemies, that is). The fort and a section of the city wall along Maha Chai Road were restored for the Bangkok bicentennial, when efforts to conserve the city's his-

toric core and exploit its tourist potential gained momentum. A controversial plan for a public park behind the fort was resisted by the site's long-established community which the authorities considered unsightly and wanted removed.

87
Phan Fa Bridge
Ratchadamnoen Klang
Carlo Allegri, Mario Tamagno, 1906

The central and outer sections of Ratchadamnoen are linked at this crossing of Klong Rob Krung. It was built and decorated in Roman style as part of Rama V's grand boulevard. There were two broad lanes for traffic which have been widened in stages since the 1950s. The present deck is supported on concrete posts embedded in the canal. The bridge was dismantled and reassembled with its cast- and wrought-iron arches, balustrades and four marble pillars retained. The balustrades are decorated with an Art Nouveau sunflower motif. The pillars have model ships bristling with armaments. The belligerent imagery evokes Rama V's military campaigns which shifted power in the regions to Bangkok.

88
Queen's Gallery
101 Ratchadamnoen Klang
c. 1975

The Phan Fa Bridge branch of Bangkok Bank was an avant-garde addition to the modernism of Ratchadamnoen, to which it responded vigorously with an exterior massed and rendered in brutalist style. The building's concrete elevations, and corners expressed as gigantic fluted columns, have a sculptural quality. At a glance it seems intrusive but it was scaled to match the avenue and the showy corner and rooftop beacon of its neighbour, the Thewet Insurance Build-

ing, once a department store. The square plan is extruded as an octagon, perhaps inspired by Mahakan Fort. Many bricks from the old city wall were unearthed during construction but the opportunity to resurrect the wall was ignored.

The Queen's Gallery Foundation was established in 2003. The building, which the bank rehabilitated, reopened that year to exhibit work by established artists and upcoming talent. Its big unobstructed spaces were given a polished makeover.

89
Old Bangkok Inn
607 Phra Sumen Road
2005

'Boutique hotel' is an overused term, often misleading but not here. The bed and breakfast inn opened as 'a model for urban ecology'. Owner Nantiya Tulyanond was an early adopter of sustainability inspired by the mantra 'reduce, reuse, recycle'. There is solar power, water and energy conservation, and furniture and fixtures made from reclaimed teak. The inn stands on land granted by Rama V to the hotelier's ancestors. The success of the enterprise inspired the family's other eco-friendly hideaway, the Bangkok Tree House (2012), a cluster of stilt house pods made with bamboo and recycled metal. It is located on Bangkrajao, Samut Prakan province, down river from the city.

90
King Prajadhipok Museum
2 Lan Luang Road
Charles Beguelin, 1906

Commanding the north end of Phan Fah Bridge this Italianate design attracts attention with its central bay rising to an octagonal cupola. The 'piano nobile' (in Italian the 'noble floor' where the main

rooms in a palazzo are) is indicated with six Venetian-style windows. The architect was French-Swiss. The client was John Sampson and Son who advertised themselves as 'Naval, Military, Court and Civil Tailors by Special Appointment to H.M. The King of Siam.' The store ceased trading in the 1920s. The Public Works Department office was here from 1933 until 2001. The building was transferred to the King Prajadhipok Institute for which it was rehabilitated as a museum to the life and times of Rama VII, the last absolute monarch.

91

Mahadthai Uthit Bridge

Boriphat Road

Carlo Allegri, Vittorio Novi sculptor, 1914

Donations from civil servants at the Ministry of Interior (Krasuang Mahadthai in Thai) funded the construction of this 'weeping bridge'. It was commissioned by Rama VI as memorial to his father. Three concrete arches support the road deck. Balustrades are embellished with festoons, laurel leaf wreaths and ghilen (a mythical creature in temple art). Pillars with pediments, two on each side of the bridge, are faced with bas-relief figures of folk grieving for Rama V. The sculptor modelled the figures from studio photographs of real people. The style is Roman, sentimental, typical of Italian cemetery art.

92

Wat Saket and Golden Mount

Boriphat Road

Golden Mount was the highest point in Bangkok until the 1960s. It sits on an artificial hill dreamed of by Rama III. His plan was for a giant prang on a brick-clad ziggurat which was pharaonic in conception and scale. Soft soil caused construction works to collapse. Rama IV restarted them in the 1850s with fill from excavations of Klong Phadung Krung Kasem. Trees were planted and brick buttresses laid to stop erosion and a small chedi was built. The present one, which glitters with golden mosaic tiles, was built by Rama V who also strengthened the hill. Erosion was finally stopped in 1957 with a concrete wrap. A pedestrian ramp with 320 steps curves to the top of the mound, 80 metres above the city.

The view is panoramic, with Wat Saket to the north spread out like a patchwork quilt. The wat dates from the Ayutthaya era and was restored around 1800 by Rama II. Its murals were painted in the third reign and redone in the seventh. It was a cremation ground, being outside the city wall (only royals could be cremated inside the old city). Cholera victims were brought here, often too many to be burned quickly. Vultures preyed on the corpses.

Across from the entrance in the soi east of the main compound is the temple's ho trai, a beautiful Ayutthaya-style teak building dating from the first reign. It has murals and decorative panels in Chinese style. The wat hosts the biggest temple fair still held in the Bangkok, during Loy Krathong.

93

Maen Si Pumping Station

Bamrung Muang at Worachak Road

Carlo Allegri, 1914

Rama V saw waterworks in Europe and built similar infrastructure to supply Bangkok with clean water. Before the

king's scheme people dug wells, collected rain and river water or got it from klongs, risking cholera. In 1898 the king established a Department of Sanitation, advised by French and Dutch engineers. Water was diverted from the Chao Phraya River at Chiang Rak upstream of the tidal limit and fed to the city by Klong Prapa, completed in 1914. A central pumping station and water treatment and filtration plant were built (at Rama VI and Nakhon Chaisi roads where two original buildings survive). Filtered water was pumped through underground pipes to Maen Si Pumping Station where it was stored in two tall concrete tanks behind the brick and stucco office building. The office is a pleasing piece of urban design, graceful at the street corner which it turns with a curved bay rising to turret.

The Metropolitan Waterworks Authority moved its HQ in 1990 to Bangkhen Water Treatment Plant. Ideas for adaptive reuse of the Maen Si building include a shelter for homeless people or a library and community arts centre.

94
Krungthai Bank
20 Yukhon 2 Road
Amorn Srivongse, 1970

Set back from the street on a landscaped site, the Suanmali Branch of Krungthai Bank is a conventional concrete, glazed box wrapped with a unique solar screen fabricated with multiple pieces of precast concrete. The screen rises organically to the building's full height on all

four sides and seems rooted in the soil, like the palm trees which complement it. Other solar screens from this period were sharp-edged, futuristic, like the one at the Indra Regent Hotel. All have a retro appeal and are back in fashion as components in energy-efficient design.

Across the street is a spectacular commercial slab block (Prawat Mongkolsamai, 1969) with a separate banking hall and plaza with a reflecting pool and public art, all in the North American corporate style of the time.

95
Manangkhasila Mansion
514 Lan Luang Road
Edward Healey, c. 1925
Western-style heritage houses that survive are often hard to find because second-generation owners sold street frontage for development as land values increased; or they are owned by the government and surrounded by offices. Manangkhasila Mansion can be seen from the street. It was commissioned by Rama VI for a head of the Royal Household. After 1932 it became a government guest house, the HQ of a political party in the 1950s and, most recently, the office of the National Council of Women of Thailand.

The mansion's Tudor Revival style is a nostalgic vision from its English architect. The composition is typically picturesque with pitched roofs, dormer windows and gables. The half-timbered exterior looks authentic but is simply wood-battened

decoration, not a wood frame. The garden is extensive. The original driveway and lamps are extant as is the gatehouse, also half-timbered style.

96
Prince Damrong Rajanupab Museum and Library
204 Lan Luang Road
Karl Siegfried Döring, 1911
Two heritage buildings accessed by an alley are hidden behind a row of shophouses. They are legacies of Prince Damrong, a son of Rama IV, revered as the father of Thai history. His house has been maintained by his descendants who completed a restoration in 1996. The second building, the Damrong Rajanupab Library (c. 1950), preserves his books and other materials given to the nation by his daughter. Before turning to literature and writing, he was Minister of Education, Minister of the Interior and Deputy Commander-in-Chief of the army

(in the garden there is a statue of the prince in uniform).

The house, Varadis Palace, is a page from the period when Western architectural styles were fashionable among the ruling class. Its German architect also designed the contemporaneous Ban Puen Palace at Phetchaburi and Bangkhunphrom Palace in similar style, which is Jugendstil, the German branch of Art Nouveau. The structure sits on a concrete raft foundation. The exterior is stucco over bricks, with pilasters decorated with a lotus petal pattern. The interiors, a mix of Chinoiserie and Western styles, are preserved much as the prince left them in 1932, when he was arrested during the coup and forced into temporary exile in Penang, then a British colony. The house stands in mature landscaping across a narrow klong from the parking lot where the library stands. Prime Minister Pridi Banomyong allocated funds for the latter, which is unconventional with two bow-shaped glazed bays rising through three floors.

97
Nang Loeng Market
Nakhon Sawan Road
Public Works Department, 1900

Floating markets survive as tourist sights. They were once the only way to shop when Bangkok was a water city of klongs, stilt houses and floating homes. Nang Loeng Market was the city's first purpose-built on land. It opened in a walkable neighbourhood which was cosmopolitan and prosperous. Migrant communities settled and traded, including Mon people from whose pottery jars the market was named. Chinese merchants occupied new shophouses, bureaucrats and soldiers were based in the emerging Dusit government quarter and aristocrats lived in nearby mansions. Klong Phadung Krung Kasem and a tram line made the market widely accessible.

Crown Properties renovated and re-roofed it in 2007, preserving teakwood parts of the structure and the shophouses which surround the market hall and are integrated with it. Restoration revealed stone markers on some buildings with notices in Thai, Chinese and English declaring their rental status. The neighbourhood is typical of Bangkok's early urbanisation. Markets and old wooden houses were tucked away in alleys. Brick and stucco two-storey shophouses lined the main roads. The streetscape on Nakhon Sawan Road is an intact example.

Next door to the market, in Trok Nang Loeng, is a barn-like, teakwood structure used as a warehouse. It was originally Sala Chalerm Thani Theatre, also known as Nang Loeng Cinema, which opened in 1918 screening silent films accompanied by a brass band. It is thought to be the oldest cinema in Thailand.

98
Rajadamnern Boxing Stadium
Ratchadamnoen Nok
Public Works Department, 1945

This was built on the order of Prime Minister Phibun who believed that sport—here Muay Thai, the martial art from 13th-century Sukhothai—would improve the moral and physical health of the nation. Work began in 1941 but the Italian contractor was unable to complete the contract due to shortages of material during the Second World War. The first kick boxing contest was held at the end of 1945, alfresco as in a Roman amphitheatre. In 1951 the venue was roofed with a trussed ring beam supporting a dome fabricated by Christiani and Nielsen, builders of the Democracy Monument. On fight nights neon blazes and fans invade the sidewalk below a 1930s movie theatre-style façade. The sport is illustrated on bas-relief panels on each side of the marquee.

99

United Nations Conference Centre

Ratchadamnoen Nok at Krung Kasem Road

Tridhosyuth Devakul, 1993

The UN bureau in Asia was set up in Shanghai in 1947 but had to be evacuated to Singapore during the civil war in China. It was moved to Bangkok in 1949 where it became the UN regional head office, located in temporary accommodation at the Ministry of Finance and Parutsakawan Palace until Sala Santitham, or Peace Hall, opened on this site in 1954. The Secretariat and other buildings followed in the 1970s. Peace Hall was demolished to make way for the Conference Centre. The design simplifies Modern Thai style, with a roof divided into visually overlapping sections fan-shaped in plan. The foyer is a four-level space with galleries set back to create a spacious, naturally lit void inside the entrance, which leads to conference halls, meeting rooms and a restaurant. The complex has been called the 'Geneva of Asia'.

Directly outside the UN is Makkhawan Rangsan Bridge (Carlo Allegri, Mario Tamagno, 1906) crossing Klong Phadung Krung Kasem. Its proportions have been altered by road widening but ornate heritage features have been kept. Nearby on Krung Kasem Road are two royal, second class temples; Wat Makutkasat west of the UN complex and Wat Somanas to the east, both begun by Rama IV to make merit and to make the banks of the canal look as Ayutthaya had been.

100

Ladawan Palace

173 Ratcha Sima Road

G. Bruno, 1908

Rama V commissioned many mansions for his numerous children. This was built for a son, Prince of Lopburi, who returned to Siam after studies in England. The interiors, which are luxurious with Euro-Asian decor, once echoed to music performed for guests by the Red Palace Thai Orchestra which the prince and his bride formed. He was Viceroy of southern Siam from 1915 to 1925, returned to be Minister of Interior and died in 1932.

The building is referred to colloquially

as the Red Palace, the colour of the compound walls which have ornate gates. The style is Renaissance, from Italy as the architect was. There is a porte cochère attached to the front elevation, which dissolves to an asymmetric composition with a three-storey wing and four-storey octagonal turret. The structure is brick, clad with stucco applied like stone; there are stucco pilasters and decorative details, fanlight windows and wide eaves.

The palace was occupied by the Japanese during the Second World War. It was briefly a base for the Allies in 1945, when it was bought from the prince's heirs by the Crown Property Bureau which is based here. The bureau, which evolved from Rama V's administration, was established in 1936. It has a portfolio of heritage buildings and, since 2000 when a special department was set up, a conservation programme for many of them. Ladawan Palace and its garden are part of a complex which has several modern buildings and contemporary landscaping. It was restored recently and houses the Library for Sustainable Development, a resource for the 'sufficiency economy' promoted by Rama IX.

101
Royal Thai Army Headquarters
113 Ratchadamnoen Nok
Public Works Department, 1909

This disciplined neoclassical façade presents itself for inspection with pilasters

like a rank of soldiers on parade, commanded by Rama V's emblem on its pediment. The building was inaugurated by the king for the Royal Military Academy which had relocated from Rattanakosin Island (its building there was taken over by the Royal Thai Survey Department). The academy (Chulachomklao Royal Military Academy since 1948) moved to a new complex in Nakhon Nayok Province in 1986. The old building was rehabilitated for the Royal Thai Army Museum in 1996, the Golden Jubilee year of Rama IX, but did not open permanently to the public. The museum was first established by Rama V at the Ministry of Defence.

Another neoclassical design built for the army can be seen in a compound opposite, on the east side of the avenue. Both show Rama V's intention to line the full length of Ratchadamnoen in European style.

102
Government House
Phitsanulok at Nakhon Phathom Road
Annibale Rigotti, Mario Tamagno, Ercole Manfredi architects; Cesare Ferro artist, 1926

Rama VI commissioned this Venetian Gothic fantasy for one of his aides-de-camp. It is a magical spectacle, like an operatic stage with loggias for arias and cupolas for serenades. The entire edifice is an echo from the stones of Venice, with references to St. Mark's Cathedral, the Doge's Palace, and the Ca' d'Oro on the Grand Canal.

In 1941 the government acquired the property, originally called Villa Norasingh, also known as the Thai Khu Fa Building, to prevent the Japanese buying it as their embassy. Luxurious marble interiors with Venetian arches and decorated ceilings host prime minister's cabinet meetings, foreign dignitaries and other state functions. The adjacent Santi Maitri Building was begun in 1954, to

host press conferences and receptions. Its interior is a covered cloister. A canopy connects it to the original structure whose Venetian style it emulates.

Nearby is Villa Phitsanulok (426–428 Phitsanulok Road), designed by the same architects for another royal aide-de-camp. The Venetian theme is the same and equally entertaining. The government took over the villa in 1942. It survived a plan to build a new Ministry of Justice on the site. It was rehabilitated in the 1980s as an official residence of the prime minister but was only used for one night because it was said to be haunted. It is not accessible to the public but Government House is, annually on National Children's Day.

103
Wat Benchamabopit
Si Ayutthaya at Nakhon Pathom Road
Prince Narisara Nuvativongse, Carlo Allegri, Mario Tamagno, begun 1900

Fame precedes this monument to Rama V's patronage. He intended that his ashes be placed here, which they are under the bronze Buddha image in the Uposatha Hall. The temple is one of the highlights on tourist itineraries, less for being the king's mausoleum and more because the hall is exotic, clad with Carrara marble (hence the popular name, the Marble Temple). The expectation is that the building will be gigantic. In reality, this concrete structure with Siamese cladding is smaller than older halls at other royal, first class wats.

Prince Naris, half brother of the king and Minister of Public Works, supervised the project. He designed the hall to accommodate a replica of a Sukhothai-era Buddha image from which molds were made in Phitsanulok province. It was cast in 1901 at the Royal Navy foundry, as was the wat's boundary fence. The prince commissioned top talent from the Fine Arts Department for the decorative scheme which is entirely Siamese. The Buddha image is framed by a flame

motif. The ceiling is coffered, elaborate with painted beams and rosettes. Doors display celestial beings embossed in copper panels or painted gold. The walls, painted in a repeat pattern during the sixth reign, show a deity with hands clasped in prayer. There are eight niches, each decorated in 1942 with a painted image of a celebrated chedi. There are two framed photographs, one of Rama V as a monk, the other of the prince.

In soft focus the hall could be in Italy, a chapel in a ducal palace which, coincidentally or not, is how the interior space is proportioned and feels. The project was a collaboration between the prince, master builder Korn Hongsakul, and the Public Works Department's senior architect and engineer both of whom were Italian. The hall is built on a cruciform plan. In addition to the Carrara marble, the coloured marble floor tiles were shipped from Italy. The stained glass windows were crafted in Florence in 1954.

There is no mistaking the exterior style, a conflation of all that is exciting and elegant in Rattanakosin architecture. Two singhas flank the main entrance which, in keeping with tradition, faces the rising sun. The five-tiered roof flows like a wave in peaks and troughs across the elevation, its golden naga boards and cho fas catching the sun. Glittering on the four gables are seals of the fifth reign. The hall's west elevation is integrated with a cloister where 52 Buddha statues collected for the king by Prince Damrong line the walls. There are two more lions, flanking a niche on the west wall where a Buddha image stands.

The temple grounds are extensive. There are row-houses for monks, a school and other halls and pavilions. Song Phanuat Hall, where Rama V entered monkhood in 1873, was moved from the Grand Palace and reconstructed here; the wat's bodhi tree was planted by him in 1900. Si Somdej Pavilion displays a rosewood drum captured when his forces crushed a Shan revolt in 1903. Water sprinkles from fountains in a pretty klong dug in 1900. The canal is crossed by three cast-iron bridges made in Milan in 1902; the profile of Rama V, elephant tusks and teacups representing medals, ivory and china distributed for fund-raising in 1900 appear on their medallions.

Wat Benchamabopit means 'the temple of the fifth king'. Merit making was among the motives for its construction. The king wished to make amends for the destruction of two old temples when

Dusit Palace was created nearby. He also wanted to showcase the best of traditional Siamese style in a city he had done much to modernise and westernise.

104
Wat Benchamabopit School
Likhit Road
Public Works Department, 1903
The school is located next door to the monks' residential quarter at the Marble Temple. It was established in 1900

by Rama V for public education. The oldest structure is the King Chulalongkorn Building, styled like a Renaissance palazzo brushed with baroque. Two wings flank a centre block in a compact composition with classical elements and wide eaves. The façade is stucco, imitating hand-carved stone on the main floor. The central elevation has twin Tuscan columns astride the entrance; pilasters have Corinthian-style capitals. The louvred shutters appear to be original. The rear elevation was pragmatic, with two recesses to maximise light and ventilation in the classrooms. At the front the entrance bay has a baroque split pediment and a plaque where the school name appears in Thai.

105
Parutsakawan Palace
Ratchadamnoen Nok at Si Ayutthaya Road
Mario Tamagno, 1906
Villa Parutsakawan on Ratchadamnoen was a gift from Rama V to one of his sons, Prince Chakrabongse, who had returned as a graduate from the army academy at St. Petersburg. Villa Chitralada at Si Ayutthaya Road was built for another son, Prince Vajiravudh. When he became Rama VI he gave it to his brother and named the mansions Parutsakawan Palace. Villa Parutsakawan has a conventional Renaissance theme. Villa Chitralada is a surprise.

Architect Mario Tamagno had arrived in Siam in 1900 with a government contract for 25 years. He joined Carlo Allegri who, from 1893 to 1916, was chief engineer at the Public Works Department. Their partnership produced many

of Bangkok's best buildings of the time. Tamagno's output ranged from classical to chic. Around 1900, Art Nouveau was the most fashionable art style in Europe. Villa Chitralada is fresh from that bohemian scene, with a sensuous porte cochère and plaster decoration in Stile Liberty. Few if any cities in Asia can boast Art Nouveau buildings of this quality.

In 1952 the National Police Department moved into the compound. Villa

Chitralada's salons and rococo ballroom later became the Royal Thai Police Museum, which is now housed nearby (Public Works Department, 2012) in a revamped 1960s concrete building to which two steel and glass boxes were added. One of the boxes has fretwork copied from the villa's rear porch, rendered as a solar screen; the other box is minimalist, elegant. Both are scaled sympathetically to the villa and its garden whose landscaping has been upgraded with care.

106

Suan Kularb Palace

Ratcha Sima and Si Ayutthaya roads

Suan Kularb has two buildings, a rambling chalet (Carlo Allegri, c. 1900) and a mansion (Mario Tamagno, 1912) both built for sons of Rama V. The chalet looks like a Victorian hunting lodge, with half-timbered gables and lookout tower; the mansion is colonial style, with an interior boasting a two-storey Moorish-style throne hall with a gallery on the upper level. From 1938 to 1941 the palace was the prime minister's office. In 1945 it was the clandestine HQ of the Office of Strategic Services (OSS) whose agents were based here, including Alexander MacDonald (founder of the *Bangkok Post*) and James H. W. Thompson (better known as Jim Thompson). The chalet was the OSS office, the hall the living quarters. After the war it became a prime ministerial residence and later the army's Internal Security Operations Command. It was restored as a royal residence in the 1990s.

107

Rama V Monument

Royal Plaza

Georges Saulo and Clovis Masson, 1908

Folklore has it that the horse on which Rama V sits is French, a wild horse he tamed by feeding and then riding it, impressing his European hosts. The horse is indeed French. The bronze statue, which shows the king as Field Marshal, was cast in Paris following his second visit to Europe in 1907. The king posed for sculptors Saulo and Masson (the former did the figure, the latter the horse).

It is a magnificent piece, the first equestrian statue of a Siamese king. It commemorates the 40th anniversary of the king's coronation in 1908. After it arrived at the port of Bangkok it was transported to punctuate the plaza in front of the Ananta Samakhom Throne Hall. The urban tableau thus created—

in the European imperial tradition of monument making—offers an insight into the king's personality and stature. When he returned from Europe in 1907 he disembarked from the *Maha Chakri*, his Scottish-built royal yacht, and rode in an automobile along the avenue, passing through nine decorative arches erected for the occasion. The statue has become a shrine—people leave offerings, cigars evidently being favoured by the king—and is where he is honoured on October 23, Chulalongkorn Day.

108
Royal Amporn Garden Pavilion
Royal Plaza
Krisda and Associates, 1972

This gleaming pavilion on the edge of a lake updates the urban design of Ratchadamnoen with monumental modernism. It suggests a new city about to be created but it was a one-off project by Crown Properties, designed as a conference hall. It looks as if it could have been the National Assembly. Perhaps it should have—it is big enough with a multi-purpose hall and it has presence. Its austere almost classical composition is enlivened by the creative engineering of the roof, a reinforced concrete slab folded like a concertina to distribute the load and cantilevered to cover the building and its upper-deck terraces.

109

Ananta Samakhom Throne Hall

Royal Plaza

Mario Tamagno, Annibale Rigotti, Ercole Manfredi architects; Carlo Allegri, Emilio Giovanni Gollo engineers; Cesare Ferro, Galileo Chini, Carlo Rigoliartists; Vittorio Novi, Rodolfo Nolli sculptors, 1906–1915

Rama V visited royal palaces in Europe, liked what he saw and commissioned this stupendous souvenir after he returned to Bangkok in 1897. It was built to impress the king's power upon all who saw it. The design team was Italian, directed by Chao Phraya Yommarat, Minister of Public Works. Blueprints were ready in 1907. Construction took eight years, too long for the king to see it finished. He died in 1910.

A concrete raft foundation was conceived by engineer Emilio Giovanni Gollo to distribute the considerable weight of the building's Carrara marble across the soft ground (this technique was not new: Wat Bot Samsen floats on a teak log raft). The exterior style is neoclassical spiced with baroque. The interior style is Renaissance, in plan derived from St Peter's in Rome. The religious typology connected the building's Western form with the divinity of the Chakri dynasty.

The interior is breathtaking. The vaulted and domed space has a decorated ceiling teeming with life, like a temple mural above the conventions of its Corinthian columns. Names of Chakri kings are surrounded by garudas, cherubs, flowers, foliage, birds, deer and elephants. The aesthetic is both Art Nouveau and neoclassical; the allegorical frescoes of dynastic themes in the domes recall those by Raphael in the papal apartments in Rome. Rama I is shown on a battle elephant returning from Cambodia; Rama II and Rama III, respectively, inspecting Wat Arun and the Grand Palace; Rama IV as the guardian of religious freedom; Rama V freeing slaves. An additional fresco was painted at the entrance to the hall, illustrating the coronation of Rama VI in 1911.

The building was commandeered by the People's Party in 1932 and rebranded the nation's parliament, which it remained until 1974 when the National

Assembly opened. Since 1992 the hall has showcased 'Arts of the Kingdom', an exhibition of the finest arts and crafts from the Queen Sirikit Institute.

110
Abhisek Dusit Throne Hall
Uthong Nai Road
Mario Tamagno, 1904

This audience chamber with an arabesque swirl of wooden fretwork and an interior which would make a sultan swoon was where Rama V received foreign ambassadors. The exterior features Art Nouveau details but essentially the effect is of Orientalism, the Western interest in Islamic and Mughal arts. The theme continues inside in a Moorish manner. The hall is a column-free space with carved brackets supporting a flat ceiling, coffered with eight-pointed stars. Restoration since 1993 has revealed the original paint colours. Contemporary cabinets display arts and crafts from the Queen Sirikit Institute. The porte cochère is the most elaborate in Bangkok.

111
Royal Elephant Stables
Uthong Nai Road
1906

White elephants are revered as auspicious. Any found must be presented to the monarch. The national flag from the second reign until 1917, when Rama VI had it modernised, was adorned with the image of one. The kingdom's prestigious honour, The Most Exalted Order of the White Elephant, was established in 1861. The traditional pavilions here

were built to house two white elephants, presented respectively to Rama V and Rama VII. After an enclosure for a white elephant presented to Rama IX was built at Chitralada Palace in 1966 the pavilions were declared a historic site and rehabilitated as a museum, opened in 1992 but since closed. A new venue, the Royal Elephants' Stable Museum, in refurbished stables at Chitralada Palace opened in 2013.

112
Vimanmek Mansion
16 Ratchawithi Road
Prince Narisara Nuvativongse 1901

This belle époque caprice, 'the world's largest golden teakwood mansion', dates from 1892 when it was begun on Koh Si Chang, a summer getaway favoured by Rama V. The island became a security risk in 1893 when French gunboats appeared in the Gulf of Siam during a political crisis that led to a short war. The king revisited the site in 1901 and ordered the partly built dwelling, which was assembled with wood pegs, not nails, dismantled for relocation to Dusit Palace where he laid the foundation stone. The master builder was Korn Hongsakul, whose family had built royal temples and palaces since 1782. Vimanmek translates as 'palace of angels in the clouds'. The architecture is refined and delicate on an L-shaped plan. There are three storeys, two in teak resting on a brick and concrete ground floor. The entrance curves outward in graceful welcome. There is a gingerbread fringe around all eaves and on an octagonal four-storey tower.

Spaces in the mansion were demarcated like the outer, middle and inner courts at the Grand Palace. The tower was the king's sanctum, with a study, bedroom, dressing room and the first European-style bathroom in Siam. Other rooms open off one side of corridors which have exterior views and were airy with natural ventilation provided by windows, and vents high on the interior walls (today there is air conditioning due to the numbers of visitors). Asian and European antiques and furniture from royal collections complement the Victorian decor. Not all pieces are original to the mansion but the past is palpable in the semi-circular throne hall, in the cabinet room where the king directed affairs of state, in the dining room decorated with royal portraits, the music salon with the original piano, and trophy room with guns and animal skulls on the walls.

The mansion overlooks a lake called the Jade Pond, part of a system of canals dug to irrigate the gardens. There are shaded promenades and a faux Siamese village built in 1904. Rama V moved again in 1906, to Ambara Sathan Villa which is still a royal residence nearby. Vimanmek was mothballed in 1932 and used for storage. Queen Sirikit had it restored for Bangkok's bicentennial. The original octagonal foundation remains on Koh Si Chang.

113

National Assembly

Uthong Nai Road

Bhol Chulasewok, Public Works Department, 1973

Parliament was housed in the Ananta Samakhom Throne Hall until this purpose-built venue opened on a site formerly part of Dusit Palace. The gate and cast-iron fence are from the era of Rama V but the National Assembly building is from the brave new world of Le Corbusier. Its brutalist concrete forms are a sculptural façade for the assembly chamber which is awesome with a concrete-ribbed roof. The building placed the nation in the mainstream of contemporary global design but it does not dominate its city as other parliaments do. It has a muted presence at the extremity of the royal and government quarter, opposite the main entrance to Dusit Zoo.

Artists were commissioned for murals and other forms of public art—there is a statue (Sanan Silakorn) of Rama VII outside—but the building was criticised for not looking sufficiently Thai. That deficiency—if it is one—may be rectified following an architectural competition in 2009 for a new parliament complex. The design chosen is a sprawling ziggurat out of some imagined past, with a golden spire suggesting the Buddhist cosmos intended for a site in Dusit overlooking the Chao Phraya River.

114

Dusit Zoo

Uthong Nai Road

Called in Thai 'Khao Din', the zoo was

a royal park established by Rama V. Its lakes were created when the site was landscaped for the royal family and guests to stroll on winding paths and enjoy scenic vistas. Special for Rama V was the prospect from the lake of the Ananta Samakhom Throne Hall being built at the time. After 1932 the city administration developed the grounds as a public zoo which opened in 1938, the first in Siam. Since 1954 it has been run by the state Zoological Park Organisation. The earliest exhibits were the offspring of deer Rama V had imported from Java, and animals from Saranrom Park. Now there is a menagerie of more than 1,600 creatures in cages and compounds.

There are traditional salas by the lake and other pavilions. The oldest of them is the Glass House (c. 1920), formerly the director's office now used by zoological associations. It is a charming period piece with a hipped roof, diamond-shaped tiles and a ridge of fretwork, located close to the secondary entrance on Rama V Road. Rama V's original scheme is evident in the lyrical synthesis of landscape, lakes and views. The vista of the Ananta Samakhom Throne Hall remains as he saw it.

115
Vajiravudh College
197 Ratchawithi Road

The college is an all-boys boarding school, originally Royal Pages College founded by Rama VI at the Grand Palace in 1910. It was renamed Vajiravudh College in his honour by his brother Rama VII in 1926. It occupies a large site with a lake. Rama VI planned it as an alternative to the tradition that every king builds a temple. He laid the foundation stone in 1915. The inspiration for the organisation and ethos of the college was British boarding schools and universities but its architecture is not a copy of Oxford where the king studied. The original scheme blended Siamese and Western built forms and decorative details, which influenced the design of several subsequent buildings at the college.

The centrepiece is the Assembly Hall (Edward Healey, 1917), a chapel-like ceremonial space raised above a ground floor which is open for ventilation like a traditional Thai house. The tiered roof is an echo of Uposatha Hall at the Marble Temple; the gables are carved with symbols of Hindu gods. Steps rise to a Gothic porch which leads to a double-height, side- and clerestory-lit hall flavoured with Gothic Revival, like a church in England from where the architect came. The architecture, contemporaneous with and similar to the early buildings at Chulalongkorn University is in the 'Royal Architectural Style of King Vajiravudh' which became known as Modern Thai.

116
Chitralada Royal Railway Station
Sawankhalok Road
Ercole Manfredi, c. 1915

The mainline railway runs past Chitralada Palace, conveniently close for a regal station. Its style is central European, neoclassical, as if transplanted from the Hapsburg Empire. It is entered by steps from a porte cochère. The structure is a square pavilion with screens for ventilation, Ionic columns around the walls, wrought iron and glass panelled doors and painted garudas below a shallow dome. The exterior has a drum-like central tower with a larger dome ringed with garlands and medallions imitating heraldry. The platform is tiled and sheltered by a colonnade. The royal train was a familiar sight here when monarchs toured the provinces by rail or travelled to the seaside palace at Hua Hin. The station is used rarely now but is well maintained by the State Railway of Thailand.

117
Chitralada Palace
Ratchawithi Road
Ercole Manfredi c. 1915

Stile Liberty. The gate on Rama V Road is the old main entrance. It is elaborate, ceremonial, guarded by two pavilions reached by a bridge with decorated lamp posts and ornamental urns. The ensemble is crescent-shaped, neoclassical in plan, flanked both sides by two more pavilions.

The main checkpoint is now on Ratchawithi Road. The palace has evolved as a showcase for Rama IX's initiatives in sustainable development to aid the rural economy. These include experimental paddy fields, a herbarium, fish pond, rice mill and dairy farm, a small refinery to produce gasohol, and a solar-powered

The main residence of the Royal Family is set in a kilometer-square, landscaped compound surrounded by a protective canal. The avenues parallel to the klong are tree-lined, as most were in Bangkok when the palace and its European-style villa were built for Rama VI. Privacy is guaranteed by the army, the canal and an iron fence. Each corner of the canal has a baroque fountain. Royal yellow flags flap like butterflies along the perimeter punctuated by ornate sentry boxes, bridges and entrance pavilions in

house. The palace is home to the Queen Sirikit Institute which attracts talent from around the kingdom to revive traditional arts and crafts.

Scala Theatre, Siam Square

4

Victory Monument to Phloen Chit

This tour follows the BTS (Bangkok Mass Transit System), also called skytrain. It started running in 1999 and re-mapped the city. Transit riders oriented their experience of time and space to the rhythm of the rails and the locations of the stations, as drivers map the city by the on- and off-ramps of the expressways. The 'skytrain' name came from similar system in Vancouver built by SNC-Lavalin which led the Bangkok project until a change of government saw it cancelled. It was revived by the BMA as the BTS with another consortium to build it, by which time the skytrain label had been used by the press and stuck.

There are two lines, Sukhumvit and Silom (see tour 5), which run on an elevated guideway on concrete columns. These stride boldly along the middle of the streets, which ensured relatively simple construction. The elevated stations were criticised because they turned the sidewalks below into gloomy strips, polluted by traffic fumes. When the more recent MRT (Metropolitan Rapid Transit) metro was planned it was decided that the tracks and stations should all be underground. But for fans of urban infrastructure—or anyone thrilled by city life—skytrain is exciting and futuristic and its stations look the part. The multilevel Siam interchange where the two lines intersect is a densely layered and peopled urban space of walkways, escalators, platforms and rail tracks supported on massive concrete posts and beams. At night in the rain it could be a film set from *Blade Runner*.

The trains whoosh above traffic but the BTS did not reduce the number of cars in Bangkok. However, congestion would have been worse without the investment in it, which was prompted by the city's reputation for having the world's worst traffic jams and their cost to the economy. And it has brought mobility and convenience. Many buildings in this chapter are within easy reach of stations, or visible from them or from the trains. Victory Monument, for example, is best seen from skytrain whose guideway curves around it (the eponymous station was initially to have been the end of the line). The monument was commissioned, and erected on a grand circular plaza laid out for it, by the government in 1941 after a short war with France, a piece of urban design intended to match anything in Paris.

Skytrain reveals Bangkok as a patchwork of global architecture from whatever source took the client's or the architect's fancy. Riders cross a cityscape of expedient and haphazard development, some of it pleasing, all of it varied. South of Victory Monument the BTS runs along a strip of hyper-consumerism that stretches east from Mah Boon Krong (MBK) to the Central Embassy project. It passes Siam Square, a dense cluster of three- and four-storey buildings on a grid of walkable sois planned in the 1960s on land leased from Chulalongkorn University. The zone, with stores and pop-up sublets paying affordable rents, has long been a hip hangout. It also has the Scala, the best preserved movie theatre in South-East Asia. A question mark hangs over the theatre's future—and the hip hangouts—because Siam Square is being redeveloped. Chula, built on land granted by Rama V for education and to provide an income to support that purpose, is exploiting its assets to fund facilities and academic programmes. Siam Square's facelift, part of a 1997 master plan for land use, is part of that strategy.

Opposite Siam Square on Rama I Road is Siam Centre (1976), Bangkok's first mall, built on land leased from the Crown Property Bureau. To the east is an up-market shopping, hotel and business district which grew around the Erawan Hotel (1956). Sandwiched between these zones is a temple, Wat Pathumwanaram, part of an older fabric that survives in places along Klong Saen Saep, 'the canal of stings', so called for mosquitoes which tormented the Laotian war captives who dug it in the 1830s for Rama III. It was a strategic canal, not only for rice and other agricultural producers to supply the city from the central plain but also as a military route to Cambodia. It also opened up this eastern edge of the old city for development. Wat Pathumwanaram and Sra Pathum Palace were built by Rama IV, followed by aristocrats who built mansions. The canal is one of the few still used for public transit. It crosses the top of Witthayu Road (Wireless Road) which was constructed in 1920 to link Phloen Chit and Rama IV roads. Witthayu got its name when the government radio station was located at its south end in 1929. It was and to an extent is still a leafy embassy quarter which remains tree-lined for much of its length despite recent high-rise densification.

Stitched into the patchwork are a few old homes and two outstanding heritage attractions, Suan Pakkad Palace and the Jim Thompson House, both collections of Siamese houses preserved in the 1950s, a time when the local vernacular was ignored by most Thais and foreigners in favour of modernity and air conditioning. Traditional houses are now status symbols; reproductions are not uncommon. Their visual style has been co-opted by tourism to lend resorts and hotels heritage character. The Siam Intercontinental Hotel (1966), demolished to make way for the massive Siam Paragon mall, was an inventive example. The look has become a cliché but the functional and eco-friendly qualities of traditional houses are being revisited by architects in search of sustainable contemporary design.

Among the new high-rises is the Ecoplex, a serious shot at sustainability with Leadership in Energy and Environmental Design (LEED) Platinum certification awarded by the US Green Building Council. It is one of an increasing number of projects which seek this international accreditation over somewhat confusing home-grown versions. The skytrain route is booming with new construction, not all of it green but often shaped oddly like the Ecoplex, or Central Embassy, a curvy high-rise on a former section of the British Embassy.

118

Ministry of Foreign Affairs

443 Si Ayutthaya Road

Architects 49, 1999

The ministry, established by Rama IV in 1840, relocated from Saranrom Palace to this purpose-built headquarters. Its scale is in keeping with the historic Dusit district on whose eastern edge it is located. Its prominent style is postmodern with contextual references to the past. The main entrance can be read as a classical pediment or a Siamese gable; the colonnades as references to Rama V's Italianate buildings or temple cloisters. A ceremonial hall and other functions are grouped in an inner courtyard as if in a palace. The office components on either side are in the architects' international modernist style. Postmodern and modernist styles seem unlikely allies but they are in accord here thanks to the development's rational plan.

119

Lecture Hall, Faculty of Science, Mahidol University

272 Rama VI Road

Amon Sriwongse, 1968

This flying saucer-shaped hall hovers above the ground where there is open space for students to gather, perhaps to be spirited away into the void at its centre. The style is brutalist with concrete that makes no apologies. The building is functional and structurally inventive. It is bowl-shaped and ribbed around the base where the texture of formwork is visible above stone-clad footings and pilotis. Clerestory-lit lecture rooms curve around the upper level, the slope of their tiered seating expressed in the building's underside where access stairs punch upward. The roof is round, fan-like with radiating striations and clad with ceramic tiles. An oculus with star-shaped glass panels lets sunlight penetrate the central void—a magical effect and a symbol of enlightenment.

Phayathai campus includes Ramathibodi Hospital, the Hospital for Tropical Diseases, and associated faculties of Mahidol University. The university's origin can be traced to Siriraj Hospital founded by Rama V in 1888.

120
Phaya Thai Palace
315 Ratchawithi Road
Mario Tamagno, Annibale Rigotti, 1922

One of Rama V's late fancies begun in 1909, originally a royal hobby farm by Samsen canal, this palace was enlarged at considerable cost by Rama VI who lived here until 1925. In 1926 it was rehabilitated by the Royal State Railways as the Phaya Thai Hotel from where Siam's first radio station broadcast. The hotel closed in 1932. Military medics occupied the site which became a hospital in 1952, expanded since 1969 as the army's Phramongkutklao Medical Centre whose office moved out of the old royal residence in 1989.

In the ever changing city it is astonishing to find the palace intact with its original melodic variations still sounding. Thewarat Sapharom Hall, built as a royal audience chamber for Rama V and used as a theatre by Rama VI is used as a concert hall. The wood and glass structure is cruciform in plan with a balcony below a barrel-vaulted ceiling and central dome. Architect Rigotti who had worked in Istanbul played a Turkish melody in its harmonious design.

The palace is an orchestration of old Europe. There are Italianate tiled loggias and belle-époque decor. There is a Bavarian fairy-tale castle tower attached to the Chakri Throne Hall (the tower is replicated in a nearby bird house). The hall's porte cochère is attached to a pavilion, Café de Norasingha, a recreation of Bangkok's first European café which opened in Dusit during the sixth reign. Outside there is an Italian fountain with a swan and cherubs, like those adorning palazzi gardens in Tuscany.

The gardens here were laid out in Italian style. Behind the palace there is a classical folly inspired by Hadrian's Villa, with Corinthian columns, a dome and statuary. It faces a pond with a fountain and sculpture by Corrado Feroci of water god Varuna. There is a teakwood pavilion in Arts and Crafts style, once Rama VI's study. His activities included building Dusit Thani, a 1/15th-scale model city, long lost. A statue of him stands at the front of the complex. The Palace Conservation Foundation conducts tours of the property at weekends.

121
Bangkok School for the Blind
420 Ratchawithi Road
Sumet Jumsai, 1973

The school is run by the Foundation for the Blind in Thailand. It was established in 1939 by an American teacher, Genevieve Caulfield, whose statue (Misiem Yipintsoi, 1983) was erected here after her death in 1972. She provided vocational training to the blind and partially sighted who were shunned socially at the time. Her mission was aided by the fact that her first pupil was a daughter of Prince Damrong. The school was a rented house in Silom until the government provided the present site. A purpose-built facility was commissioned from a young Thai architect fresh from study in France and England.

To minimise costs the concrete structure was system-built. All components were prefabricated and assembled onsite. The structural concept and its resolution are visible still, although the two-storey box was originally raised on pilotis après Le Corbusier to create naturally ventilated open space at grade, since filled in. The elevation's vertical brise-soleil were angled to provide solar shade and to catch the wind. The composition was anchored by a central pylon with a stairwell between vertical ribs from which corridors flowed with floors painted brightly to aid partially sighted navigation. The building is still used as the school's classroom block.

122
Xavier Hall
Soi 12, Ratchawithi Road
Krisda and Associates, 1972

The chapel's sermon is a subtle blend of modern design and traditional Thai style by Krisda Arunvongse, one of a new generation of Thai architects whose members refreshed the local scene after study in Europe or North America. Built for the Catholic Jesuit order, the chapel has a tiled, tent-like roof with concrete ribs visible inside. Both sides of the roof climb steeply to meet at a flat lateral ridge which is skylit to let light penetrate the sanctuary and illuminate the altar's cross. The building sits on a podium where the concrete ribs form colonnades open to natural ventilation. The front elevation is glazed, set back under the roof's curved eaves creating a Thai-style

overlap; the fish-scale pattern of roof tiles is also Thai.

The adventurous use of concrete is typical of late modernism, a breakaway from purist rectilinear and modular architectural theology which can be seen in the other buildings in the compound. The first Jesuit mission to Siam began in 1607 and lasted until the fall of Ayutthaya. At the chapel entrance is small pond where two bricks are embedded in the wall. They are relics, the smaller thought to be from the ruins of a Jesuit church in Ayutthaya and the larger from Lopburi. The present mission has been at this leafy location by Samsen canal since 1958.

123
Victory Monument
Intersection of Phahonyothin, Phaya Thai and Ratchawithi roads
Pum Malakoul, Corrado Feroci sculptor, 1941

This rocket-like monument around which skytrain loops was commissioned by Field Marshal Phibun following a brief war with France in 1940-1941, to regain territory in Laos and Cambodia. Neither side gained an upper hand but the land was returned to Thailand after the Japanese brokered a treaty. Phibun's war was supported because parts of Laos and Cambodia had been part of Siam before French colonial expansion in the 19th century. At the end of the Second World War the disputed territory reverted to France after the defeat of Japan, with which Phibun's government was an ally.

A vast traffic circle was created for the five-sided obelisk on a plinth showing the armed forces as the guardians of the nation state. Sculptor Corrado Feroci, following his success at the Democracy Monument, was Phibun's choice for its bas-relief panels and statues of a soldier, sailor, airman, police officer and a civilian volunteer. Their style is national socialist, similar to the fascist work commissioned by Mussolini in Italy to which Feroci had returned on a visit in 1938. Feroci later disowned the project. When erected, it was the tallest structure in the area which was a low-rise suburb at the time.

124
Discovery Learning Library
Ratchawithi Road, at Soi 4
2007

The Soi Phra Nang branch of the public library services was the second to open as part of the Discovery Learning Library Network (the library at Lumpini Park was the prototype). This clean design is makeover of an existing 1970s library building. It stands on a plaza, is set back from the busy road and has an inviting civic presence. The plaza is a landscaped activity area paved and planted with shade trees which form a short avenue to the entrance where there is a café.

The intervention is multi-purpose, a one-stop centre which fits global ideas of how public libraries must respond to technology. There is internet available and traditional book lending. There is a

playroom for kids, traditional stacks, a study room and a mini theatre, all variously on three levels. Natural light from the plaza is admitted to the interiors which are uncluttered. The image presented is progressive—the facility is intended to improve the quality of community life. Across Ratchawithi Road is Santiphap Park, a green space opened in 1998.

125
King Power Complex
Rang Nam Road
Architects 49, 2007

Four functions define this complex built on land leased by Crown Properties to the biggest duty and tax free retailer in Thailand. Each is expressed as a simple shape: a dome, a cube, a rectangular box and a vertical slab. The dome, or Crown Atrium, houses client Vichai Srivaddhanaprabha's museum of Buddha images; the cube is corporate headquarters; the rectangle a retail, restaurant and entertainment mall with a theatre block attached; the slab is a hotel with a garden courtyard. The architecture is modernist, functional, high tech like Suvarnabhumi Airport terminal where the client's activities are also focussed.

There is an airport-style drop-off for buses which bring tourist groups to shop. Traditional Thai productions are put on at the Aksra Theatre. The Buddha images can be seen at the VR Museum (Architectkidd, designLAB, 2011), distributed around the ground floor perimeter and mezzanine of the dome, a contemplative space in commercial surroundings. The dome also functions as an information centre and circulation node with a gathering space, escalators and a glazed elevator. It is the landmark feature and the most visibly high tech structure, articulated with steel bracing and an exterior space frame which secures the curtain wall. Louvres inside act as solar shades. On the HQ block nearby,

solar shading is external; the foyer is a full-height steel and glass atrium, square in plan and impressive. The sidewalk on Rang Nam Road was repaved and planted with trees, a public benefit of this development. The grounds are landscaped and there is a soothing, linear water feature at the entrance to the mall.

126
Suan Pakkad Palace
352–354 Si Ayutthaya Road
Suan Pakkad means 'cabbage garden' which is what the site was before 1952

when Prince and Princess Chumbhot started a museum of heirlooms and acquisitions. These are displayed in several traditional rural dwellings, most owned by the prince's family since the 19th century and relocated to this beautiful garden. The princess landscaped the site which includes a lake and a boathouse which exhibits the royal barge of the prince's father. Next to the barge is the exquisite Lacquer Pavilion, believed to have been part of a 17th-century royal residence at Ayutthaya from where it was moved to Bangkok for reconstruction and conservation. Its panels illustrate Buddhist lore and the Ramakien; the gold-on-black lacquer painting is of exceptional artistry.

The property was donated in 1987 to the Chumbhot-Pantip Foundation whose Centre of Arts displays the Ban Chiang Collection of ancient artifacts, stumbled upon by an American student in 1966 at what is now a Unesco World Heritage Site in the northeast. The centre is a discreet contemporary design (MLTD and Associates, 1995), scaled to fit the site.

127
Baiyoke Sky Tower
Soi 3, 222 Ratchaprarop Road
Plan Architect; Arun Chaiseri engineers, 1997

At 85 storeys Baiyoke Sky Tower (also known as Baiyoke Two) was the first skyscraper in Bangkok to exceed 300 metres, the tallest building in Thailand. It was the pinnacle of the 1990s real estate and construction boom. Its vertical volume is mixed use, including a hotel. Pilings were driven 60 metres below grade to support the structure which is reinforced concrete painted in sandstone colour.

The style is faux Art Deco imitating the glamour of 1920s New York. It opened just before the Thai economy tanked in 1997. It had the country's first open-air, 360-degree revolving roof deck, from where the skeletons of numerous high-rises left incomplete after the crash could be seen. Its height, which reached 327 metres when an antenna was added in 1999, soars above Baiyoke One (Plan Architect; Arun Chaiseri engineers, 1987) nearby which had been tallest building in the city.

128
Indra Regent Hotel
120–126 Ratchaprarop Road
Jira Silpakanok, 1971

The Indra arose on the Pratunam retail strip like a white god of tropical modernism, with prefabricated concrete sunshades covering the entire slab-block structure raised on a gigantic podium. It was a prestigious development, built to cater for long-haul, mass tourism which started after the Boeing 747 made its first flight in 1969. Queen Sirikit was guest of honour at the inauguration of the hotel. Behind the futuristic façade the lobby was finished in teak and Italian marble.

The resort-style deck on top of the podium was a novelty, with a replica of 'a typical Thai aristocrat's house' fitted out as a restaurant, with food accompanied by classical Thai dancing, a combo which has since become a staple of local hospitality. The Indra also combined banquet and conference halls, a business centre, a shopping arcade, a department store and a movie theatre. It was the template for Bangkok's now ubiquitous malls.

129
Siam Commercial Bank
131 Phetchaburi Road
1931

Once owned by a provincial governor, this villa shows the lingering taste in high society for the belle-époque spendour of the fifth reign. It was rehabilitated with a banking hall and offices after being bought by SCB in 1971. The hall's tiled floor is original as are the tiles on the porch which is given a sense of occasion by a classical-style balustrade (the tiles are English Minton pattern, found often in Bangkok's Euro-style heritage buildings). The elevation is roofed in Dutch colonial style with a central dormer window set in a rococo gable. There is a porte cochère behind which an extension can be seen. This is an unobtrusive glass box built in 1995, when the villa was refurbished with meeting rooms upstairs and the banking hall redecorated in heritage style. The balcony above the entrance displays the royal Garuda, a symbol adopted by Rama VI which indicates the bank was established by Royal Charter.

130
National Stadium
Rama I Road
Jittasen Aphaiwong, Chareon Visawakum engineer, 1936

National Stadium, also known as Suphachalasai Stadium, was named in 1941 to honour Commander Luang Suphachalasai, Minister of Education for the People's Party which promoted physical education as part of its nationalist agenda. In architecture the régime's style was generally a humourless Art Deco. The effect here is monumental and decorative. The entrance gate has two fluted and curved pylons on Rama I Road from where a short avenue leads to stadium. The main bay on the façade, designed to support a scoreboard on the reverse side, is defined by a modernist clock and fluted pilasters topped with sculpted elephants and mahouts. More pilasters, also fluted, run along the elevation which is terminated at each end with corner towers.

The stadium was built on the site of 'Windsor Castle', the nickname of an

English-style palace of Prince Vajiravudh (Rama VI) which was demolished. A few fragments of it were excavated in the 1990s and displayed at Chulalongkorn University Faculty of Sports Science next door. The stadium hosted Pope John Paul II who addressed more than 40,000 people assembled for Mass in 1984. It was the nation's premier sports venue for athletics and soccer until superseded by Rajamangala National Stadium built for the 1998 Asian Games.

131

Jim Thompson House

Soi Kasemsan 2, Rama I Road

Jim Thompson, an American intelligence officer in the Office of Strategic Services (later the CIA), arrived in Thailand at the end of the Second World War. He ran the OSS office in Bangkok and reinvented himself as the saviour of Thai silk handicrafts after leaving the military in 1946. His legacy is the Thai Silk Company and his house or rather, houses—six traditional teakwood dwellings. They sit in a compound directly across Klong Saen Saep from Baan Krua where the oldest house was built around 1800. It belonged to a silk-weaving family. In 1958 Thompson bought, dismantled and rebuilt in it in the centre of the compound where it is oriented to face the klong. Others were sourced from Ayutthaya province and Bangkok.

Thompson was assisted by a Thai architect friend and carpenters from Ayutthaya who knew how to build with pegs, no nails. The houses were raised above ground in the traditional manner but connected in a spatial sequence to Thompson's liking. The red exteriors were caused by creosote wood preservative, not a traditional feature. In 1959 he moved in with his collection of Asian objets d'art. In 1962 he opened a silk store at Sala Daeng (see entry 174).

The uninhabited interiors give little sense that this was a gathering place for Bangkok's high society and jet-set visitors. The property has evolved with its popularity as a tourist spot. A water feature separates the house from the Thompson Bar and Restaurant, which contrasts silk and concrete in a finely judged interior design. Across from this is

the Jim Thompson Art Centre and shop, new structures in traditional style. The garden was restored in the mid-1990s.

Sustainability was not a buzz word when Thompson saved these homes but they are an example of it, demonstrating the eco efficiency of traditional Thai architecture (the study was the only air-conditioned room). Thompson's connoisseurship is evident in his superb art collection which can be viewed by a guided tour of the interiors.

132
Henry B. Thompson Building
Soi Kasemsan 2, Rama I Road
Sakran Punyatalung and Ratchada Burunchai, 2007

This recent building next door to the

Jim Thompson House is named for his nephew, who carried out his uncle's wish that the Jim Thompson house and its collection be donated to the Thai people. Since 1975 the bequest has been administered by the James H. W. Thompson Foundation.

The new building includes facilities for artists and curators and, on the double height top floor, the William Warren Library and offices for the Jim Thompson Art Centre. It is contemporary Thai in form and style, sympathetic to its historic context and eco friendly. The architects studied the original house, its materials and colours. The structure is traditional post and beam, in concrete with some steelwork and bricks. Vernacular-style wooden shutters open to a wood deck, linear like the internal organisation of the interior spaces which are open-plan. Floors are polished concrete acting as a heat exchange, cool air being released during the day. Natural ventilation is encouraged, with air conditioning supplementary.

133

LIT Hotel

Soi Kasemsan 1, Rama I Road

VaSLab Architecture, 2011

The name refers to the hotel's lighting design which is varied in colour and mood. 'Lit' is also the French word for 'bed', a cute play on words for a boutique hotel, a type that has to jump out from the crowd. This one has an aluminium composite wrap angled off the perpendicular, patterned with laser-cut openings. This 'detached façade' and solar screen veils the rooms in the L-shaped structure. There is a lively spatial interplay of circulation decks and a poolside plaza. Transparency in the lobby diffuses the open-air and interior public spaces which are slightly retro. Structural columns are exposed. Parking is hidden underground. The plaza is accessed by a stairway that provides a connection to the soi, which is a typical Bangkok mish-mash in which LIT's bizarre appearance is not out of place. An artwork ('Fisherman' by Thaweesak Srithongdee) sits on the steps.

134
Bangkok Art and Culture Centre (BACC)
939 Rama I Road
Robert G. Boughey and Associates, 2008

This concrete palace of culture in Bangkok's premier shopping strip was built after years of campaigning. The project was announced in 1995. Resident American architect Boughey won an architectural competition for it and construction started in 2000, but stalled with régime change at City Hall. Commercial use proposed for the site was opposed by the Thai Artists' Network. A municipal election in 2004 saw the project restarted, the design unchanged.

The building was intended as an icon to propel Bangkok into the big league of art and design centres with iconic architecture inspired by the Guggenheim galleries in New York and Bilbao. Entry is at street level and by a bridge from a skywalk link to the BTS and malls nearby. The internal focus is a full-height atrium crossed by escalators and wrapped with a ribbon of spiral ramps for circulation

and exhibition spaces, like those in the Guggenheim in New York.

The interior, casually dressed in wood, concrete and glass, contains exhibition and performance spaces, meeting rooms, computer labs and coffee shops arranged at angles off the atrium and a library and study area on the lower floor. Escalators stop at level seven where the building becomes less like a mall. The upper galleries, accessed by elevator or spectacularly by the spiral ramp, are peaceful and spacious, top-lit with diffused daylight. The exterior elevation extrudes a half-moon of the atrium's circular plan, set back from the corner of Phayathai and Rama I roads to create a plaza for public art.

135
Mah Boon Krong
Rama I at Phayathai Road
CASA, 1985

When it opened this was the biggest mall in Asia, a megastructure with a high-rise office block, hotel tower, parkade, cineplex, supermarket, department store and shopping centre. The horizontal façade was later re-clad with colourful, off the shelf postmodern components which were trendy at the time, and the giant MBK sign added. The complex is best known for its shopping centre, an eight-storey souk with a food court on the sixth floor and some 2,000 kiosks and shops with eager vendors distributed along aisles off an enormous atrium. Renovations completed in 2004 maintained MBK's popularity with tourists and locals.

136
Hard Rock Cafe
Soi 11, Siam Square
Architectkidd, Montree Sayabovorn engineer, 2011

This funky façade was a response to fashion conscious Siam Square and its streetscapes which are loud and competitive. A musical metaphor was devised—a 'sound wave' of 1,800 reflective black panels on a screen of horizontal ribs attached to vertical steel trusses bolted to the building's concrete frame. The trusses were fabricated with curved profiles which the ribs and panels follow to create the wave effect. Musical rhythms were an inspiration, with real sound waves digitalised and visualised for the new look. The panels are Shera ply, a fibre cement composite tile. Spaces between the angled panels show the old structure, to make the distinction between it and the attachment clear; the spaces also make the screen appear weightless despite it being black.

The interior was redone with some reclaimed wood, most of it from demolished houses. Wood is applied in the soffit between the base of the screen and the façade. Signage is restrained by Siam Square standards—the sound wave

panels do the work. Retrofits like this are the new vernacular. The architects are right on with their experimental, often eco-conscious re-claddings which use unconventional materials creatively.

137
Scala Theatre
Soi 1, Siam Square
Jira Silpakanok, 1969

Bangkok was once cinema city with dozens of stand-alone, big-screen picture palaces. They have faded away, replaced by cineplexes in malls. Also gone are artworks, as epic as the movies they advertised, which were hand-painted from publicity photos to decorate every cinema marquee in the nation. Siam Square had a trio of those theatres, the Siam, Lido and Scala. The Siam (1966) was destroyed by arson during political unrest in 2010. The Lido (1968) was reconfigured as a cineplex. The Scala is untouched by change. Its name recalls La Scala opera house in Milan. It is a unique architectural spectacle.

The exterior style is a flamboyant modernism with columns flowering in vaulted sections which continue inside in an array of fan-like vaulting below the roof slab. The split-level foyer, day lit from an open-air vestibule and double-height windows with Gothic tracery, dissolves in a spatial and decorative montage of retro chic that is more glamorous than anything in Siam Square's hipster hangouts. A five-tier chandelier like a stalactite hangs among the columns and lotus-like rosettes. The auditorium is announced by a bas-relief like a story board featuring performing arts. The only concession to update the venue was a digital projection makeover in 2013 by owner Apex Theatres.

138
Siam Paragon
991 Rama I Road
J + H Boiffils, Design 103 International, 2005

A paragon of conspicuous consumption, this dazzling mall has an outdoor performance plaza and a stepped walkway with waterfalls below the street-facing façade. The public space is generous by local standards. Inside the drum-shaped atrium at the main entrance there are more waterfalls, and a vertical garden by French eco guru Patrick Blanc. Shopping avenues wide enough for skytrain tracks penetrate the multilevel interior. A sky-walk to the BTS was provided at the east end of the mall.

Paragon's site was occupied by the Siam Intercontinental Hotel (Joseph Salerno, 1966). Its lease was not renewed and the building was demolished in 2002. It was a low-rise resort noted for

its Thai-style roof which evoked old Siam without pastiche (how to do this tastefully is a conundrum that still challenges architects). It was set in luxuriant grounds and won an award for environmental protection in 1999, which was not enough to save it or much of the environment. The land, part of a royal estate established by Rama IV, includes the Siam Kempinski hotel and Sra Pathum Palace behind the mall. The palace has a fine Italianate mansion (Mario Tamagno, 1915) restored in 2008 as the Queen Savang Vadhana Museum.

139

Siam Kempinski

991 Rama I Road

Tandem Architects, Brennan Beer Gorman architects, 2010

The hotel's high-rise mediates the gap between it and the adjacent bulk of Siam Paragon. The other components step down to a porte cochère flanked by two pavilions. The style of the buildings is postmodernism, faintly Art Deco in their massing and on a fluted fringe around the tops of the towers. The foyer evokes a palatial classicism and formality. A picture window reveals a resort-style courtyard with a pool, wooden decks and landscaping. This can be seen only from inside the hotel, an inward focus of exclusivity and privacy. The design brief contained the unusual condition that rooms should not overlook Sra Pathum

(Lotus Pond) Palace. There are artworks and much lotus-themed decor.

140

Wat Pathumwanaram

969 Rama I Road

The temple was planned by Rama IV in 1853 and featured a landscape design with lotus ponds for ritual alms giving by boat when it opened in 1857. The land was royal retreat known as the Lotus Pond (Sra Pathum) Palace, a pleasure garden and a place of worship for the king, for monks he sent from Wat Bowonniwet, and for residents of the palace and

aristocratic homes built either side of Klong Saen Saep.

The ubosot and viharn have similar roofs, two-tiered, with cho fas, bai raka and tiles in Chinese style, but the lotus was the decorative theme for the whole project. The ubosot and viharn stand in line, separated by a white chedi which rises from a square base with a four-tiered lotus on each corner; in the viharn there are lotus-painted columns; gold-painted lotus carvings interspersed with mosaic glass tiles decorate the doors, windows and shutters. A baldachin houses two Buddha images (Phra Saen, below it Phra Soerm) originally taken from Vientiane when Rama III's army laid waste to the city in 1827. Murals show witty folk tales of Sri Thanonch.

Lotus plants appear on the gables of the ubosot. Two naga sculptures are posed outside. The interior is an intimate space. The Buddha image (Phra Sai, also from Vientiane) sits on a tiered altar behind which is a mural with angels and more lotuses, big ones. The side walls are decorated with murals of the king's boats in the lotus ponds and, between the windows, scenes of monastic life. Window shutters and doors have mosaic

glass and gold-painted carvings of water buffalo, farmers and fishers. These were commissioned to record village life as it was when the temple was built among ponds and paddy fields. The original residents of the village were Laotian war captives brought here in the 1820s.

Paddy fields and lotus ponds have vanished but a small shanty town at Klong Saen Saep has its roots in the old village. The temple grounds are leafy and have a turtle pond. Directly north of the historic buildings there is museum hall and a garden landscaped for meditation. A new school building (2007) was sponsored by Princess Sirindhorn. The wat is overshadowed by shopping centres but it retains its spiritual power. It was a refuge during the political unrest in 2010. Six people in the temple were shot and killed by snipers, still unidentified, when the army dislodged demonstrators camped on Central World Plaza.

141
Central World
Ratchadamri Road
Various architects, 1987–2007

From shophouse to megastructure is the story of Central's retail rise. The shophouse was in Thonburi where the Chirathivat family's Chinese patriarch settled in 1927. The megastructure is Central World (Architects 49, Altoon + Porter Architects 2006), a multi-use mall with huge floor plates spread out over multiple levels. Abutting the mall are a convention centre and 505-room high-rise hotel, Centara Grand (Tandem Architects, Brennan Beer Gorman architects, 2007) and an office tower (Palmer and Turner, 2005). The office tower is

conventional except for the lantern-like roof; the hotel has two concentric stacks with a wrap-around sleeve which opens at the top like lotus petals.

The massive development, on land leased from Crown Properties, was launched by the Wang Petchaboon Group as the World Trade Centre (CASA, Thai Group Yamazaki) but got stranded by the 1997 economic crash. Central Group acquired the hulk in 2002 and completed the towers and renovated the mall. Its interior is punctuated with atriums to help shoppers navigate the promenades. Two department stores anchor the structure which is bigger than the navy's aircraft carrier. The main elevation was clad with the longest glazed curtain wall and media screen in Asia. Part of the wall was destroyed when the centre was torched and Zen department store gutted during political protests in 2010. A trellis of steelwork supporting a new glass wall marks the reconstruction. The elevation is aligned to a wide linear plaza, the largest public space of its type in Bangkok.

142

Erawan Shrine

Ratchadamri at Phloen Chit Road

Department of Fine Arts, 1956

Several sumptuous shrines at Ratchaprasong are the work of property owners hopeful of good fortune and publicity. The main reason for them is to appease the spirits of the land (small spirit houses generally serve this purpose and most homes have one). The Erawan Shrine is the oldest here, erected to stop mishaps which plagued construction of the Erawan Hotel. An astrologer said the foundation stone had not been laid on an auspicious day and that a shrine would solve the problem. The hotel, a four-storey Modern Thai-style government project to attract international business, opened without further incident.

The four-headed figure of Phra Phrom, the Thai version of the Hindu god Brahma, is the focus of the shrine. Its power is thought considerable. Drivers 'wai' it as they pass. People pay respect and request blessings, and classical dancers are

hired by those whose wishes come true. In 2006 the statue was restored after being smashed by a deranged man who was beaten to death by witnesses. The original hotel was replaced by the Grand Hyatt Erawan Hotel (Rangsan Architectura, 1990), a postmodern reincarnation of ancient Sukhothai, on steroids.

143
Peninsula Plaza
153 Ratchadamri Road
Four Aces Consultants, 1986

The mansard-style roof on this shopping centre could be in Ho Chi Minh City or Hanoi, but Peninsula Plaza's Indochine styling is equally at home in Bangkok. European-themed architecture has retained its cachet since it was popularised by Rama V. The plaza's French colonial-style design was to lure aristocratic and aspirational shoppers to the mall's luxury boutiques. These are set in galleries around a spacious atrium, an arrangement which recalls the typology of early

department stores which were built in Paris in the 19th century.

144
Four Seasons Hotel
155 Ratchadamri Road
Dan Wongprasat Architects, 1983

The design of this mid-rise development is timeless, as fresh now as when the building opened as the Peninsula Hotel. Its blend of traditional Thai and international five-star style is elegant and unaltered. Its soothing water features and landscaped courtyards influenced subsequent developments, but few match its spatial syncopation or the artistic quality of its decor. The lobby is a fusion of belle-époque grandeur and Thai arts and crafts. Ceiling murals like mandalas, with mythological and astrological elements of the Buddhist cosmos, were designed and hand-painted on silk by Paiboon Suwannakudt, a master of temple mural art. On the wall of the lobby's grand staircase is a spectacular image of royal pageantry, 'The Coronation of a King', also by Paiboon, which represents the ascent of the Chakri dynasty. It recalls the world of Rama V, as does the palazzo-like architecture.

145
Royal Bangkok Sports Club
1 Henri Dunant Road

Rama V granted a royal charter in 1901 for the club which had been lobbied for by local and foreign residents. A horse racing track opened in 1903, followed by cricket and rugby grounds, swimming pools and an 18-hole golf course—all very British, the nationality of many foreign residents at the time. The grounds were used as the city's first airfield until Don Muang became the base of the Royal Siamese Air Force in 1914. The first airplane flight in Siam was made by a Belgian aviator from the club's racetrack in 1911. Rama VI attended the event. The Japanese military occupied the site during the Second World War. Many additions have been made since, including a multi-purpose indoor sports complex (Architects 49, 2002). The RBSC is private but horse races and betting are open to the public. A panorama of this green space can be seen from BTS Ratchadamri station.

146

The Hansar Bangkok

Soi Mahatlek Luang 2, Ratchadamri Road

WOHA, Tandem Architects, Warnes Associates engineers, 2011

A follow-up to the Met on Sathorn Road, this condominium and hotel combo was designed to fit a tight site. The floor plans and spatial arrangements were a response to that. As at the Met, the building programme was eco friendly. The site was short of green space, but the condo has sky gardens on every fifth level where structural interventions tie together its four slim towers. The towers, clad with bronze-coloured, metal mesh solar and privacy screens, are sited at the edges of a square footprint. The hotel component is a modular-looking slab block, lower than the towers and offset

from them. It faces the street and is distinguished by a green wall (or vertical garden) around the parking podium on which there is a swimming pool, above the entrance.

147
Amarin Plaza
496–502 Phloen Chit
Rangsan Architecture, 1985
Architect and real-estate developer Rangsan Torsuwan, Bangkok's emperor of postmodernism, built several neo-Roman projects of which this was one of the earliest and most influential. Roman-styled shophouses and villas soon appeared around Bangkok and in provincial towns, constructed by developers, or any local builder with a cement mixer, who saw Amarin Plaza's fake classical façades as a sign of metropolitan sophistication. The Roman theme is replicated

inside the plaza's shopping mall where there is an atrium with more fluted Ionic columns and classical cornices. Fortunately or not, these stop short of the project's office block which is modernist, clad with glazed curtain walls.

148
Central Chidlom
Chit Lom at Phloen Chit Road
CASA, 1974, 1998
Central Group's showpiece, somewhat diminished by the BTS elevated guideway, was billed as 'the finest department store between Hong Kong and Singapore' when it opened in 1974. It was one of Bangkok's biggest developments, with American-influenced monumental elevations. The concrete structure was clad in tiles set in regular bays. Each bay was defined by concrete fluting which curved outwards above the sidewalk to create a pedestrian-oriented canopy. The main entrance was a faceted corner, also concrete. It would be appealingly retro now, but for fashion. The overall massing is all that survived a postmodern makeover in the 1990s. The store was revamped internally in 2012 and a new exterior wrap is planned, as a visual link to the group's Central Embassy project.

149
Mercury Ville
Lang Suan at Phloen Chit Road
Supermachine Studio, 2013
This is a redesign and renovation of

retail units below the postmodern Mercury Tower (1999). It has an improvised temporary quality, the sort of pop-up novelty which makes Bangkok's design scene lively and unpredictable. The interior, a lifestyle shopping mall with stores arranged around an atrium, is slightly curvy but was necessarily more conventional than the cladding, where the architects were evidently unafraid of colour and experimental forms.

150
Mater Dei School
534 Phloen Chit Road

Four sisters of the Ursuline Order arrived in Bangkok in 1925 to serve with the Catholic Mission in Siam. They taught at Holy Rosary Church before moving to Mater Dei (Mother of God) School when it opened in 1928. The school, primarily for girls, was a social success because two boy pupils were briefly the brothers Ananda and Bhumibol Mahidol, educated later in Switzerland before becoming respectively Rama VIII and Rama IX.

The compound is one of the few green spaces left in central Bangkok. The oldest building is a colonial-style chalet with an open ground floor, two turrets and fretwork gables. Modern Thai and postmodern structures were built as the school expanded. Trees give the compound privacy, which became an issue when Chit Lom skytrain station was being built in 1998. Its south platform overlooks the school. Protests were organised. The BTS refused to move the station but deleted a stair to it planned for the intersection outside the school

(where it would have been most useful for transit riders) and installed a screen on the platform to prevent passengers seeing the girls in compound.

151
Vanicha Park
Soi Lang Suan
Ong-Ard Architects, 1985
Rama V made European architectural styles socially acceptable. They remain popular, imitated en masse in heritage-themed suburban gated communities and show-off villas. There is no need to visit the 'burbs to see the effect. This postmodern ensemble downtown has it all: a street of faux belle-époque townhouses framing a view of an apartment block complete with penthouse pediments like a Roman temple on the roof.

152
British Embassy
14 Witthayu (Wireless) Road
Ministry of Works, London, 1926
The first British Consul was appointed after an Anglo-Siamese treaty was negotiated in 1855 by Rama IV and the Hong Kong-based British envoy Sir John Bowring. Property was rented in Bangkholaem until the king granted land for a permanent consulate in 1876, in a compound next door to the Portuguese Embassy. In the fifth reign Britain became Siam's most significant trading and investment partner. The British symbolised this by erecting in the compound their tallest flagpole in Asia, sent from Hong Kong in the 1890s and, in 1903, by importing a statue of Queen Victoria who sat holding a globe and sceptre at the gate. For many years she was the most visible monarch on Charoen Krung Road, where the General Post Office now stands.

The Legation, as it became in 1895, moved to the present site in 1922. The Residence (1926), with a porte cochère and pediments with lion and unicorn heraldry on identical elevations front and back, is typical of the East-of-Suez colonial style: neoclassical, stiff like a starched white collar. The Legation was refurbished after Japanese occupation during the Second World War and upgraded to an embassy in 1947.

The front garden was sold for redevelopment in 2006. The gate on Phloen Chit and a vista of the War Memorial (1923) and the Residence were lost, but the compound was so large that many trees and a lake have been retained. Enough space remained for new amenities and accommodation blocks (MJP Architects, 2009). These are refreshingly post-colonial, rectilinear with visible concrete posts and floor slabs, and solar shades. The flagpole, War Memorial and Queen Victoria were reinstated. The Residence was refurbished along with the barracks for Gurkha guards. There is a defensive-looking new entrance on Witthayu Road. Perimeter security was strengthened.

The embassy occupies the southern half of the old Nai Lert estate which had six stone boundary markers. One survives, an oddity on the corner of Phloen Chit and Witthayu roads.

153
Central Embassy
Phloen Chit at Witthayu Road
2014

The British Foreign Office made its most lucrative sale of property ever when one-third of the British Embassy compound, said to be the most valuable land in Thailand, was sold to the highest bidder in 2006. The site is adjacent to the BTS on the city's primary downtown retail strip. The buyer was Central Group which wanted a look-at-me building and got one.

The architects conceived this organic form to emerge glistening from the backdrop of Bangkok's postmodern urbanism. Its aluminium-tiled skin covers a tower and podium concrete structure. The podium is a seven-storey retail and lifestyle base from which a 30-storey hotel rises. Its utilities are distributed off

light wells; there are terraces and gardens; guest-related facilities overlook Nai Lert Park, and public areas the city centre. Parking is underground.

The typology is familiar in Bangkok. This is the first project to exploit it creatively. The free-form massing morphs glazing with the aluminium wrap, integrating the podium and tower as one. It is polite to the British Embassy which is not entirely eclipsed. The podium's retail galleries in two connected atriums reflect the building envelope's looped form. This was achieved by digital design but construction was typically labour intensive. The tiles glitter with a moiré pattern, like sunlight on the tiled roofs and gilded gables of temples. Tile effects aside, there are no obvious traditional elements to this biomorphic building other than its poise, which is graceful like a classical Siamese dancer.

154
Spa 1930
42 Tonson Road
Vodhyakarn Varavarn, 1948

Dormer windows on a pitched roof, half-timbered gables and informal composition show the influence of the Arts and Crafts movement on this rustic cottage. Its wood floors, plaster-walled rooms and the interior's irregular spaces and levels are characteristic of the style. The spa is a 1990s intervention, with the building's original features conserved. There is a basement, unusual in Thailand, and a garden. Windows imitate leaded glass, roof shingles at the gables are curved to soften edges and exterior walls are plaster on wood battens. The architect/owner studied in England in the 1920s, worked for the State Railway of Thailand and taught at Chulalongkorn University. This teak wood house was his retreat. A tiny Gothic-arched door inside adds a monastic touch.

155
Royal Netherlands Embassy
15 Tonson Road
Bierman Henket architecten, Architects
49, 2005

Two contrasting buildings stand on the embassy site: the new Chancery and the Ambassador's Residence, a picturesque villa (c. 1900) first occupied by Dr. Alphonse Poix, a French doctor who was physician to Rama V. From 1913 it belonged to Prince Bovoradej until he was exiled after he led a revolt against the 1932 coup. It was acquired by the Dutch in 1949 for their first ambassador (previously there had been consuls). The style is Victorian gingerbread with fretwork gables rising to a turret. In 1985 the Dutch government, tempted by rising land prices, proposed redevelopment of the embassy site. This would have sacrificed the historic Residence. Intervention by Sumet Jumsai and Ambassador Peter van Walsum saved it.

The Chancery is an expressive modernist concrete building with a delicate footprint on an island created for it, surrounded by little klongs. The water effects are as much Dutch as Thai, the Netherlands being laced with canals. The building is oriented to Soi Tonson, parallel to Witthayu Road but quieter, between the United States Embassy and its Ambassador's Residence. Like the American compounds, the Dutch outpost is a tranquil green space.

Modern security is typically tight but the building does not look like a fortress. There are imprints of Dutch modernism (transparency, utility and restraint) adapted to the tropical setting. The composition is shaded and held together visually by a canopy supported by thin steel columns, to which Teflon brise-soleil programmed to respond to

the movement of the sun are attached. Working areas feature energy-efficient thermal flow. The building's salubrious atmosphere is complemented by the landscape design. It creates a positive first impression of the diplomacy of the Dutch. They were among the earliest Europeans encountered in Siam, trading in Ayutthaya in the 17th and 18th centuries.

156
Holy Redeemer Church
Soi Ruam Ruedi 5, Witthayu Road
Giorgio Acinelli, 1954

Redemptionist missionaries arrived in Thailand from United States in 1948. They lodged at the Archdiocese and held Mass at Assumption Cathedral before heading upcountry. The mission in Bangkok was established in 1949, a time when the number of English-speaking residents was increasing.

The style of the church, a simulation of Rattanakosin style in concrete with typical roof tiles, was suggested by a visiting American prelate. The traditional tiered overlay was simplified and ornament reduced, aside from a panel with the Madonna and Child on the gable and golden filigree around the openings on each side of the exterior aisles. Air conditioning was not needed because the openings allowed natural ventilation.

The focus of the nave is a gilded image of Jesus Christ above the altar. The ceiling is slightly coffered, with lotus flower motifs like rosettes. Two fonts for holy water are marble, each sculpted as an angel holding a sea shell. Six confession boxes have Siamese gables. The walls are animated by the Stations of the Cross in unusual orientation on two linear friezes (framed panels usually suffice). The building was controversial initially but proved influential. Several modern Catholic churches were built in Thai style.

157
Japanese Embassy
177 Witthayu Road
Kume Sekkei, 2010

This new embassy and consular complex was the result of a move from Petchaburi Road, where the buildings were demolished and the site cleared for sale. The embassy was re-established in Bangkok's traditional diplomatic zone. Its concrete austerity is a result of the architects' restrained, rational style and of security concerns. Few embassies today avoid the fortress look. Governments demand it, a 21st-century paranoia. A checkpoint leads to the Embassy Building. A second checkpoint accesses a surface parking lot for the Consular Office and Japan Information Service. The Embassy Building is a five-storey block dignified by a porte cochère and cornice. Behind it is a garden with old trees retained and staff accommodation.

The soi on the southern boundary of the embassy compound leads to another new building of diplomacy and culture, sans paranoia, the Alliance Française (see entry 292).

158
GPF Witthayu Towers
93 Witthayu Road
Robert G. Boughey and Associates, 1992

Originally called Diethelm Towers, these two buildings were a creative response to the zoning of the time. The development was site-specific, in sympathy to the leafy urbanism of Witthayu Road. Both towers were angled at 45-degrees to the road, a plan which retained existing trees and which extends to the sidewalk where there are two triangular plots, each with a reflecting pool. The taller tower has granite cladding at ground level where the scale is humanised by a covered walkway; the shorter one rises from a parkade which has monumental postmodern elevations. These enrich the urban texture and contrast with the towers' glass curtain walls. The juxtaposition of extremes is surprisingly effective. The project's spirit house is unconventional, pyramid-shaped in granite.

A heritage house, Vidyu Palace (1925), built when Witthayu was a leafy suburb, can be glimpsed from the parkade. It was designed in half-timbered chalet style for Prince Rangsit, a son of Rama V.

159
Rolex Centre
89 Witthayu Road
Robert G. Boughey and Associates, 1996

This was designed with the precision of the product it represents. The entrance is announced by a drum with a double-height cutaway. The drum is a striking feature, separated visually from the rest of the structure by narrow vertical recesses which make it seem larger. It was expressed inside as a void above the showroom where the floor was etched with a watch dial and the ceiling with

a circular mural (Panya Vijinthanasarn) illustrating Eastern and Western myths of time and astrology. A stair was cantilevered from the wall to access offices. At the rear a fire stair was fitted, also in a circular void, lit from an oculus. The building's sculptural form and interior spatial effects, scaled up considerably, are echoed in the design of the Bangkok Art and Culture Centre by the same architect.

160
V House
89/1 Witthayu Road
Vin Varavarn Architects, 2007

This rehab took a generic row house and expelled its dated interiors. Partitions and walls were removed to create an open-plan live/work space. Wood floors were retained and re-stained. The exterior elevations were reclad, partly with a perforated solar screen. A parking space was inserted into the ground floor next to the entrance. Energy-saving was not considered in the original design in the 1980s when air conditioning was the conventional answer to climate control. The unit was part of a small-scale, European-style development around a square. The rehab shows how all the units (and similar structures on other sites, especially shophouses) could be modernised modestly with environmental sustainability. The building was not

torn down. The energy credit from its original construction remains and the debit of new construction was avoided.

161
All Seasons Place
87 Witthayu Road
Palmer and Turner, 1997–2002

This mixed-use complex was designed and marketed as a self-contained mini city whose inhabitants could live, work and shop in a controlled, air-conditioned safe environment. Not that Bangkok is particularly dangerous outside. Many of those working here commute.

Five towers are grouped en masse but with elevations angled to maximise daylight and views of and from each building. The site plan is essentially X-shaped, with the 55-storey China Resources Tower at the centre. There are two 35-storey towers, a 28-storey condominium and a 400-room hotel, whose pool and other amenities are on the roof of a five-level retail podium. Landscaping reflects the leafy streetscape of Witthayu Road. The office towers' cone-shaped peaks, which are illuminated at night, brought instant pizzazz to 'Embassy Row' and marked its shift to commerce. The project was delayed in 1997, when only the 35-storey office towers were complete. Eco factors were not much considered then, but the project's density and proximity to the BTS gains it points for sustainability.

162
American Ambassador's Residence
Witthayu Road
1914

The house was built by Horatio Victor Bailey, a British engineer and automobile agent. It was bought by the Siamese government in 1926. Japanese troops occupied it in 1942. After the war it was transferred by the Thais to the United States in a gesture of reconciliation.

The structure is teak, the style Arts and Crafts, adapted to the climate. The living spaces, raised above an open ground floor, were well ventilated. There is an English half-timbered gable and a porch where Bailey reputedly slept with his three local wives. The interior retains high ceilings, gingerbread screens and parquet floors. Ambassador Edwin F. Stanton and his wife restored the house and grounds which were littered with Japanese army junk after the war. A guesthouse was added in similar style. The Residence, with its little klongs and garden, shows how this part of Bangkok used to be.

Diplomatic relations between Siam and the United States date from 1833 when a Treaty of Amity and Commerce was signed, the first between an Asian nation and the United States. The embassy (south of the Residence) is one of America's largest, a legacy of the Vietnam War era and a response to current geopolitics. The Consular Section (1952) is on the east side of Witthayu Road; the new Chancery (120-122 Witthayu Road; Kallmann McKinnel and Wood, 1996) is on the west side. The building programme for the Chancery was driven by security risk assessment which resulted in a five-storey office block which looks like a fortress. Its style is postmodern, somewhat classical. The master plan preserved trees and water features by locating the building at south perimeter of the site.

163

Park Ventures Ecoplex

57 Witthayu Road

Palmer and Turner, PLA (PLandscape), Vision Design lighting, 2011

The building's shape is said to have been inspired by the 'wai' and lotus buds. The convex curtain walls suggest curvy interiors but the floor plates are rectangular with column-free office space around a service core. The offices are reached from a double-height, modernist lobby at the corner of Witthayu and Phloen Chit; above them is a five-star hotel accessed from Witthayu Road. The hotel pool and a bowl-shaped lounge are cantilevered from structure where they look like they should retract flush with the building envelope in bad weather (which would have been clever but costly).

The building has a wide waistline but its bulk is mitigated by the reflective quality of its glass. The shape is animated at night with LED lighting. The glass is energy-saving, low-emissivity, which reduces solar heat transfer and helps reduce air conditioning. Carbon dioxide sensors control ventilation fans when offices are occupied; daylight sensors and motion detectors adjust indoor lighting.

Waste water is recycled for landscaping on the podium roof and on the project's plaza. There is a shrine of course, but also public art and Norfolk pine trees which complement the patterns on the building's elevations. A ramp leading to the shrine is inlaid with the words 'reduce, reuse, recycle' and other epigrams which reflect the eco-friendly stance of developer Park Ventures. To encourage transit use, there is a link to BTS Phloen Chit station. The energy-efficient building programme and management system, green space, density and transit connection gained the Ecoplex the first LEED Platinum certification in Thailand for a mixed-use development.

164
Bhakdi Building
2/2 Witthayu Road
Robert G. Boughey and Associates, 1983

This futuristic low-rise structure on Witthayu Road was built as the main branch of the Bank of America. It was designed with clarity and sensibility to the local setting and climate. Horizontal overhangs shade all levels, which step back in ziggurat form.. The entrance is set deep in the structure, covered by a floor slab which acts as a porte cochère. Wide steps lead to a terrace and a water feature with public art; a ramp descends

to an underground parkade. The frame is concrete, post and beam; the cladding is travertine, a material favoured by the Romans, here projecting the American commercial empire's image abroad, but courteously. Trees were spared and, like the adjacent Swissôtel, it fits comfortably in Nai Lert Park.

The Bank of America was the first bank from the United States to locate in Thailand, when an office was opened opposite the GPO on Charoen Krung Road in 1949.

165
Swissôtel Nai Lert Park
2 Witthayu Road
Design 103 International, 1983

Formerly the Hilton International Nai Lert Park, this was a significant local development by the American chain in a city awash with US aid during the Vietnam War. The 300-plus-room hotel in international modernist style was a sign of a maturing travel and tourism market. The building's jet-age glamour anticipated the resort-style accommodation that changed the look of downtown Bangkok over the following two decades. What makes this development almost unique now is its scale. It is low-rise, as most of the city was when it was planned in the 1970s. Like the now demolished Siam Intercontinental it was a good fit with that all but vanished, often verdant urbanism.

The entrance at Witthayu Road is landscaped. A ramp leads to the hotel's raised forecourt where a sala contains a statue of Nai Lert, a business baron during the fifth reign, hence the name of the park. The Hilton was leased on a portion of the Nai Lert family estate which extends to the klong on Soi Som Khit. The hotel's centrepiece is the lobby atrium, with elevators for four floors which extend in two angled wings. Two vertical concrete panels cast as abstract artworks screen the lifts from the lounge and bar. The atrium diffuses into a luminous space that leads to the park which is embraced by the hotel's wings, which are stacked in exterior step backs. There is a deck and a pool in the park; trees and plants are labelled for their botanical interest. Alterations to the building over the years have been cosmetic. The original concept was inspired and is still evident.

166

Vanit Building

1126 New Phetchaburi Road

Plan Architect, Arun Chaiseri engineers, 1993

This high-rise, also called Vanit 2 (there is an adjacent lower block, Vanit 1) towers above the Swissôtel Nai Lert Park. It is located on Phetchaburi Road, the poor relation of Phloen Chit. Vanit 2 raised the profile of the street with distinctive architecture. The lobby is approached from a landscaped plaza and a spacious covered deck with open sides which acts as a grand porte cochère. A parking podium is offset to the canal side of the site. The tower is clad with reflective glass. Facets catch the light and step back at the top where there is an octagonal cupola. The facets and step backs relieve the monotony of the glazed curtain wall and add a Thai element which can be likened to a Khmer-style prang.

167

The Park Chidlom

1 Soi Som Khit, Phloen Chit Road

Palmer and Turner, 2007

Advertised as 'super-luxury condominiums . . . inspired by the Art Deco skyscrapers of New York', these apartment blocks are crowned with Gotham city-style pinnacles which erupt at night with light, like a backdrop in a Batman movie. The Art Deco is pure escapism, gated and landscaped like a resort. The structures are concrete, in simple forms any competent contractor could handle. Architects do the packaging, and will comment privately that this is all some clients want or understand. Ritzy styling aside, or maybe because of it, the Park's units sold before completion, to a mix of Thai and foreign buyers.

The Robot Building

5

Suriwongse, Silom & Sathorn

Suriwongse, Silom and Sathorn roads, like most of Bangkok's network of highways and sois, began as canals. Klong Silom was dug in 1858, Klong Sathorn in 1888 and Klong Suriwongse in 1897. They were branches of Klong Hua Lamphong, dug in 1857, which was connected to the Chao Phraya River by Klong Sathorn. Since the 1950s these and other canals have been paved over or completely filled in to widen the roads. Klong Sathorn still exists, as a culvert and open drain separating North and South Sathorn roads, as the two sides of the boulevard are called.

The three roads—Suriwongse, Silom and Sathorn—were laid along their respective klongs on earth excavated when the canals were dug. They are parallel, each connected by sois which were originally smaller klongs. The pattern of modern development in Bangkok is an overlay on those small klongs and the water transportation they provided. They were not dug with the modern city in mind and were an unsuitable template for it, like the medieval street pattern in central London which has defied rational town planning. The little klongs irrigated the area's vegetable gardens and orchards which stretched north to Chinatown and south to the European business district at Bang Rak. Windmills (Silom means windmill) were built to pump water from the canals to irrigate the crops. A metal windmill sculpture erected in 1998 at the intersection of Silom and Narathiwas roads recalls that time when the area was agricultural, residential and low-rise. Hydro power is now delivered by electric cables. Silom is one of the few streets in the city where these are underground.

Silom Village, a pioneering 1980s preservation effort which turned a group of old houses into a shopping and entertainment venue, captures some of the old ambience, as does the M. R. Kukrit Heritage Home although its collection of traditional Siamese-style houses (similar to the Jim Thompson property featured in tour 4) is not authentic architecturally to the district. More representative are the heritage homes from the fifth and sixth reigns which can be found in sois off Suriwongse, Silom and Sathorn. Some have been preserved, rehabilitated as restaurants or embassies. The most conspicuous is the former Russian Embassy, an Italianate mansion built in 1914 facing Sathorn Road.

It was the family home of Chao Sua Yom, a Chinese immigrant who was commissioned by Rama V to construct Klong Sathorn and its roadways. Mr Yom was rewarded with an aristocratic title, Luang Sathorn, and is remembered in the name of the road. Its arrow-straight length and unusual width give it an urban grandeur but it was a suburb, a result of Luang Sathorn being granted ownership and development rights either side of the canal. He took advantage of these by selling large lots to the Siamese ruling class and Western merchants for mansions. The road was graded, tree-lined and lit by oil-lamps. The area became an exclusive residential district, 'one of the healthiest, coolest, and quietest in Bangkok'. Lumpini Park, conceived by Rama VI as a site for an international expo in the 1920s, added to the area's salubrious garden-city appeal.

Luang Sathorn's mansion was rehabilitated as part of Sathorn Square, a mixed-use development with a high-rise hotel and office tower flanking the old house. If this project had happened several decades ago, the house would have been torn down because it sits on prime land where profit dictates urban planning. Its adaptive reuse is a significant success for heritage preservation which has taken many decades to take root in Bangkok. Sathorn Square is also notable for providing uncommonly generous public space. The office tower gained LEED Gold certification, mainly for adding density to and being on an urban site with connectivity to mass transit.

Sathorn Square—and MahaNakhon, under-construction and set to be the city's tallest building—can be seen as a culmination of a conventional pattern of development which began in the 1960s when Suriwongse, Silom and Sathorn roads became business and tourism strips. The Dusit Thani Hotel and the Bangkok Bank head office are icons of that trend which created a central business district (CBD) in North American style with office and retail workers commuting from the suburbs by minivan, bus and car, and more recently by BTS skytrain and MRT metro. CBDs attract iconic architecture but are not known for eccentricity, except in Bangkok which has the Robot Building, an amusing take on modern life as much as it was the head office of the Bank of Asia. It loomed large on Sathorn Road but now seems toy-like surrounded by taller towers, an irony because a Japanese toy was the inspiration for it.

The city's growth has been achieved with maximum free enterprise and minimum urban planning—few planning officers in other cities would have given the Robot Building a green light. Bangkok's municipal planning office (now the Department of City Planning, part of the Bangkok Metropolitan Administration which was created in 1972) was established in 1953. In 1958 the Thai government hired US consultants Litchfield Whiting Browne and Associates for advice. The Litchfield Plan, a 30-year strategy for land use, transportation and infrastructure, was delivered in 1960 but not implemented until after 1992, when the BMA's first City Plan was published. Those missing years were when Bangkok sprawled with unrestrained urbanisation.

Political and administrative conflict, complexity and corruption are a challenge to regulatory enforcement. Planning for 21st century sustainability demands it, but concern for the health of the planet is not mainstream in the Thai development industry. However, planning is taken more seriously now that climate change is evident. The 2013 City Plan shows 'sub-cities' in the suburbs accessible by rail mass transit. Residential and commercial development and density are already evident along the BTS and MRT lines. But the planning goal of efficient, eco- friendly 'compact cities' accepted elsewhere remains elusive and green space is still scarce. The beautiful (and planned) Lumpini Park is an exception.

168

Lumpini Park

Rama IV at Ratchadamri Road

This was Bangkok's first public park, founded in 1919 by Rama VI who chose the site, donated the land and named it after the birth place of the Buddha in Nepal. It was designed to host the Siamese Kingdom Exhibition, an international expo to boost the economy after the First World War. Ornate gates, an ostentatious avenue, an exhibition hall and a Chinese clock tower were completed, and villas for foreign VIPs (three are in a compound on Ratchadamri Road).

The expo was cancelled after the king died. The park was completed, with an amusement park to help pay its way, during the seventh reign. Today it is Bangkok's 'central park'. It has similarities to Central Park in New York, not only with its backdrop of skyscrapers but also in its European landscape design. There are pavilions and architectural curiosities, and a parterre arranged as a clock at the main gate. The avenue is wide, straight and formal; the layout of lakes and woodland is more natural, in the English manner. There are activities and there can be solitude. People do tai chi,

walk, jog, go boating on the big lake, and attend concerts in the cool season. The Miss Siam beauty contest was held on an island in the lake, where there was a restaurant to which diners were ferried.

Lumpini is Rama VI's most popular legacy—'the park the King gave to his people'—and he is honoured with a statue at its main entrance.

169
Rama VI Monument
Rama VI Plaza, Lumpini Park
Corrado Feroci, 1941

The statue was commissioned by the nationalist government of Field Marshal Phibun. It shows Rama VI standing on a massive plinth at the entrance of the park he created. The figure is three-times life size and shows the king in full military dress, from polished boots to plumed hat, holding a sword and sceptre. The militaristic pose was in step with the times. The monument is an assertion of 'Nation, Religion, King', the trinity appropriated by Phibun which had been coined by Rama VI. Sculptor Feroci had been invited to Siam in 1923 to work for the king and he crafted the figure with affection.

170
Lumpini Discovery Learning Library
Lumpini Park
1956

This well proportioned, concrete and stucco neoclassical pavilion was built as the People's Library of Bangkok, a name which appears on the entablature. The pediment above the porch bears the city's official seal (Indra on a white elephant), drawn originally by Prince Narisara Nuvativongse. The pediment is supported on columns which have Thai-style capitals. Wings were added later. The library was rehabilitated by the BMA recently, the first to open as part of the Discovery Learning Library Network, a public access programme which promotes community libraries as multimedia knowledge centres.

171
Dusit Thani Hotel
946 Rama IV Road
Kanko Kikaku Sekkeisha Architects, 1970

Sala Daeng was the name of the residence of Chao Phraya Yommarat, a mandarin during the fifth reign. His former compound is the site of the Dusit Thani Hotel. Its architecture is sophisticated and brought global metropolitan style to Bangkok. The hotel was advertised as 'Thailand's newest, most luxurious . . .' and was one of the tallest buildings in the city until the 1980s.

The tower tapers slightly as it rises on a triangular floor plan from a two-level podium with a vehicle ramp to the entrance. The exterior and interior design evoked traditional Siamese forms. The triangle motif, suggestive of temple gables, appears on the canopy around the base of the building, where there are saw-tooth arches and columns which splay out like fans. The rooftop spire looks like a futuristic cho fa. A courtyard deep inside has a secluded garden with a waterfall, a feature which has survived periodic renovations to the interior. Outside at the front of the hotel palm trees sway in the garden whose landscape design has been maintained, as are the building's essential architectural features.

172
Abdulrahim Place
990 Rama IV Road
Interdesign, Wong Tung and Partners, 1997

The bulk of this granite-clad office tower is stepped back as it rises to a pyramid peak, reminiscent of Art Deco skyscrapers in North America. The step-backs comply with a zoning requirement that floor plates get smaller on the upper floors to allow sunlight light to reach the ground. They lend the tower a retro-deco vibe because the origin of this type of zoning was a 1920s by-law in New York (the step-back massing of skyscrapers was a result of it). The plaza at the base of the tower and the big, public lobby are also North American forms. The landscaping of the driveway is attractive, with a park-like palm grove similar to the grounds at the Dusit Thani Hotel.

Behind a wall in the shadow of the tower is a fragment of the original garden in which Abdulrahim House was built in 1908 for an Indian merchant whose father immigrated during the fifth reign. The house is a gingerbread bungalow. It was retained by the family after the tower was built on the property and has been restored. A larger house was added in 2013.

173
U Chu Liang Building
968 Rama IV Road
Tandem Architects, 1999

Floor plates here were recessed at the edges to increase daylight and views from corner offices. The tower steps back at the top like Abdulrahim Place but without an Art Deco hat. The two buildings are complementary. Both are confident pieces of urban design. Abdulrahim Place stands alone, set back from Rama IV Road to preserve a heritage home. The U Chu Liang Building, also known as the HSBC Tower, engages more with the street. An eight-storey annex to the east matches the tower's materials and massing.

174
Jim Thompson Thai Silk
9 Suriwongse Road
James H. W. Thompson, 1962

Fabled American silk king Jim Thompson opened the Thai Silk Company store on Suriwongse Road in the early 1950s. The company gained international recognition, especially after Queen Sirikit appeared on overseas trips attired in the company's garments, designed by a Paris couturier. Thompson revived silk making and supported rural communities by paying village weavers to work from home. His contribution to the well-being of the kingdom was recognised in 1962 when he was awarded the Order of the White Elephant.

Production shifted to a factory in Korat after his disappearance on vacation in Malaysia's Cameron Highlands in 1967. He was an intelligence asset for the CIA, until criticising US policy in South-East Asia. His fate, still unsolved, added to his and the company's mystique. His taste

for exquisite design and craftsmanship was nurtured when he was as an architect in the United States. That heritage is evident in this store, an architectural composite with a Thai-style roof, ogee windows on the main floor and a front elevation which echoes the Federal-style proportions of his native land. His residence, the Jim Thompson House on Klong Saen Saep, is preserved as a museum (see entry 131).

175
Montien Hotel
54 Suriwongse Road
Mitaroon Kasemsri, 1968

The hotel has been extended but it remains a 1960s classic with a rhythmic concrete solar screen well preserved. The neighbourhood, known as Patpong, attracted jet-age business travellers, tourists and US military personnel. There were airline offices and banks, and the Jim Thompson Thai Silk store. Montien Plaza, a 1960s shopping centre with Thai style roofs, was built next to the hotel's parking lot. Patpong was once a banana plantation off Suriwongse Road. In the 1940s it was developed by Udom Patpongpanit, who built Patpong Soi 1 to connect Silom and Suriwongse roads. The area became a sexy bar scene for US troops on leave from Vietnam. It has cooled off a bit, better known now as a night bazaar for bootleg products and bargain clothes.

176
Bangkok Bank
333 Silom Road
CASA, 1974

Established in 1944, the bank filled a vacuum after European banks closed during the Second World War. The biggest casualty was the Hong Kong and Shanghai Bank (HSBC) which had financed much British imperial trade in Asia since it opened in Hong Kong in 1865. A branch was opened in Bangkok in 1888. It was the first commercial bank in Siam, whose first banknotes it printed. It also was the

first foreign bank to lend money to the Siamese Government, for railway construction, and thus underpinned much of Rama V's economic modernisation.

Bangkok Bank became Thailand's premier commercial bank. This head office was the tallest and largest corporate building in the kingdom when it opened. The structure is a giant multi-storey slab block with offices above a podium which contains parking and a spacious banking hall. The hall is announced by a concrete canopy stretched across the elevation. Landscaping is linear, with water features.

The hall has a superb tiled mural with historical scenes of the Chao Phraya River and Bangkok (these subjects also appear on some 19th-century murals in temples). It is the only decorative element, aside from the bank's royal Garuda on the front elevation of the podium. The mural shows influence from North America where architects and their corporate clients commissioned artworks to lend prestigious projects cultural cachet. Here the art alleviates the austerity of the architecture.

177
The British Club
189 Suriwongse Road
1910

Founded in 1903 by a band of expatriate diplomats and company directors, this was a gentlemen's club modelled on those in London. It had an all-male, all-white membership, since opened to women and all nationalities.

The present clubhouse is the second. It has the personality of a Georgian country house, complete with a front lawn where the original clubhouse once stood. Membership increased and the old house was demolished. The construction date of the new and larger building appears in a cartouche on the pediment above the porte cochère. The land leased was later donated to the club by Rama VI in 1915.

The edifice is an echo of empire, from a time when Britain was the dominant foreign power in South-East Asia. On the staircase there is a portrait of Queen Elizabeth II. There are sporting trophies and panels with names of distinguished past members. A function room retains ceiling fans; there is a pub, the Churchill Bar. Outside there are tennis courts, cricket nets and a poolside terrace. An 'oasis in the heart of Bangkok', it is one of the few green spaces left in the Silom area.

178
Neilson Hays Library
195 Suriwongse Road
Mario Tamagno, 1921

The *Bangkok Times* described this Beaux-Arts essay as 'a grand palace on a small scale', which is how its symmetry, gleaming stucco, and a rotunda roofed by a dome looked when it was built on semi-

rural Suriwongse Road. The building looks small from the outside. The surprise is the interior which is spacious and luminous in Beaux-Arts style intended to evoke European antiquity and learning. The style was popular in the US, the client's rather than the architect's heritage.

The library was the gift of Dr. Thomas Heyward Hays in memory of his wife, Jennie Neilson Hays. He was an American physician, a consultant to the royal court and a friend of Prince Damrong Rajanupab; she was a Danish-born Protestant missionary who arrived in Siam in 1881. From 1895 to 1920, as a plaque in the rotunda has it, she 'was the inspiration and mainstay of the Bangkok Library Association', a book club 'for ladies' formed in 1869.

The building is a lively social centre where users browse among teak cabinets beneath classical columns, decorative plasterwork and vaulted ceilings. The rotunda, once the entrance vestibule (the canopy remains attached outside) is now an intimate art gallery. The Garden Gallery and Café (Peter Harper, 2006) is a neat contemporary glass box built in the parking lot where there is a gate to the adjacent British Club.

179

Mirasuddeen Mosque

Soi 20, Silom Road

The mosque was founded in a wooden house by a local land owner around 1912.

The property was bought by a benevolent businessman in 1983. He funded the construction of this new mosque designed in Indo-Saracenic style, with a tiered minaret and an onion dome above the prayer hall. Next door is Talad Soi Prachum, an old wet market. The style is 1930s concrete modernism but it was built later, in 1969. The row of two-storey shophouses across the soi dates from the 1960s. With the market, they form a typical vernacular streetscape from that time.

180

Sri Maha Mariamman Temple

2 Pan Road

This Hindu temple was founded by immigrant traders from southern India and Ceylon (now Sri Lanka) in the 19h century. The first site was in the Hua Lamphong area and the original building a simple sala. The temple was relocated here during the fifth reign, around 1880. Its present form is an accretion of construction. The architecture is Dravidian, rooted in the ancient India. There are elaborate domes but the most visible and typical feature is at the entrance. This is a gopuram, a tower tapering from a rectangular base, alive with five tiers of plaster mythological figures and deities. Mariamman is a powerful mother god worshipped for protection against the vagaries of life. Buddhists can be seen at this temple, a reminder that Buddhism in Thailand is a conflation from several sources which include Hindu beliefs.

181

Silom Village

286 Silom Road

1980

Adaptive reuse of heritage buildings is an accepted method of preservation, and an eco-friendly sustainable option. They can be revitalised and pay their way instead of being torn down. That was unknown territory when Prasongsak Aksoramat rehabilitated this cluster of teakwood houses dating from the fifth reign on family property, as arts and craft shops, an inn and restaurants. The vision—to create a shopping and entertainment venue featuring Thai food and culture which would appeal to the growing tourist trade—was achieved by using the houses to recreate old Silom's village ambience. The project was influential and has been much imitated. Its alfresco walkable spaces, perfect for evenings out, created a template which has been adopted recently by developers of community malls.

182
Sueb Samphanthawong Church
Si Wiang Road
1903

The church was the idea of the Presbyterian Mission Board in New York, to serve the mission's Bangkok Christian College which was the first private school for boys in Siam, founded in 1853. The school moved from Thonburi to Sathorn in 1902. The church was funded by Thain Hee, the first student from the kingdom to study in the US where he was sponsored by a missionary. He became the first Siamese medical doctor and worked with Rama V's military expeditions to Laos. He was awarded an aristocratic title, Phraya Sarasin Sawamipak. He was also a rice merchant and co-founder of Siam Cement. He owned land in Silom and, in memory of the missionary who had helped him as a child, gave this site for the church.

The building is wood with delicate fretwork and a trussed roof. It was restored in 2007. The style is Carpenter Gothic, like the picturesque pioneer and mission churches built by settlers in the United States in the 19th century.

183
Blue Elephant
233 South Sathorn Road
1903

This commercial palazzo was originally the offices of the Bombay Burmah Trading Company, established in 1863 by Scottish merchants who traded tea and teak wood from Burma and had logging concessions in Siam. The Italianate building has a noble entrance with an arched porte cochère projected upwards

through all floors. There is a typical cornice, round-arched windows and delicate plasterwork.

Above the entrance bay is a curved gable added by the Thai-Chinese Chamber of Commerce (founded in 1910) which bought the building in 1930. The association further asserted its identity by attaching the pagoda arrangement of bracketed solar canopies which project from the façades. During the Second World War the Imperial Japanese Army commandeered the building. The Chamber of Commerce reoccupied it in 1946. In 1995 the organisation moved to the newly completed Thai CC Tower behind the old building, which was rehabilitated in 2002 for the Blue Elephant Cooking School and Restaurant.

184
Saint Louis Catholic Church
215 South Sathorn Road
1957

The leader of the Roman Catholic Mission in Siam, Monseigneur Jean-Louis Vey, set aside land for this church in 1898. Its Arts and Crafts style is of that time but it was built some 60 years later. It has a pitched roof, pretty belfry, slightly buttressed brick walls and a brick gable end. Windows are Gothic style, echoed inside where brick arches bestride a cruciform plan. The brickwork is precise, beautifully laid. A plaza separates the church from the clergy house, a recent building with gables and brickwork in keeping with the scale, texture and style of the church. The Vatican Embassy stands in a leafy compound next door.

185
Saint Louis Hospital
215 South Sathorn Road

Monseigneur Jean-Louis Vey established Saint Louis Hospital in 1898. The Sisters of Saint Paul de Chartres were assigned to run it. It was named after King Louis IX of France, the only French king to be elevated to sainthood. A statue of him here is now a shrine, with garlands placed on its pedestal by visitors. Bangkok is a blend of cultures. The conflation of a European saint and Siamese spirits is not an anomaly.

The hospital's original colonial-style buildings do not survive but green space does, facing Sathorn Road. The main entrance block (c. 1973) is concrete, sculptural in the manner of Le Corbusier, as is St. Mary's Chapel with its spiralling spire and convex, ribbed ceiling. Behind them is a gigantic postmodern tower (c. 1998) on a parking podium which dominates the complex.

186
Sala@Sathorn
Soi 11, South Sathorn Road
Hassell architects, Meinhardt engineers, 2009

The development brief was for office space with views of the city and the river. In the past that would have meant lots of glass and total reliance on air conditioning for climate control. This project used environmental design to achieve a salubrious workplace.

A pre-construction 3D sun study determined the tower's various elements. The west elevation has a double-skin curtain wall with fritted (ceramic-coated) glass to minimise solar glare and heat penetration; flexible internal blinds further restrict solar gain. The fritted outer screen projects visibly from the main structure creating a vertical void into which midday sunlight is absorbed (the void has a steel catwalk for maintenance on each floor).

The south elevation is layered with brise-soleil; the north, street-facing façade has thin vertical solar fins. The tower's east elevation is patterned randomly with metal composite cladding. Vertical strips reveal elevator movement, a result of the electrical and mechanical services being located inside this wall instead of in a central core, an orientation which created wide-span floor plates.

The parking podium is at the rear where aluminium grills and a precast vertical bas-relief inspired by bamboo leaves add texture. The street elevation is articulated to a human-scale where it meets the ground. There is a generous sidewalk detailed with paving and wood decking. The building does not shout 'sustainability' or any particular style but on the right side of climate change it is an efficient performer.

187

Robot Building

191 South Sathorn Road

Sumet Jumsai, 1986

It took several years, numerous sketches and discussions with the client, the Bank of Asia, before this robot came to life, inspired by a Japanese toy the architect spotted his son playing with. The 'machine' concept fitted the bank directors' desire that the building symbolise their new computerised services, and the

building's humour gave their head office a friendly face.

The building as a machine echoes Le Corbusier although the great modernist never thought 'robots'. There are stylised caterpillar tracks and nuts and bolts on the side elevations; the eyes function as panoramic windows on the executive office level. There are two communications antennae on the roof which also act as lightning conductors.

Styling aside, this was, as the architect has said, 'a sensible building', rational and economic. Construction is reinforced concrete with glazed curtain walls front and back and side elevations clad in ceramic panels. Its 20 storeys seemed high when it crawled on to Sathorn Road which it dominated for several years. Its massing with floor plates reduced in stages was not only to resemble the Japanese toy but also the result of municipal setback regulations of the time.

The urban design is well mannered. The tower stands firmly at the sidewalk where the entrance plaza is formal, originally with a colonnade leading to the portico and banking hall. The hall is glazed to the street, accessible, double-height, informed by classical proportions. There is an eight-level parkade at the rear linked to the tower with pedestrian ramps. The Bank of Asia was acquired by the United Overseas Bank in 2005.

188
H Gallery
Soi 12, North Sathorn Road
c. 1900

This attractive colonial-style house with a verandah on the upper floor is patterned with fretwork. Ventilation panels at ceiling height on both levels, also patterned with jigsaw woodwork, allowed air to circulate, an example of how buildings of the pre-air conditioning era were adapted to the climate. It was rehabilitated in 2002 for H Gallery, with

the structural qualities of the house—wood posts and beams, ceiling joists and polished floors—exposed as a neutral backdrop for exhibitions of Thai and Asian contemporary art. The gallery was one of the first small spaces to refresh the city's art scene.

189
Plan Toys
Soi 10, North Sathorn Road
Plan Architect, 1988

Opened as Ruklook Kindergarten, this free-form building was planned with

interconnected spaces open for natural ventilation. It is a miscellany of decks, turrets, balconies, arches and windows, like a toy castle for children to explore and enjoy. The picture book imagery is very postmodern but the influence was traditional village temple schools which blend sheltered and open-air learning facilities. Much of the original kindergarten has survived conversion as offices. There is a book and toy store, and a café on a deck outside, formerly the playground, under foliage which has greened the site.

The architects' offices, Plan House (1987), are next door across a lane. A prominent column anchors the composition. A landscaped external stairway serves each level. Internal circulation is by lift and a spiral staircase lit by glass blocks. Like the nursery design, the style is postmodern and the spatial organisation imaginative. The building extends into the lane where it is visibly supported on pilotis. The lane has two more 'plan houses' which continued the architects' idiosyncrasies and feel for urban design.

190

Sathorn Square

North Sathorn and Narathiwas roads

Palmer and Turner, Warnes Associates engineers, 2012

Sathorn Square filled the last unexploited corner at the Sathorn and Narathiwas intersection and gives a focus to the Central Business District which is strung along Sathorn Road. The development is a blend of heritage preservation, contemporary architecture and urban design. Its office tower and high-rise hotel frame an Italianate heritage house around which the project's ground plan evolved. Developer Golden Land's adjacent Infinity Condominium (Palmer and Turner, 2008) was part of the mixed-use concept.

The heritage house was built in 1914 for aristocrat Luang Sathorn. It is decorated elaborately with plasterwork inside and out. It became the Royal Hotel in 1927. In 1948 it was leased by Crown Properties to the Soviet Union as an embassy. After the Russians relocated in 1999 it became a spooky relic, abandoned to the ghosts of Cold War spies.

It stands in its original position but with a plaza and pond where there was a garden. Two wings at the back enclose a courtyard where trees were retained to shade the outdoor space. The house was rehabilitated for the hotel, W Bangkok. The hotel's elevations, like those on the office tower, are sleek; its interiors are ultra hip, design-themed.

The office tower's elevation turns the corner into North Sathorn Road with an exclamation mark. The transition is

dramatic with a curving vertical cleave shooting up from a steel and glass cone to the roof. The cone is transparent, to provide a viewpoint from the lobby to a water feature on the plaza and the urban landscape.

191
MahaNakhon
Narathiwas Road
The name of this 77-storey, 314-metre-high icon means 'great metropolis' in Thai. Designed as a luxury condominium and boutique hotel, it will be the tallest tower in Bangkok on completion, scheduled for 2015. It deconstructs the typical tower-on-podium typology. Stepped terraces give it human scale where it meets the ground. There is a plaza with a retail annex, the seven-storey Cube.

Above the 150-room hotel are 200 condos 'inspired by the grandeur of historic Manhattan apartments'. Some units are 'skyboxes' variously recessed and cantilevered to offer panoramic views; sky terraces diffuse indoor and outdoor spaces. A penthouse was listed as the most expensive residential unit in Bangkok. The tower's structure is concrete, the styling a baroque modernism. The mannered elevations appear eroded, an instant ruin, as if in a city after environmental meltdown. Press releases and commentary explained the look as 'pixilated', a reference to digital imaging and computer-aided design.

192
Empire Tower
195 South Sathorn Road
ACT Consultants, Wong Hobach Lau engineers, 1997
This mammoth, 58-storey block opened as one of the city's most technically advanced buildings, wired with the now essential fibre optic cables for data transmission and communications. The column-free office floors serviced by

45 high-speed elevators are above a parking podium. It is the biggest office tower in the city. Its mass is minimised with reflective glass curtain walls which are facetted in recessed vertical shafts rising to an irregular roofscape to break the bulk.

A recent renovation gave it a connection to BTS Chong Nonsi station and the Bus Rapid Transit (BRT) loop. The BRT, opened in 2010, runs from Sathorn across the Chao Phraya River to BTS Talat Phlu. The BMA commissioned an upgrade to the existing four-way pedestrian bridges at the Sathorn and Narathiwas intersection to create an elevated public plaza (Asian Engineering Consultants) connected by covered skywalks to transit.

193
Bangkok City Tower
179 South Sathorn Road
Kenzo Tange Associates, 1999

A sleek piece of international modernism, this building's two triangular segments meet in a thin vertical recess at the street corner. The segment on Sathorn is taller, responding to the street's prestige as a business address. The lobby is luminous with spider-clamped glazing, and twin entrances defined with classical proportions. The curtain walls touch the corner with knife-edge precision. The architecture is elegant, precise, in keeping with traditional Japanese architecture and arts and crafts.

Across the road is Sathorn Thani Complex (90 North Sathorn Road; CASA,

1997), divided into three high-rises with bold, almost brutalist, concrete verticals but lacking Bangkok City Tower's grace and corner definition.

194
Sathorn City Tower
175 South Sathorn Road
Palmer and Turner, 1994

Nothing could contrast more with the Japanese restraint of Bangkok City Tower than this hulk next door, clad in glass and granite. Built at the high point of postmodernism in Bangkok, it features the stylistic kleptomania of that era, in this case grandiose Art Deco with step-back massing and a rooftop like some ancient temple. It is entered from a plaza set back from the street. The lobby is grand, retro, like a commercial palace in 1930s Shanghai. There are two large and typically vigorous artworks by Thawan Duchanee.

195
M. R. Kukrit Heritage Home
Soi Phra Phinit, South Sathorn Road

Behind the wall of corporate towers on Sathorn Road is this relic of aristocratic refinement, the work of Oxford-educated polymath and politician M. R. Kukrit Pramoj. Among his many interests was Khon classical theatre, and masks are displayed in a pavilion he built for performances. The pavilion opens to a Khmer-style garden and Kukrit's private quarters. These are composed of five, single-room teakwood stilt houses, one from Bangkok, the others found in Ayutthaya province. The oldest structure, opposite the pavilion, dates from around

1810 and was originally sited near the Giant Swing. Their arrangement around a deck was inspired by traditional compounds, where accommodation would be added when required and the deck extended. Each of his rooms had a different function: formal reception, sitting room, library, bedroom, shrine.

As with the Jim Thompson House, this traditional architecture is durable, adaptable, comfortably proportioned and pleasing to the eye. The ambience is personal. Kukrit's acquisition and relocation of the houses was a 20-year project begun in 1960. The houses, their antique contents and the site plan are as he left them.

196
Singapore Embassy
129 South Sathorn Road
Chan Sau Yan Associates, 2005

This new building was commissioned by Singapore's Ministry of Foreign Affairs following a design competition. It is a carefully crafted tropical modernist box with wide aluminium eaves and a horizontal solar wrap, composed with rectilinear clarity. The structure is steel, glass and concrete. There is a reflecting pool and textured stone at the entrance. A transition from the busy street to the interior is created in a courtyard. The defensive metal gate is an inevitable installation, typical of contemporary embassy design and security. The building is orderly, functional, like the city-state it represents.

197
The Met
125 South Sathorn Road
WOHA architects, Tandem Architects, Worley engineers, Cicada landscape design, 2009

The Met is a 66-storey, 370-unit residential development built in the tower and podium typology that is familiar in Bangkok. Structural ingenuity and a green agenda raise it above the crowd. The eco idea took the traditional Thai house and adapted its sustainable qualities to high-rise living. The structure is a lateral offset—essentially two towers, each composed of three vertical stacks, sandwiched and perforated for air and views. It is articulated with vertical fins and balconies which provide solar shade.

Units are cross-ventilated by breezes to minimise air conditioning. Vertical and horizontal gaps in the elevations allow air to rise in the voids, and decrease the wind sway to which tall buildings are exposed (a model was wind-tunnel tested; the Met also has a seismic rating). Structural bracing was necessary to stabilise the six stacks at every fifth level. Green 'creeper' screens were intended to cultivate living walls all the way to the top, and balconies have planters. The idea was that the project be bio-sustainable, festooned like a hanging basket. That this has not quite happened may

be due to not all condo owners having green fingers, but the podium has a vertical garden. The project won the 2011 Lubetkin Prize from the Royal Institute of British Architects, for excellence in international architecture by a member of the institute.

198
Christ Church
11 Convent Road
James S. Smyth, 1905

In 1861 Rama IV gave land to foreign residents led by the British Consul to build the Protestant Union Chapel on Charoen Krung Road. An Anglican chaplain, Reverend Herbert de Courcy Blakeney, was sent from England by the Society for the Propagation of the Gospel. He condemned the chapel 'an architectural monstrosity' plagued by noise from the Bangkok Dock Company next door.

Rama V granted land for the parish to be relocated to Convent Road. Reverend Blakeney oversaw the construction of this church which is brick and stucco in Gothic Revival style. Similar parish and garrison churches were built across the British Empire. Many were designed by engineers, as architect James Smyth was (he worked for the Royal Railway Department).

In plan the building is conventional, with a porch at the base of the tower. Inside there is a choir and apse reached from a nave flanked by columns from which Gothic arches spring. There is an aisle on each side, expressed externally as Gothic arcades. In the nave, clerestory windows let in high light below the teak roof from where ceiling fans cooled the congregation, until air conditioning was fitted in 1994.

There were no bells in the tower, to avoid disturbance to Bangkok Nursing Home and St Joseph's Convent nearby. Traffic became noisier than bells, so one was installed in 1955. Stained glass windows were imported from Britain. One survives from the original chapel. Fourteen new windows were commissioned in 1991. The pipe organ, made in London in 1904, is the oldest in Thailand.

199

The Sukhothai

13 South Sathorn Road

Kerry Hill Architects, Ed Tuttle, 1991

A tree-lined avenue leads to this luxury hotel set in landscaped grounds in a walled compound. There are several interconnected buildings, understated and functional with unadorned four- to nine-storey elevations. They are mask for an inner plan enlivened by colonnades and courtyards which recall the colonial style of the fifth reign, as do the interior spaces decorated with traditional artwork. The courtyards are serene spaces, one with a reflecting pool with five brick pagodas inspired by ancient city of Sukhothai. There is a cluster of Thai-style pavilions by a klong in the garden. Heritage lends the hotel its identity but the overall feel is contemporary.

The design team returned to the site for the Sukhothai Residences (2012), a neo-modernist high-rise with modular-looking elevations. The structure's footprint steps back politely from the hotel's personal space.

200

Family Condominium

Soi 1, South Sathorn Road

Open Box architects, Tierra landscape design, 2008

Low- to mid-rise density in Bangkok used to mean rows of concrete shophouses. Recently a new form of mid-rise

has emerged. Architecturally it is more imaginative, appeals to design-literate young professionals, requires less investment than high-rises, less time to build, and potentially makes a quicker return. The new formula is common in Europe and North America, with open-plan, loft-style live-work spaces. Modular or modular-looking units are stacked, often irregularly; elevations are patterned with perforated or slatted solar shades.

Family Condominium is an example at the luxury end of the market, with 32 apartments (21 duplex) arranged in connected clusters. The development has a strong street presence, with the structure massed above the main entrance from where it turns through 90 degrees to stretch back, enclosing a landscaped inner courtyard.

201
The Goethe Institute
Soi Goethe, Soi 1, South Sathorn Road
Habita Architects, 1985

The cultural institute of the Federal Republic of Germany promotes its nation's language and culture and international cooperation. Historic links between Thailand and Germany go back to 1862 when a treaty of friendship, commerce and navigation was signed. The institute is located in a compound which was leased to the Thai-German Cultural Foundation from Crown Properties in 1984. There are three adjoining buildings, their elements a mix of renovation and new build. The structures are two-storey, post and beam colonial-style raised on columns with ground floors partly open. The middle building has an inner courtyard. The compound is leafy; the entrance to it has a wooden gatehouse, gates and fretwork fence.

Such compounds were common around Sathorn, Soi 1, also known as Soi Attakarn Prasit, the name of a senior official during the fifth and sixth reigns. He built 10 houses, some for members of his family; others were sold to foreign or local merchants. The Danish Embassy (10 Soi Attakarn Prasit; 1910), was one, bought from the Borneo Company by the Danish Ministry for Foreign Affairs in 1954. Any leafy compound left in central Bangkok is likely to hide an old house.

Chinese-style Buddha images, Wat Leng Nei Yee

6

Chinatown to Bang Rak

Chinatown, or Sampheng as it is also known, developed after Rama I moved an established Chinese community out of Rattanakosin Island when he began to build the Grand Palace in 1782. There was no land tenure in Siam: all land belonged to the king until 1908 when Rama V introduced Western-style title deeds. During the first reign and later, a suspicion lingered that the Chinese, who had been clients of King Taksin who himself was half Chinese, were not entirely loyal to the newly formed Chakri monarchy. But they were needed for their labour and enterprise which thereafter helped build Bangkok.

In the 19th century migrants fled wars and poverty in China. Many headed for Bangkok where there were opportunities and existing networks of trade and settlement, and where a better life was possible. The migrants were divided by five rival languages: Cantonese, Hainanese, Hakka, Hokkien and Taechiu. As in other overseas Chinese communities around the world these clans were insular and self-reliant. In the absence of hospitality from the host society each group formed benevolent associations, schools and businesses. Overcrowding in Sampheng became so bad by the 1890s that collective efforts were made to improve the quality of life. The Thian Fa Foundation Hospital is an example. Solidarity was promoted by Dr. Sun Yat-sen, the pro-democracy activist who visited overseas Chinese communities to raise funds for the revolution of 1911 which created the Republic of China. A soi off Ratchawong Road was renamed for him in 2004 and an ornamental gate erected. Sampheng people cling to their culture (witness the area's many shrines) but have also adapted to Siamese supremacy and integrated over the years. Merchants forged alliances with the Siamese ruling class, some gaining titles when their daughters became royal consorts. Many of Bangkok's biggest and most successful private companies today were founded by Chinese immigrant entrepreneurs.

Sampheng is one of the oldest, possibly the oldest, of the Chinatowns around the world, and one of the largest and most densely built and populated. The old focus of the community is Sampheng Lane, the original northern boundary of the Chinese settlement in the 18th century. Wats Chakrawat and Sampheng respectively were the western and eastern edges; the Chao Phraya River and docks off Songwat Road marked its southern extent. After a fire consumed part of the neighbourhood in 1891—the alleys prevented firefighters getting in with water pumping carts—Yaowarat and other new roads were built as wide streets, in part to act as firebreaks with new buildings constructed in brick and concrete. In the 1950s Yaowarat blossomed with a forest of neon signs rising from an undergrowth of gold shops with gaudy, 1930s-style interiors. Either side are souk-like alleys and sois with shrines, old-style shophouses, restaurants, street food vendors and long-established family-run stores.

Old Chinatown is threatened with redevelopment as property values rise with the arrival of the MRT Blue Line extension which has a station on Charoen Krung Road. The metro is the first serious improvement to the infrastructure since Rama V had Yaowarat and other main roads built. It will bring public benefits: ease of access to the area, a cleaner environment with new buildings and an alternative to sitting in gridlocked traffic. However, as the Siam Society has warned, it will erase the authenticity of the historic neighbourhood because the 2013 City Plan allows high density and tall buildings zoned around transit stations, and people will be evicted to make way for them.

Bang Rak was a mangrove-edged jungle with scattered villages before the Bowring Treaty with the British in 1855. Rama IV assigned the area to Europeans for their legations, businesses and dwellings. The spine is Charoen Krung, or New Road, an elephant track until foreign residents petitioned the king to pave it in the 1860s so they could take the relatively cool evening air on foot, on horseback or in carriages. During the day rickshaws were hired, like tuk-tuks. Public transportation improved when a tram line from the City Pillar Shrine to Bang Rak was inaugurated in 1887, with streetcars hauled by horses until the line was electrified in 1894.

In 1902 there were only around 1,000 European residents in the city. They had a disproportionate influence, not only due to the extraterritorial treaties the British, French and other foreign governments had negotiated, but also because Rama IV, and especially Rama V, welcomed their expertise and technology to modernise the kingdom. Teak logging, mining and shipping concessions, and diplomatic, religious and residential privileges granted to the British, other Europeans and Americans made colonisation less likely. Bangkok was open for business, as the architecture from that time shows. New Road was lined with Sino-European shophouses and the prime riverfront sites with colonial-style legations, banks and the Oriental Hotel, 'the largest and best appointed hotel in Siam'.

Britain, the leading imperial power of the time, had colonised Malaya and Burma bordering Siam and it dominated trade and investment in Bangkok and up-country. Portuguese and French Catholic missions, active in the Ayutthaya era, continued to introduce education and Christianity—the French-built Assumption Cathedral is a spectacular example. Dutch, Scandinavian and German companies were active in shipping and commerce. Italians were the leading foreign architects and several settled and lived many years in Bangkok. Of the European nations, Italy seems closest socially to Thailand: a love of family and food, the blend of superstition and religion, the culture of patronage, and the view of regulation as advisory and etiquette mandatory. 'Advisory' could be said of Bangkok's approach to urban planning but much of Bang Rak's historic fabric survives, especially around the Oriental Hotel.

Some buildings from Chinatown to Bang Rak that are best seen from the river are featured in tour 7—the Chao Phraya River and Thonburi—as cross reference between maps 6 and 7.1 will clarify.

202

Chinatown Gate and Wat Traimit

Odeon Circle

The name of the traffic circle recalls the 1950s Odeon cinema, since demolished. The roundabout got a makeover in 1999 when this heritage-style arch was erected as a gateway to Chinatown and named Chalermphrakiat Arch (King's Birthday Celebration Arch). The central panel reproduced calligraphy meaning 'Long Live The King' penned by Princess Sirindhorn.

In the background is a marble podium and a mondop with a golden spire. This is the pinnacle of an ostentatious redevelopment (2009) of Wat Traimit, which includes the Chinatown Heritage Centre. The wat's outstanding attraction is the Golden Buddha. The image, long thought to be stone and stucco, was brought to Bangkok by Rama I. It was moved to Wat Traimit in the 1930s where it remained unremarked for two decades until it was moved within the compound in 1955. A rope broke, the image fell, the plaster cracked and gold was exposed. The image was, reputedly, disguised during the Ayutthaya period to hide it from marauding Burmese. It was made in Sukhothai in the 13th century, is over three metres tall and weighs five and a half tons. It is the largest solid gold Buddha in the world.

203

Thai Watana Panich Building

Maitrijit Road

c. 1955

Founded in 1935, the Thai Watana Panich Company printed school textbooks and grew to be one of the most advanced print shops in Thailand. Hot metal type-

setting technology was imported in 1957 from the Monotype Company in London. The machines, for which a new Thai typeface was designed, enabled typesetters to cast type automatically rather than setting each character by hand. The building is imprinted on the street corner with an Art Deco, wedge-shaped profile of glass blocks. The elevations are emphasised by wide eaves in the modernist manner. The building was damaged by fire and vacated some years ago but its frayed edges could be repaired.

204
Thian Fah Foundation
606 Yaowarat Road
1905

This is the oldest charitable society in Bangkok. It was established in 1903 to provide traditional Chinese medical care, given free to the poor. Western health care was introduced as an option later. Rama V attended the inauguration.

The foundation's buildings enclose three sides of a plaza which is entered through an old-style gate built in 2003. In the centre of the square is the Thian Fa Pavilion, traditional, decorated elaborately. It is a Buddhist shrine to Guan Yim, goddess of mercy, whose gilded wood figure in a frame above the altar appears theatrically out clouds of incense smoke. The image is Chinese, Tang dynasty, installed here in 1960. The alter is flanked by portraits of the hospital's six founders who united Sampheng's five ethnic groups in this mutually beneficial enterprise. The hospital was named for Tian Fa, the protector of sailors and fishers, with whom the Guan Yim figure has been conflated in the popular imagination. The pavilion was rebuilt for the foundation's centenary.

205
Art Deco Building
Yaowarat at Charoen Krung Road
c. 1950

Pilasters, eaves, balconies and a bullish projecting corner butt into the confluence of Charoen Krung and Yaowarat roads. The style of this assertive apartment and commercial block is Parisian Art Deco, via Shanghai. The exterior is unaltered above the storefronts on the ground floor where the original caged elevator can be glimpsed in a lobby. The building replaced a pitched-roof shophouse, once a branch of Kiam Hoa Heng, an import-export company founded by Low Khiok Chiang (also known as Jacobe Low), a leading benefactor of Assumption Cathedral in Bang Rak.

206

Tang To Kang Gold Shop

345 Sampheng Lane (Soi Wanit 1) at Soi Mangkon

1921

Chinatown has been a centre for gold and gem trading since its earliest days. This family owned store was named for its founder, dates from the 1870s and is the district's oldest goldsmith and retailer. The business moved from deepest Sampheng to a shophouse at this corner. The founder's son was appointed by Rama VI to serve the royal household, the firm was granted the Garuda symbol of royal patronage and this building erected to reflect the good fortune. The style is Sino-European. The structure is concrete, stuccoed to imitate stone on the elevations which have wrap-around balconies with classical balusters, heritage-style shutters, and the store's name on plaques. The building, originally five storeys, was constructed to fireproof standards, a necessity in the cramped environment. A museum about the shop and the tradition of gold crafts opened after a restoration in 2002.

207

Bangkok Bank

Sampheng Lane (Soi Wanit 1) at Soi Mangkon

c.1910

Thailand's biggest commercial bank started trading in 1944 with 23 staff in this building across Soi Mangkon from Tang To Kang Gold Shop, whose Sino-European style it shares. The façades are embellished with stucco details in Renaissance style, which is emphatic at the entrance with Tuscan columns and finely formed faux stonework. Balcony ironwork was cast in a Chinese pattern. Both buildings are essentially shophouses, taller and more richly decorated than others built during the fifth and sixth reigns.

208

Leng Buay Ia Shrine

125 Trok Isaranuphap (Soi 6, Yaowarat; Soi 16 Charoen Krung)

The alley is packed with vendors, cheap and cheerful eateries and shoppers seeking the variety and quality of freshly prepared food and delicacies. There is a century-old wet market, Talat Mai (new market); Talat Kao (old market) is across Yaowarat Road.

The shrine lies on a plaza behind two tenements on the east side of the alley. According to a heritage plaque it dates from 1658, which would make it the oldest Chinese shrine in the kingdom. It might have been founded in Ayutthaya. The origin is unclear. A bronze bell is dated 1843. The architecture is traditional, with wooden posts and beams and a tiled roof with ceramic dragons on the ridge. Two more dragons leap from the columns at the entrance which is flanked by painted panels illustrating folk scenes. The main altar is arranged like a stage set from a Chinese opera, with miniature figures of 14th-century scholar Koe Yi (whose shrine this is), warlord Guan Yu and other deities.

209
Wat Leng Nei Yi
423 Charoen Krung Road
1879
Rama V ordered the land cleared for this temple in 1873. It was built for the Chinese Mahayana Buddhist sect whose patriarch in Siam took up residence here. Construction was financed by government officials and Chinatown merchants. Known as the Dragon and Lotus Temple, or Wat Mangkon Kamalawat in Thai, it is the neighbourhood's largest and most important religious site.

The main entrance on Charoen Krung Road is an ornate gate with dragon and lotus imagery. A passage through the nine-storey temple school (1978) opens to a plaza and a walled compound. The temple entrance is Chatulokaban Hall, named for its four Buddhist guardian figures. Above its door is the temple name, painted on a red plaque in calligraphy by the first abbot.

The layout of the wat's halls, abbot's garden and monks' quarters follows Chinese imperial palace precedents with a hierarchy of ceremonial spaces and courtyards connected by corridors. Here the main inner area is the Buruphachan (Founding Fathers) Hall. This is a lofty wooden post and beam structure open on two sides, adorned with painted panels, delicate screens, and artistic carvings of flowers and animals, all supported by stem-like columns with lotus bud capitals.

Through clouds of incense smoke, three Chinese-style Buddha images sit and look out from an alcove where

they are flanked by figures of disciples displayed in glass cases. An adjacent courtyard with a single tree in a miniature rock garden is a peaceful space next to the abbot's garden, which is private.

210

Siam Commercial Bank, Chaloem Nakhon branch

269 Charoen Krung Road

c. 1910

The structure of this building is ferroconcrete, an early use of reinforced concrete in Bangkok, clad by its architect with stucco to look like stone, Italianate

style. There are Tuscan columns at the entrance, wide eaves, a balcony and a pediment at the corner where the façade turns gracefully. Originally this was a shop called SEC Store. Siam Commercial Bank, whose royal garuda is on the pediment, rents the building from Crown Properties. Recent exterior and interior restoration included the banking hall which has classical columns and a tiled floor.

A twin across Worachak Road created a well balanced urban design. Its original owner, Societié Anonyme Belge, left its name at the intersection, called SAB Junction. The building was constructed as an outlet for SAB's import business. The company, by royal appointment, was noted for jewellery and an inventory of upscale European and American products.

211

Sampheng Lane

Soi Wanit 1

Sampheng Lane is about six metres wide but the pedestrian way is much less because retail displays spill out from the storefronts, a characteristic not only of Chinatown but also of many Bangkok sidewalks. The alley is sweltering, packed with shoppers, food carts, porters with rolls of fabric, and delivery drivers on beat-up Vespa scooters. In the past the lane was animated with sailors and immigrants fresh from China who disembarked at Sampheng docks; there were

goldsmiths, traders and opium dealers, gamblers, pawnbrokers and prostitutes. They inhabited a maze of wooden houses along the lane which stopped at Saphan Han, the bridge over Klong Rob Krung just short of the old city wall and wealthy residential compounds along what is now Chakphet Road.

212
Wat Chakrawat
225 Chakrawat Road

The temple lies south of Sampheng Lane between Chakrawat and Mahachak roads. Shophouses (which provide income for the wat) and a modern compound (formerly where cholera victims were cremated) hide the oldest part of the temple, which is close to Sampheng Lane. The historic compound has a complete range of traditional structures, picturesque on what is now a tight but green urban site. The wat dates from the Ayutthaya era but was reconstructed radically during the third reign, having received royal second class status in 1825. The Khmer-style prang was erected as a monument to Rama III's victory over a rebellion in Laos. The rebel leader, brought here in a cage, died of exposure.

The king's army was led by Chaophraya Bodindecha who renovated the temple for the monarch.

Four water fountains with animal heads surround the ubosot (1829) which has handsome porticos, Sino-Siamese decorated gables and murals much restored. It faces west in the direction of Wat Phra Kaew rather to sunrise. Its size was determined after Rama III noted that the floor of a new viharn (1827) was, contrary to hierarchy, raised above that of the existing ubosot, which was downgraded but still stands. The viharn, built to house a Buddha image taken from Vientiane, is small but exceptional for its chinoiserie and walls decorated with a repeat pattern of a type usually applied inside such buildings.

There are two enclosures for the wat's live crocodiles. Keeping these reptiles started as merit making, captured reptiles being donated to the temple. Grotesque specimens are preserved in a glass case. Italian traveller Salvatore Besso wrote: 'We went to the Chinese quarter of Sampan [sic] to see the Temple of the Crocodiles where, in a stagnant pool, together with two enormous tortoises, vegetate two decrepit examples of the race.' Besso was writing in 1911. Much of the crocodile pond had been filled in the 1890s when an artificial hill was raised at Rama V's command for the prang-topped pavilion which houses a replica of the Buddha's footprint. A grotto in the compound has a painted shadow of the Buddha, recalling a long lost mirror on which a vision of the deity is said to have appeared.

213
Chao Krom Poe Pharmacy
229–231 Chakrawat Road

Chinatown has numerous old shops run by the same families for generations. Education and upward social mobility, air conditioned convenience stores and supermarkets make their future uncertain, as does real estate development. There is still a large resident population, and many people who move out return with their children to favourite temples and stores.

This pharmacy, next door to one of Wat Chakrawat's three gates, is the oldest purveyor of Thai herbal medicines in the kingdom. The shop is open to the street, on the ground floor of a concrete shophouse which replaced the wooden one where the business was founded in 1894. The atmosphere is informal, the store cluttered but organised, a metaphor for the city. The most prized medicines are kept in wooden cabinets that look as old as a portrait of the founder, Chao Krom Poe, which hangs at the back of the store.

214
Songwat Road Shophouse
Songwat at Ratchawong Road
c. 1900

Sampheng docks were developed in the 19th century by Chinatown's import and export entrepreneurs who built their own (or shared) piers. Some merchants owned junks, and later steamships for coastal services. Ocean-going ships anchored downstream; passengers and cargos were transferred on shallow-draught boats. The docks became so busy that a tram line from Chakrawat Road served Ratchawongse Pier which was built in 1892 by the Public Works Department, as was Ratchawong Road. Songwat Road was paved in 1897. Western and Indian trading companies established premises. Sois perpendicular to Songwat led to the docks and were lined with godowns.

Changing patterns of trade and transportation made the docks redundant by the 1950s. Shipping companies moved

to the new port at Klong Toei, leaving Songwat Road with many heritage buildings. It should be a conservation area (it would be in many other cities). One of the most striking relics is this brick and stucco shophouse with classical pilasters, wooden balconies and fretwork. With its showy corner, the building evidently was once the office of a merchant keen to display his success. The style is Gothic Revival with a whiff of the British Raj.

215

Lao Pun Thao Kong Shrine and Peiing School

831–833 Songwat Road

A Chinese gateway on Songwat Road leads to this shrine, also called San-chao Kao, thought to have been built in the early Rattanakosin period around the time Sampheng was founded. It is dedicated to the deity Pun Thao Kong, a guardian god of communities in south-east China from where immigrants to Sampheng came. The present building, a reconstruction following one of the periodic fires in the neighbourhood, dates from 1868. Decorative features are typical: red (to ward off evil but also the colour of happiness), celestial warriors, dragons, phoenixes and turtles. The plan and decoration are similar to Leng Buay Ia Shrine, also of antique origin.

Pei-ing School, established in 1916 by local merchants to match the facilities and quality of education at Christian mission and leading Siamese schools, was opened in 1920 after a construction period interrupted by shortage of materials during the First World War. The building is Italianate with loggias, balustrades, a galleried atrium and stone effects in stucco. The front façade is partly visible behind the shrine and the west elevation can be seen in Rong Khom Lane.

216

Fruit Building

900 Songwat Road

c.1900

The Sino-Portuguese shophouse style evolved in the 19th century. It is characterised by European architectural details and bas-relief decoration overlaid on the traditional Chinese shophouse form. It was and is still popular in South-East Asia notably in Singapore, Penang and Phuket where there are many well preserved examples. The style is Portuguese because the first European navigators, traders and missionaries encountered in Asia were and their florid architecture followed; Chinese because the building type suited the communal and commercial life of overseas Chinese. Old shophouses in Sampheng and on Rattanakosin Island display that cultural blend and sociability. Few are as fully ripe as this row. The fruits symbolise good fortune.

217
Luang Kocha Isahak Mosque
979 Songwat Road
c. 1895

The mosque stands in a courtyard in a short alley at the east end of the Fruit Building. Established in the late 18th century it is the only mosque in Sampheng. It was named after its founder, a government official and Malay interpreter whose ancestors from the south arrived in Bangkok during the first reign. The original wooden structure was used by resident Muslims, and Malay and Indian sailors and traders. A graveyard was laid out. As Sampheng docks grew, more people required a bigger building which was evidently designed by a locally based Western architect. The style is Palladian. Neoclassical plasterwork enriches the main pediment, its entablature and the smaller pediments above the upper windows. Ground floor doors and windows have arabesque screens substituting for fanlights.

218
Wat Sampheng
1620 Songwat Road

Dating from the Ayutthaya period the wat was rebuilt from a ruin during the first reign when it was named officially Wat Pathum Khongkha, or Lotus of the Ganges. The name refers to the holy river in India in which ashes of the dead are

scattered. The temple was a way station for Siamese royal ashes. It was also a burial site for white elephants and an execution ground for disloyal princes (an execution stone is displayed). Like Wat Chakrawat, this temple had a charnel ground where victims of cholera were cremated, or left to vultures if firewood ran out during epidemics. The ubosot and viharn stand side by side in a cloistered quadrangle around which is a display of Buddha images. The ubosot's eight bai sema take the form of small Khmer-style prangs. In the parking lot outside is a row of 19th-century reliquary chedis. The temple school and some of the monks' quarters are across Songwat Road which bisects the wat's original compound.

219
Wat Maha Phruettharam
Mahaphruttharam Road

This is a third class royal temple built on the site of an Ayutthaya-era monastery called Wat Tha Kwian, said to have been a layover for wagon (kwian) travellers, or because of a legendary visit by the 14th-century King Uthong of Ayutthaya. The temple was rebuilt and renamed by Rama IV. There are three main structures: the ubosot, viharn and a pavilion which houses a reclining Buddha. Murals in the ubosot painted in the fourth reign blend Siamese temple style with landscapes and buildings showing the influence of Western art. There are charming cameos of daily life. One panel shows monks receiving alms; another illustrates a Siamese junk of the type modelled at Wat Yannawa. The gables have a gilded stucco royal seal of Rama V; those on the viharn are similar, but with the emblem of Rama IV.

220
Captain Bush House
Captain Bush Lane (Soi 30, Charoen Krung Road)
c. 1890

Opposite the Sheraton Royal Orchid Hotel is a plot of land granted by Rama IV to Captain (later Admiral) John Bush who built this villa on it. Bush and his wife arrived in Bangkok in 1857 after the

Bowring Treaty of 1855 opened Siamese ports to British trade.

Bush, an experienced English navigator, became the king's harbour master, a post he retained for 30 years. His business interests included the Bangkok Dock Company. He also skippered royal yachts In 1868 he took Rama IV to Prachuap Kiri Kan province where the king had predicted and wished to view an eclipse of the sun. Bush served Rama V until 1890, when he ran the yacht aground en route to Singapore. Evidently he was forgiven: he died in 1905 and is buried in the Protestant Cemetery where his grave has an obelisk with a royal inscription 'For his long and faithful services'.

His house is a brick structure, stuccoed to look like stone, an effect noticeable at the corners which are turned with rusticated faux quoins. Traces of past elegance filtered through years of decay before Crown Properties began to restore the house in 2014. The composition

is Palladian with an arcaded entrance and a pediment dominating the hipped roof. Bush could look down a soi to the river, a view now obscured by the hotel.

221
Bangkok Folk Museum
Soi 43, Charoen Krung Road
Three old teakwood buildings in a leafy compound form this fascinating museum, surprisingly peaceful in the shadow of the expressway. It was established in 1992 by Varaphon Surawadee, daughter of the original home's owner, Sa-Ang Surawadee Tanbuntek. A second house was relocated here. The third building is a row house. Artifacts are displayed on the ground floor and a Bang Rak history gallery is upstairs.

The main house (1937) is a Western design with high ceilings, varnished wood floors and jigsaw patterned ventilation screens. The front porch lends it a North American feel, as if somewhere on the prairies. Furniture and fittings are original. The structure is wood frame, with board siding, a pitched roof and gables, and crawl space under the porch and ground floor. This assists air flow as do the high ceilings and screens inside, and windows which let breezes in from the leafy compound. These features and fans rather than air conditioning sufficed, when Bang Rak was more open than built up.

222
General Post Office
Charoen Krung Road, between sois 32 and 34
Jittasen Aphaiwong, Sarot Sukkayang
1940

When the Post and Telegraph Department outgrew its original head office near Memorial Bridge, it moved to this monumental Art Deco building built on land occupied previously by the British Legation. It is one of Bangkok's most dignified heritage buildings. A marquee stands out above doors recessed in a projecting central bay designed to command the elevation, which has a tall wing at each end. Pilasters divide the façade with classical regularity. The main doors are decorated with metalwork and garudas in Art Deco style.

The central bay is topped either side with garuda sculptures. Local folklore has it that when the Allies bombed Bangkok during the Second World War the garudas took flight and saved the building from being hit. They were sculpted by Corrado Feroci, who designed stucco panels in the style of postage stamps in the main hall and, on the plaza outside, the statue of Prince Bhanurangsi Swangwongse, the department's first director.

The plaza was repaved in 2013, part of an extensive restoration and adaptive reuse of the building as an events venue, operated by Impact Exhibition Management. The main hall is a function suite; the postal outlet has moved to a smaller space in the north wing. A new name came with the makeover—the Grand Postal Building.

223

Trocadero Hotel

343 Suriwongse Road

1922

In 1950 the *New Guide to Bangkok* described this as 'one of the largest hotels in town . . . in the business centre'. It was built to rival the Oriental, with Italianate grandeur which would not be out of place in Rome. Its façade retains a bracketed cornice, balconies and fenestration. At some point unrecorded a two-storey addition on the roof destroyed the original balustrade, which ran the full length of the elevation, and an ornamental gable above the entrance bay. On the ground floor subdivision for retail units has disrupted the linear formality of round-arched windows. The grandeur is faded but not beyond repair.

224

OP Garden

Soi 36, Charoen Krung Road

2009

Concrete balconies and solar screens (some new with slatted wood) enliven this 1960s shophouse and former clinic rehabilitated as part of a mini mall with boutique stores, an art gallery, restaurant and café. The development is a pleasing fusion of old and new. Set back from the

soi are intimate landscaped courtyards with several houses, also refurbished, some dating back to the fifth reign.

225
Oriental Place
Soi 38, Charoen Krung Road
1908

This was one of the largest foreign-

owned commercial buildings in Bangkok. It was built for Falck and Beidek, importers, wholesale and retail merchants who provided 'practically everything which a resident in Bangkok needs'. The firm was established in 1878 on an adjacent site. The architect of this second and palatial emporium is not known but the clean-cut colonial neoclassicism suggests British. Around 1980 the store was converted to an upmarket shopping centre, one of the first ventures of its type to adapt a heritage building. The specialty is Asian arts and crafts and antiques, in outlets distributed around an atrium which has an old-style caged elevator.

226
Oriental Hotel
48 Soi Oriental (Soi 40, Charoen Krung Road)
Cardu and Rossi, 1887

Two establishments preceded this iconic hotel. They were of no lasting consequence other than bearing the now legendary name. The first, a seamen's hostel run by an American, Captain Dyer, burned down when a fire destroyed almost 70 buildings in the neighbourhood in 1865. The second was run by a Danish mariner who sold it in the early 1880s. The buyer was fellow countryman

Captain Hans Niels Andersen who hired Stefano Cardu, a Bangkok-based Italian architect, contractor and sawmill owner to design the 'new' Oriental. Andersen bought a steam launch to transfer guests from ocean-going ships, recruited the appropriately named George Troisoeufs, a chef at the French Legation, and hosted a garden party to mark the opening in 1887. He sold the hotel a few years later, developed much of the land between it and Charoen Krung Road, and established the East Asiatic Company. He lives on—the fan on the hotel's publicity was his original logo.

The hotel is known for its Authors' Wing, named after famous writers who have visited or lodged in the original two-storey structure. It is Italianate, somewhat Venetian, with round-arched windows, wooden fretwork, pilasters, and a central gable with a rising-sun motif below a split pediment. The hotel

name can be seen below the gable as it appeared in 1887. Shutters open to a riverside garden where two neoclassical statues stand like detached caryatids. Inside, there is a central courtyard, now a café and tearoom, originally open-air. The 19th-century scene is shown in a painting in the Authors' Wing. The hotel gained the highest seal of approval in 1890 when Rama V made a personal inspection and judged it fit for Prince Nicholas, later Czar Nicholas II of Russia, who was the king's guest the following year.

The Tower Wing was built behind the original structure in 1958. In 1972 the Oriental merged with the Mandarin Hotel Group which built the River Wing (Palmer and Turner, 1976). It is linked to the older structures by a luminous Thai-themed foyer entered from a porte cochère. The hotel has since been voted regularly among the best in the world.

Outside on Soi Oriental is the colonial gingerbread-style China House, formerly home to a Chinese merchant, rehabilitated as restaurant for the hotel in 1990.

227

Assumption Cathedral

23 Soi Oriental (Soi 40, Charoen Krung Road)

1910

Across Soi Oriental from the hotel is an alley dividing the two parts of the East Asiatic Company building which are connected by a Venetian-style bridge. The alley opens to an urban space resembling a provincial square in France,

dominated by the west front of Assumption Cathedral which is overwhelming, completely unexpected.

The cathedral replaced the original smaller church of 1821. Its Romanesque Revival style, complete with a round-arched entrance, rose window and two flanking towers, is carried into the nave where arches in the aisles, and a grand one at the altar, are banded in a two-tone stone effect. This is a typical Romanesque feature, as is the cathedral's basilica plan. The architect, said to have been French, embellished this historical vision with Renaissance-style: the arches spring from Corinthian columns and the ceiling is barrel-vaulted, coffered with stars. A triptych and a gilded statue of the Assumption of the Virgin Mary into Heaven fill the apse. The figure of Saint Peter stands outside, along with Pope John Paul II who visited the cathedral in 1984. The tension rods crossing the nave were fitted after the Second World War when there was some damage from bombs falling nearby. Extensive restoration was done in 2014.

228

Assumption Press

23 Soi Oriental (Soi 40, Charoen Krung Road)

The first French Catholic Mission to Siam arrived in Ayutthaya in the 17th century. French and other missions based in Bangkok grew during the reigns of Rama IV and Rama V, indicated by the medley of architecture around Assumption Cathedral square—Assumption College and Convent, the Rectory and Assumption Press.

Assumption Press, formerly the Roman Catholic Mission Press, was established in 1795 at Santa Cruz Church in Thonburi by Monseigneur Garnault, who had travelled from Pondicherry to Penang in 1788 to spread the gospel. He had a printing press from France and it arrived with him in Thonburi. His book of Christian teachings, printed at Santa Cruz in 1796, was the first printed in Siam using Romanised Siamese language (the first printing press using a Siamese typeface was introduced in 1835 by Daniel Beach Bradley of the American Protestant Mission at Thonburi).

The press moved next door to Assumption Cathedral in 1837 and later, to make way for a high-rise built for the college, to this former bishop's residence in 1970. The building dates probably from the early fifth reign. The architecture is neoclassical, proportioned beautifully, reminiscent of the tropical neoclassicism favoured by British colonial administrators. The pediment above the porch displays bas-relief heraldry representing the Bishop of the Archdiocese.

229

State Tower

1055 Silom Road

Rangsan Architecture, 2004

The project, called Silom Precious Tower, bullied its way into the neighbourhood in 1993 during economic boom times. It was intended as a 'jewellery business condominium' containing hundreds of residential and commercial units. It turned out to be fool's gold. The crash in 1997 stopped construction and the plan was changed to mixed use. The building was said to be the largest reinforced concrete structure in Asia. It is one of

the most absurd architecturally, with a parody of a classical porch, balustraded balconies and a trio of fake pediments which step back to a neo-Roman rooftop dome. A gigantic parking podium looms above a row of 100-year-old shophouses which include Nguan Ha Cheang, a long-established pawnbroker at the corner of Silom and Charoen Krung roads.

230
Wat Suan Phlu
Soi 58, Charoen Krung Road

An arch between shophouses on Charoen Krung Road is the only clue to the existence of this wat in the shadow of the Shangri-la Hotel. The temple was founded in 1797 by the Chinese community, on a betel leaf (ton phlu) farm.

Its compound contains a temple school, century-old monks' dwellings with delicate fretwork, a chedi, viharn, and an ubosot dating from 1798. The ubosot, rebuilt recently, is decorated with tiles and cho fas; aspara and naga figures perform on the gables. The viharn (1934) contains a statue of Rama V and a reclining Buddha. A scripture hall was built in a pond, as in the past when libraries were placed over water to prevent termites damaging the wood and eating the books.

There were eight kuti until 2011 when three were torn down for a new building, although they had been restored and received a conservation award from the Association of Siamese Architects in 2002. The demolition highlighted land use issues that face many urban temples. 'Nothing lasts forever' the abbot here said, not only invoking Buddhist passivity but also implying that temples must evolve to attract visitors in changing times. The trouble is that old buildings and shade trees make wats welcoming but they are vulnerable to new construction and parking for which their compounds were not designed.

231
Centre Point
1522 Charoen Krung Road
Sumet Jumsai Architects, 1994

This project was intended to float lightly on the site at Bang Rak market. The first sketch showed a yacht-like building, the nautical notion expressed in curving sail-like profiles on the tower which has serviced apartments and a helipad. The podium contains a retail anchor (Robinson Department Store) and a parkade. The tower is set back to minimise its visual intrusion on the historic streetscape. The main entrance to the store is a concave curve which created public space for shoppers, street traders and tuk-tuk and taxi drop-offs. The air conditioned cafeteria was quickly colonised as a social centre by Bang Rak's shophouse-dwelling, mahjong-playing Chinese senior citizens.

232
Saphan Taksin Shophouse
Charoen Krung Road and Sathorn intersection
Jok Premthada, 2008

This urban loft-style, live-work space recycled a humble heritage building, and shows how the shophouse typology can be reinvigorated in a contemporary, sustainable way. The original two-storey elevation (c. 1920) is accessible from an alley off Charoen Krung Road. The sliding doors on the ground floor, typical of shophouses of the period, were refurbished and the narrow interior was opened up. An internal steel and teak stair follows the footprint from old front through to a three-storey extension. A brick party wall was exposed and restored. The rear elevation has a wall of glass louvres which provide ventilation, privacy and a modernist decorative pattern. It overlooks the soi which serves the BTS station. In contrast, the trok off the soi has an old tree and an antique, eight-unit wooden row house.

233

Sathorn Unique Tower

Soi 51, Charoen Krung Road

Rangsan Architecture

Urban adventurers blog their visits to this hazardous ruin from the financial meltdown of 1997, when nouveau riche were reduced to penury, selling noodles on the streets, their Mercedes flogged at knock-down prices on parking lots. Hundreds of projects across the city were abandoned after bankrupt developers walked, leaving contractors unpaid and investors with heavy losses. For a decade, skeletal silhouettes stood as a reminder of dashed hopes or dented hubris. Most have since been revived and refurbished.

Sathorn Unique, uniquely for its size, remains stuck in the year of the crash. It was to have been a neo-Roman extravaganza, like State Tower, crowned with a dome. It has little chance of refinancing. The style is past its sell-by date. It is a spectacular ruin and a daunting demolition project. If structurally sound it could be productive, as a vertical garden and urban farm.

234

Wat Yannawa

1648 Charoen Krung Road

The temple was founded during the Ayutthaya period and restored around 1845 by Rama III. The ubosot, originally built by Rama I, has beautiful doors with guardian figures, and window shutters

showing Buddhist folk scenes. Other Rattanakosin-style buildings in the wat are recent.

The name translates as 'Temple of the Junk', specifically the full-size model of a Siamese junk with two chedis as masts that seems to have been beached broadside in the compound. Rama III ordered its construction instead of the usual royal pagoda. He anticipated that this type of vessel would become obsolete. His inscription says, 'For those who wish to see what a junk looks like . . .' It recalls Siamese seaborne trade with China. His statue stands next to it. Its prow has two enormous eyes to ward off sea devils and guide seafarers to safe harbour.

Between the temple and Saphan Taksin there was a pier called May Chin Port where immigrants from China seeking work and wealth in Bangkok disembarked in the early 1900s. Directly downstream, Captain John Bush opened the Bangkok Dock Company in 1865. It was the city's first modern ship building yard and dry dock, where Western sea-going vessels, which replaced the Rama III-era junks, were repaired.

235

Protestant Cemetery

Soi 72, Charoen Krung Road

The cemetery lies between Charoen Krung and the Chao Phraya River, hidden behind a gate in the soi and by a flood wall on the riverbank. There are around 1,000 graves of government officials, missionaries, mariners, fathers, mothers and children, many of whom expired from cholera which made no social distinction. The land was granted by Rama IV in 1853 after an appeal by foreign residents for a cemetery. It was accessible only from the river until New Road (Charoen Krung) passed its east side a decade later.

The site is not immediately picturesque but many of the grave markers are, with cherubs and angels, Celtic crosses, obelisks and neoclassical columns. The most elaborate structure is a triple-tiered Gothic Revival memorial to British consular official and aide to the Siamese royal court, Henry Alabaster. It is inscribed with the words of Rama V: 'In recognition of faithful service'. An obelisk recalls the 'long and faithful services of Admiral Sir John Bush', the king's royal yacht captain and harbour master. A plain marker notes John Clunis, the architect of the Chakri Maha Prasat Throne Hall, buried apparently penniless in 1894. Daniel Beach Bradley, the American Presbyterian missionary and medical doctor to the royal court, is buried here. Jews were interred before an adjacent plot was created for them, and there are graves of Chinese and Thai Christians. The cemetery registrar is held at Christ Church and records can be found online. There is a pleasing, partly open-air chapel by the river where a flood wall was built a decade ago.

Wat Arun, the Temple of the Dawn

7

Chao Phraya River & Thonburi

For centuries the Chao Phraya River has been Bangkok's link to the outside world. It was where travellers by sea gained their first impressions of the kingdom and its Buddhism, as proclaimed by Rama II when he built Phra Samut Chedi at Paknam (the mouth of the river). The channel that created the white chedi's island has since silted up and the chedi now stands on the river's west bank. Foreign ships waited outside a notorious sandbank (or bar) for high tide, then cleared customs at Paknam and continued to Bangkok. In 1888 mariner and writer Joseph Conrad recorded in his novel *The Shadow Line* his first sight of Phra Samut Chedi glowing at sunrise, and of the city:

> *'One morning early, we crossed the bar, and while the sun was rising splendidly over the flat spaces of the land, we steamed up the innumerable bends, passed under the shadow of the great gilt pagoda, and reached the outskirts of the town. There it was, spread largely on both banks, the Oriental capital . . ; an expanse of brown houses of bamboo . . . a vegetable-matter-style of architecture . . . like the nests of an aquatic race, clung to the low shores. Others seemed to grow out of the water; others again floated in long anchored rows in the middle of the stream. Here and there in the distance, above the crowded mob of low, brown roof ridges, towered great piles of masonry, King's Palace, temples, gorgeous and dilapidated, crumbling under the vertical sunlight . . .'*

Herbert Warrington Smyth, an English mining engineer who arrived in 1891 was less enchanted, writing in his memoir *Five Years in Siam*:

> *'But where was the Bangkok I had read of—that Venice of the East . . . with its gilded palaces and gorgeous temples? Before us lay but an eastern Rotterdam: mud banks, wharfs and jetties, unlovely rice mills belching smoke, houses gaunt on crooked wooden piles, dykes and ditches on either hand, steam launches by the dozen, crowded rows of native rice boats, lines of tall-masted junk-rigged lighters, and last, most imposing . . . British steamers, and Norwegian and Swedish barques . . .'*

The water city observed by Conrad accommodated nature and its annual floods which today's metropolis does not. Modernisation required roads, flood walls and locks which prevent natural drainage. In 2009 the Bangkok Metropolitan Administration lost a case brought by klong communities in Thonburi protesting against such works, which now require environmental impact assessment (as does any large-scale construction). The low-rise aquatic city has vanished on the Bangkok side of the river, but in the backwaters of Thonburi klongs, greenery, neighbourhood temples and wooden houses can still be found.

Thonburi, merged with Bangkok in 1972, was the capital founded by King Taksin after the fall of Ayutthaya in 1767. There are traces of multicultural communities from that period, south of his riverfront palace Wang Derm. The palace site is now occupied by the Royal Thai Navy. Conservation work won a Unesco award in 2004 but the site is generally not accessible to the public. The navy compound is bisected by Wat Arun, the Temple of the Dawn, which punctuates its stretch of the river. Both banks here are clear of high-rise intrusions, thanks to the preservation of Rattanakosin Island and respect for historic sites like Wang Derm, Wat Arun and the Grand Palace. In 2013 the BMA proposed the heritage zones on the east and west sides of the river be listed as a Unesco World Heritage site.

Much the city's riverfront is off limits, being owned by the Crown or privately for residential or commercial use. There are few public parks or promenades but cross-river ferries, the Chao Phraya Express boats or long-tail boat trips in Thonburi reveal remnants of the past. Temples by the klongs of Thonburi are evidence of community life connected to the canals and to the river. It looped round Thonburi before a shortcut to reduce travel time to Ayutthaya was dug in the mid 16th century. The river widened the cut which is now the main channel; the loop became klongs Bangkok Noi and Yai.

The old horizons change downstream from Memorial Bridge. Dockyards and rice mills were built by European and local Chinese entrepreneurs in the 19th century. Most of the industrial activity noted by Warrington Smyth has moved beyond the city limits. Even the once extensive Port of Bangkok at Klong Toei has been downgraded by deep water facilities on the Eastern Seaboard. Despite these shifts in shipping and industry the Chao Phraya River is still a significant transportation route with express boats and ferries, and bulbous rice barges towed by tugs, a common sight. Some old teakwood barges have been converted for sightseeing and dinner cruises for tourists. High-rise hotels have been built by the river since the 1970s. Condominium developers have followed, even on the once unfashionable Thonburi side.

The removal of docks and industries provides opportunities for urban renewal and heritage preservation. Among the significant historic sites needing attention are the Customs House and the East Asiatic Company Building, both crumbling from neglect. Recent examples of adaptive reuse include Asiatique the Riverfront, a rehabilitation of the East Asiatic Company godowns and wharf as a heritage-themed mall, and The Jam Factory, a mixed-use makeover of an abandoned workshop compound in Thonburi. Other industrial sites with heritage potential include the Bangkok Dock Company—its historic dry docks could be the nucleus of a maritime museum. The waterfront from which the city turned away when the business district in Bang Rak shifted inland in the 1960s seems ready for a revival.

236

Rama VIII Bridge

Buckland and Taylor engineers, 2002

Rama IX spurred this new crossing of the Chao Phraya River to ease traffic gridlock. The engineers designed the asymmetric cable-stayed bridge, with traditional decorative touches. A gigantic, inverted Y-shaped concrete pylon distributes the royal yellow-coloured cables which support the steel and concrete road deck. Its shape recalls antique prangs, like the centrepiece at Wat Arun. The top of the pylon has a lotus bud-shaped beacon; twin beacons flank the east and west approach ramps. Directly downstream there is a waterfront park, a statue of Rama VIII (Fine Arts Department, 2012) and a museum dedicated to him. The adjacent two-storey neo-Italianate building (2011) houses the Royal Development Projects Board and the Chaipattana Foundation for royal projects.

237

Praya Palazzo

Soi 2, Somdet Phra Pinklao Road

1923

This was a waterfront wreck when it was acquired by Wichai Pitakvorrarat of Rangsit University's architecture faculty. Enough remained of the structure, the garden and grand steps from a private boat dock to justify investment which funded conservation and rehabilitation, as a restaurant and boutique hotel. The villa, first named Baan Bang Yee Khan (a reference to the neighbourhood), was the family home of an aristocrat who ran the Royal Customs Department. The style is Palladian, popular with clients of the Italian architects working in Bangkok at the time. The property was sold to a school foundation in 1946 and aban-

doned 50 years later. Following its rescue from decay, the villa was renamed Praya Palazzo; a restaurant opened in 2009, followed two years later by the hotel.

238
Wat Dusitaram
Trok Dusitaram, Somdet Phra Pinklao Road
This is a mix of wats from the Ayutthaya era. One was destroyed in an air raid in 1945 and the buildings seen today were damaged. They are bisected by the trok. On one side is a modern compound which replaced the bombed area. On the other is an ubosot built by Rama I. It is centred in a quadrangle with two prangs and two chedis, each to its own corner. Cloisters contain 64 Buddha images, once gilded, and fragments of murals. The paintings date from the first reign, as are those in the ubosot. They too are fragmentary but more extensive and in better condition. The cloisters are post and beam with tiled roofs. The ubosot roof is two-tiered with painted beams inside, and is gabled with a porch at either end. The full range of decorative features is here, from fish-scale tiles and hongsa brackets to naga motifs and cho fas. The structures are brick and stucco. The murals are delicate and beautiful.

Directly north round the bend in the trok are an older ubosot and viharn flanking a ho trai pond. The bot has a high porch with columns and a big standing Buddha in bas-relief, like the smaller ones in the cloisters. A much needed conservation programme began in 2014.

239

National Museum of Royal Barges

Klong Bangkok Noi

The Fine Arts Department upgraded this dock as a national museum in 1974. The building is a functional steel-arched shed which protects a fabulous a collection of long, narrow, gilded barges used traditionally for river ceremonies, and merit-making after the annual monsoon when temples were visited by kings to offer robes and gifts to monks. The custom is thought to have started in Sukhothai in the 13th century.

During the reign of King Narai the Great (1656-88) in Ayutthaya, the Royal Barge Procession was witnessed by Europeans who recorded it as a magnificent spectacle. Royal comfort was ensured by parasol bearers, safety by pilots and helmsmen, and propulsion by up to 100 oarsmen. Ayutthaya's barges were lost when the Burmese sacked the city in 1767. The performance was revived after 1782 by Rama I and has continued periodically since then.

The barge dock, shed and some barges were damaged in the air raid that destroyed Thonburi Station across the klong in 1945. In 1947, the Bureau of the Royal Household engaged the Fine Arts Department to repair and maintain the barges. The *Suphannahongsa*, designed with a graceful bow and carved hongsa, was modelled in 1911 on a barge built in the first reign. It was hollowed out from a single teak log and is the largest dugout vessel in the world. The *Ananta Nagaraj*, built in 1914, has a seven-headed naga figurehead; the *Anakchat Bhuchong* from the fifth reign has no figurehead but is decorated with a pattern of nagas. The *Narai Song Suban*, its prow carved as Narai riding the Garuda, was launched for the Golden Jubilee of Rama IX in 1996.

240

Wat Suwannaram

Soi 32, Charan Sanitwong, Klong Bangkok Noi

This Ayutthaya-era temple was rebuilt by Rama I. The ubosot's interior is decorated with murals of masterly quality depict-

ing Jataka tales painted during the third reign, when the wat was refurbished (c. 1830). Their humanity, in delicately painted vignettes, often humorous, shines through the conventions of the genre. Recent restoration by the Fine Arts Department conserved original brushwork—the repainting is distinct but does not overpower the earlier artistry. The space below a magnificent wooden ceiling is dominated by a Buddha image believed to have come from Sukhothai at the end of the first reign because of its similarity to the grand image at Wat Suthat. The proportions of the hall are satisfying, similar to the interior of Buddhaisawan Chapel at the National Museum whose murals are kin to those here. The wat also has a viharn, chedi, a Chinese-style belfry and kuti in a peaceful setting beside the klong.

241
Thonburi Locomotive Depot
Suttawat Road, Klong Bangkok Noi

Until recently the State Railway of Thailand's yards extended along Klong Bangkok Noi as far as the Chao Phraya River where Thonburi Station was built in 1903. The site had a mosque which was relocated across the canal where it can be seen today, and Wat Amarintraram whose compound was reduced to make room for Rama V's trains. During the Second World War this was the start of a rail route to supply Japanese troops in Burma, via Kanchanaburi where trains cross the River Kwai. The line to Burma was built by the Japanese using slave labour from South-East Asia and Allied prisoners of war. Thousands died building it. In 1945 Allied planes bombed the station and yards. The rebuilding programme included this maintenance depot, which attracts rail fans because some SRT heritage steam locomotives are kept in working order here.

242
Siriraj Bimuksthan Museum, Siriraj Hospital
Phiran Nok Road
Design 103 International, 2013

The museum, the latest of several at Siriraj, features medical and local history. Archeological excavations revealed the

remains of brick walls thought to have been part of King Taksin's fortifications of Thonburi, and timbers of an old riverboat were found and displayed.

The project was an adaptive reuse of Thonburi Station, first built for the Phetchaburi Railway in 1903 to a design by Karl Siegfried Döring. It became the Bangkok base of the Southern Railway, which opened when the first express train to Malaya, then a British colony, steamed out of here in 1919. After the Rama VI bridge was completed in 1927 the Southern line's trains were routed in and out of Hua Lamphong, but Thonburi continued with local services. The station building was redesigned and rebuilt (Vodhyakarn Varavarn, 1950) after being bombed in 1945. The structure is concrete, faced in brick; the style is Italian modernist from the 1930s.

The station closed in 2003 to accommodate a massive expansion of Siriraj Hospital. The old building, its clock tower and two wooden warehouses were retained for the museum. A riverfront park initiated by the SRT, which had planned to keep the station open and restore it, was landscaped. There is a royal sala. A steam locomotive is displayed on a short length of track. A no-frills new station was built near the locomotive depot a kilometre west along Klong Bangkok Noi.

243
Siriraj Hospital
Phiran Nok Road

In 1886 Rama V established a committee for public health following an outbreak of cholera in Bangkok. Two years later a medical school, now Siriraj Faculty of Medicine (administered by Mahidol University), was founded on the site of Wang Lang, a palace during the first reign.

Siriraj is the oldest and biggest public hospital in Thailand. It is a city within a city, with much recent development crammed onto its site. There is a variety of buildings in many styles: Italianate, modernist, brutalist and postmodern. Until Memorial Bridge opened in 1932 access from the Bangkok side of the river was by ferry—the pier serving the hos-

pital is still a busy stop on the express boat route. Just upstream is the first pier, rebuilt (Chua Patthamachinda, 1927) in Italianate style. It was the formal entrance to the hospital. A pedestrian way from it leads through the Italianate-style Administration Building (1925) to Centennial Hall Plaza where there is a statue of patron Prince Mahidol.

244
Sri Savarindhira Building, Siriraj Hospital
Phiran Nok Road
SJA+3D, Architects 110, 2011

Nicknamed 'The da Vinci Building' this is the most idiosyncratic of the recent additions to Siriraj Hospita—15 storeys of reinforced concrete with a curvy and colourful, rib-like elevation. According to lead architect Sumet Jumsai it was inspired by the sketches of the dissected human body by Leonardo da Vinci. The precision and depth of those sketches is reflected in the building's surface and volume. The ribs express the floors; the body has a huge incision for natural ventilation and the ground floor mini mall, where there are fast food and other services, is open front to back. The mall's four-storey space is partly occupied by a

600-seat auditorium, above which is the main laboratory. Other facilities include several smaller laboratories, an information technology centre, lecture theatres and classrooms. Hanging gardens were provided on the fourth and sixth levels. The building replaced the old four-storey Anatomy Building with a design of cheerful clarity for a serious purpose and 21st-century student life.

245

Wat Rakhang

Arun Amarin Road

At the end of Trok Wat Rakhang is the Temple of the Bell. It dates from the Ayutthaya period. King Taksin established it as a royal temple for his capital at Thonburi. The bell which gives the wat its name was found during excavations in the first reign for a scripture hall. Rama I was enchanted by its resonance, took it to Wat Phra Kaew and compensated Wat Rakhang with five other bells.

The temple's structures, varied in their styles and decor, include gates with mondops, and a muscular Khmer-style prang with Buddha images in niches and a troop of guardian figures around its mid level. The murals in the ubosot, painted in the sixth reign, blend Western perspective with Renaissance and Chinese landscape styles and Siamese architecture and characters. A battle scene shows a royal war barge.

The most historic structure—the oldest dwelling in the city—is the teakwood, red ochre scripture hall, originally the house of future monarch, Rama I. In 1768 he gave it to the wat where it was rehabilitated by the crown prince as a library on the king's orders in 1782. Its three rooms, expressed externally with gables, were originally raised on wooden stilts, now concrete. Conservation of the structure, its murals and fittings, which include magnificent gilded, lacquered cabinets for scripture texts, began in 1968 and was completed for the Bangkok bicentennial in 1982.

246

Royal Thai Navy Headquarters

Arun Amarin Road

This waterfront naval zone bisected by Klong Mon and Wat Arun extends from the Naval Dockyard Department, where there is a historic dry dock (c. 1913), to Wichaiprasit Fort at Klong Bangkok Yai. The fort's battlements inspired the modern gates to the complex, originally the

site of King Taksin's palace, Wang Derm, where Rama V established the navy's academy. The northern half is dominated by the dry dock's travelling crane, industrial sheds and workshops. Two identical colonial-style buildings grace the riverfront north of Klong Mon, which is crossed by a Venetian-style bridge. The bridge leads to the contemporary (with a traditional entrance) Royal Thai Navy Convention Hall in the southern and most historic part of the complex.

A 10-year restoration of the surviving royal buildings, which include a throne hall, was begun in the mid 1990s by the Phra Racha Wang Derm Restoration Foundation. Decades of inappropriate modifications and structural erosion were reversed. Accretions were removed and original features revealed and restored, or replicated with traditional materials and craftsmanship. The work was rewarded with Unesco heritage award in 2004.

NOTIFICATION

247

Wat Arun

34 Arun Amarin Road

Legend has it that King Taksin arrived at this spot one day at sunrise, when the temple looks most enchanting. It seemed a significant omen, since he had just fought and escaped from the Burmese who were besieging Ayutthaya. After he established the new capital in 1767, he had the temple renovated and named Wat Jaeng, the Temple of the Dawn. During his 15-year reign he made merit by enlarging it. The Emerald Buddha, taken from Vientiane in 1778 by one of his generals, the future Rama I, was exhibited here.

The present size and appearance of Wat Arun date from the second reign. The tallest feature is a Khmer-style prang rising from the centre of a podium, decorated with step-backs, the structure seemingly supported by ranks of guardian figures. Above these are niches with Indra riding Erawan. Steep steps symbolise the quest for enlightenment; the prang itself represents Mount Meru. Each corner of the podium has a peripheral prang with niches for Vayu, god of the wind. Between each of these is an elaborate mondop; the podium gates are guarded by Chinese stone figures.

Rama II, who attached the name Arun (referring to Aruna, the Indian god of sunrise), planned to heighten the prang and build the four smaller ones, work which was completed in the third reign (the prang rose from the original 16 to 67 metres on a tiered base). Stability on the soft ground was achieved with a raft-like foundation of logs on inverted ceramic water jars. Rama III added to the picturesque glow of the prangs by cladding them with broken china.

The ensemble can be studied from a riverside plaza which is landscaped with topiary and dotted with Chinese-style salas. As befits a royal first class temple there is a panoply of colourful architecture—not only the prangs but also an ubosot with murals painted in the second and third reigns, restored in the fifth and more recently. There are chedis, cloisters, Buddha images, and Chinese sculptures aplenty (one guards a sign warning visitors to wear 'appropriate polite dress'). And there is a shrine to King Taksin who started it all.

248

Wichaiprasit Fort

Wang Derm Road, Klong Bangkok Yai

Two 17th-century forts guarded the river

approach to Ayutthaya against hostile foreign ships. Wichaiprasit Fort was built on the Thonburi side; a second fort, part of a French mission, was built on the Bangkok side where the Grand Palace now stands. The forts were garrisoned by Siamese soldiers, and at various times French and Portuguese in royal service. In 1688 the fort on the east side was besieged by a nationalist army of King Phetracha. The French destroyed it when they retreated across the river and eventually left Siam. The kingdom was closed to farangs for a century.

Wichaiprasit Fort is a Western design with north and south turrets and crenellated walls guarding an inner bastion with an upper level; the lower outer walls are also crenellated. Cannons were sited to fire through the gaps in the parapets. In the 1770s the fort guarded King

Taksin's palace and the approach to Rattanakosin Island. A ship's mast was raised as a flagpole when it was transferred by Rama V to the navy, which restored it in the 1980s.

249

Chakrabongse Villas

396 Maha Rat Road

Ercole Manfredi, 1908

Prince Chula Chakrabongse and his Russian wife Katya lived in this villa, originally called Tha Tien Palace. The couple married in Istanbul in 1906. The prince told neither his father, Rama V, nor his host in Russia, Tsar Nicholas II, of the marriage, a deviation from protocol. The villa was a refuge for Katya, the only European at court, and for the Prince when not engaged in royal duties. His official residence was Parutsakawan Palace in Dusit.

The couple's grand-daughter rehabilitated the property recently as Chakrabongse Villas, an exclusive boutique hotel. A traditional Ayutthaya-style wooden house augments the original house which was restored along with the garden. The top floor is a 1920s addition, by architect Edward Healey. A peculiarity is the 'captain's lookout', a feature usually found on seaport villas in the West. The tower was intended as the family shrine for Buddha images and royal relics.

250

Sunanthalai Building, Rajini Secondary School

444 Maha Rat Road

1880

Rama V commissioned the Sunanthalai Building — the Royal Seminary for Girls — as a memorial to Queen Sunandha and her daughter who drowned when their boat sank at Nonthaburi en route to Bang Pa-In. A story has it that they could not be saved because it was forbidden for commoners to touch royals. The Palladian elevation, octagonal dome and cupola are visible from the river, but the elevation seems slightly distorted because its ground floor arcade is hidden by a concrete flood wall. A statue of the queen is in the compound. She founded Rajini School (the Queen's School) in 1904, at Asadang Road near Pak Klong Talat. In 1906 it was relocated to this riverfront site which was enlarged over the years with new buildings around the old seminary.

251

Rajini Secondary School

444 Maha Rat Road

Architects 49, 2009

This four-storey addition for 1,500 students of the venerable school fits the scale of its historic neighbourhood. The building is a surprise among Rattanakosin Island's shophouses and prestigious heritage buildings, like the school's Sunanthalai Building whose architectural

quality it matches in a manner which is bold, refreshing and contemporary. The structure is reinforced concrete on pilings 28 metres below grade. Cladding materials and glazing facing Maha Rat Road emphasise a rectangular administration box, a drum-shaped tower and a rectilinear wrap. The wrap continues along Klong Ku Muang Derm to the river. Classrooms extend around a courtyard; student dormitories near the river are open at ground level to allow views. Other parts are also opened up in this way to maximise natural ventilation. Solar shades create a pleasing, functional pattern on the elevations.

252
Wat Hong Ratchaworawihan
Soi 28, Itsaraphap Road, Klong Bangkok Yai

The klong-side temple in an old-style neighbourhood got its name from a wealthy Chinese who built it during the Ayutthaya period. King Taksin became its patron and declared it a centre for religious education. Next to the wat is a shrine roofed in Modern Thai style where he sits impassively in statue form above a flight of steps. Legend says this spot is where his corpse was brought for cremation after he was executed. In 1954 an equestrian statue of the warrior king with sword raised was sculpted by Silpa Bhirasri and erected at Wong Wien Yai roundabout.

The wat was renovated in the third and fourth reigns. Framed paintings on the walls date from those times and are said to show the story of the Emerald Buddha. The murals in the ubosot were repainted recently. The sitting Buddha image had a cement coating which cracked in 1956 and the image was revealed as gold Sukhothai style, a year after the better known example at Wat Traimit was revealed.

253
Kuan An Keng Shrine, Wat Kalayanamit
Soi 6 (Soi Wat Kalaya), Arun Amarin Road

The shrine is just south of Wat Kalayanamit, from where there is access by a riverfront walkway. Two shrines were built by Chinese followers of King Taksin, but were abandoned in the early Rattanakosin period when many Thonburi Chinese moved to Sampheng. During the third reign their Hokkien heirs reconstructed the shrines as one building, installed a likeness of goddess Guan Yin and gave the shrine its present name.

The decorative scheme, animated with wood carvings, bas-reliefs, murals and dragons, survives due to the intervention of Prince Damrong. When he visited Wat

Kalayanamit in 1932 to see the installation of its bronze bell, the biggest in the kingdom, he saw the shrine next door was decayed. He wrote to Prince Naris that it was a national monument and should be preserved.

Wat Kalayanamit was founded in 1825 by a Sino-Siamese official. It has Thailand's largest sitting Buddha image and tallest viharn, built by Rama III to house the image. The wat's name, 'good friend', was given by the king in appreciation of its founder. The murals show the neighbourhood to have been multicultural.

254
Bang Luang Mosque
Klong Bangkok Yai, Arun Amarin Road

South of Klong Bangkok Yai are the Kudi Jeen and Kudi Khao communities which

were peopled in the Ayutthaya and Thonburi periods by Siamese, Chinese, Portuguese and Muslims. That diversity is evident in the area's religious architecture: there are Buddhist temples, Chinese shrines, a Catholic church and mosques.

A heritage sign on the west side of Arun Amarin Road, just south Klong Bangkok Yai, identifies the alley leading to this brick and stucco mosque, built by a Muslim merchant during the third reign. It has the structural form of a Buddhist ubosot with porches at either end and a gabled, tiled roof extending out from the hall to supporting columns.

Being Islamic there is no imagery other than floral plasterwork on the gables. The Siamese called it Kudi Khao, 'kudi' meaning religious building and 'khao' for white, which the building is. The community was founded by Malay immigrants, raft-dwelling traders in the Ayutthaya era. The oldest mosque, Tonson, first called Kudi Yai, was founded in 1688. It too was Siamese style, in teak. The mosque today, on the north bank of Klong Bangkok Yai, visible from the bridge on Arun Amarin Road, dates from 1952. It is concrete in neo-Mughal style with a dome and Indo-Saracenic arches.

255
Santa Cruz Church
Soi 4, Arun Amarin Road
Mario Tamagno, Annibale Rigotti, 1916

Portuguese Christians gathered here after the fall of Ayutthaya and built a teakwood church in 1770 on a site granted by King Taksin. The settlement was destroyed by fire in 1833. A brick and stucco replacement opened the following year. It was succeeded by this neoclassical design, basilica in plan with a Renaissance-style interior.

The aisles are separated from the nave

by arches which spring from Corinthian columns; the barrel-vaulted ceiling is coffered. A statue of the Crucifixion is raised above the altar which has a fresco-like sky as a backdrop framed with gilded palm fronds and a pediment with the Lamb of God. The front elevation is lively with Italianate touches: a porch with three arches, Ionic columned mullions, an entablature with festoons, a balustrade and a rose window. The octagonal bell tower and dome rise to a cupola. The dome is replicated on a modern building at the nearby convent, founded in 1906. The church, known as Wat Kudi Jeen, faces the river where there is sala in Rama V gingerbread style and a walkway to Kuan An Keng Shrine and Wat Kalayanamit.

256
Wat Prayoon
Soi 4, Arun Amarin Road

Here is a great pagoda, a colossal, bell-shaped Ayutthaya-style white chedi which rises over 60 metres from a circular neoclassical base. It was built as the reliquary of the Bunnag clan which founded the wat in 1828. The clan's origin is Persian. In the 19th century it was influential, highly placed at the Grand Palace.

In 2005 Abbott Phra Brahmapundit noticed that the central brick pillar inside the chedi was leaning by one metre off the vertical, measured by a survey team led by architect Somsak Thammavatevittee from King Mongkut's Institute of Technology. The Fine Arts Department was consulted and local people involved, recognition that the temple is not only a historic relic but also a life-enhancing community asset. The structure was stabilised and conserved. Traditional techniques (such as sugar cane and rice mortar) and modern engineering (a vertical, steel box truss around the central pillar, with radiating struts to the inner walls) emulated the original wood cross beams, some of which were retained. The structure was revealed as an octagon—the internal void's spectacular ascent of brickwork has eight vertical ribs.

Outside in the shadow of the pagoda, beside its circular outer screen tipped with 10 small chedis, is a neoclassical pavilion (1885), also restored, which houses a museum of Buddha images and relics found inside the chedi. The conservation won Wat Prayoon an Award of Excellence in the 2013 Unesco Asia-Pacific Heritage Awards, the highest award and first for a Thai project.

The pagoda dominates the ubosot and viharn in a compound surrounded by a cast iron fence imported from Britain. The fence is decorated with weapons and was intended as a gift from the Bunnags for Rama III to install at the Grand Palace. The king preferred it be used at the temple, which is known locally as Wat Rue Lek (iron-fenced).

Adding to the variety that makes this temple a delight is Khao Mo (1835), a miniature mountain surrounded by a turtle pond and a path in a park-like setting. There are niches and grottos, shrines and replica temple structures, variously Siamese, Chinese and Gothic. Its surreal quality is due to its inspiration, which was Rama III observing the accumulation and solidification of wax dripping from candles. Similar artificial hills existed in Ayutthaya, in temples and royal parks. The desire of their creators, like gardeners everywhere, was pleasure in the restorative powers of Nature.

257
Memorial Bridge
Dorman Long engineers, 1929–1932

Memorial Bridge, or Saphan Phut (Rama I Bridge), was built and opened by Rama VII to commemorate the 150th anniversary of the Chakri Dynasty and the city. A monument to the dynasty's founder, Rama I, was erected on a plaza on the Bangkok side. Companies from

Europe and the United States bid for the contract which was won by British engineers, who designed and built the Sydney Harbour Bridge at the time. They shipped steelwork from the UK and supervised construction in Bangkok. It is a bascule bridge with two centre sections which opened like a drawbridge, required for warships to reach the navy base and dry dock upstream.

The bridge was damaged by an Allied air raid in 1945. It was repaired and reopened in 1949. The navy's big ships are now based elsewhere and the bridge has not been raised since the adjacent Phra Pokklao Bridge was built with no lifting mechanism in 1984. In 2011 the BMA installed lights to accentuate its steel truss structure and Art Deco pylons which flank the approach on both sides of the river. Commemorative inscriptions survive on the pylons' plinths. It was the first road crossing of the Chao Phraya River. Rama IV railway bridge (1927) north of Bang Sue was the first bridge across the river.

258

Post and Telegraph Building

Saphan Phut Road

Bangkok's first post office was located on the bank of the Chao Phraya River at the southern end of Klong Rob Krung. The building was originally the home of an official charged with embezzlement. The government expropriated the house, which was enlarged for the Post Office Department established by Rama V in 1883. In 1889 the Post Office merged with the Telegraph Department and the building became the joint headquarters.

It shimmered in the sun like a Venetian palazzo, with pilasters, balustrades and loggias, and a clock tower centred above a grand exterior stair leading to the postal hall. It was torn down in the early 1980s for approach roads to Phra

Pokklao Bridge. Some green space was created on which Sumet Jumsai, who campaigned for the building's reconstruction, resurrected the façade and tower in 2004. The facsimile was based on old photos. Costs prevented recreation of the original volume.

259

Bangkok River Park Condominium

Trok Saphan Yao

Rangsan Architecture, 1993

This was the last and most likable of Rangsan Torsuwan's neo-Roman high-rises. It is composed like a classical column, with a base (the parking podium), shaft (condominiums) and capital (a penthouse dome). The podium's river elevation has a neoclassical façade complete with Ionic columns, a pediment

and—this is the weirdest bit—a gigantic neo-Gothic rose window. The mix of styles was audacious as was the tower's location: it stands alone, close to the edge of historic Rattanakosin Island.

260

Princess Mother Memorial Park

Soi 3, Somdet Chao Phraya Road

Nond-Truengjai Architects, 1994

The land here, formerly a Bunnag estate owned by a minister of commerce in the fifth reign, was donated to Rama IX who established this community park in honour of his mother, whose childhood neighbourhood this was. She was the daughter of a goldsmith and lived in a modest house, long demolished, which was reconstructed in the park. Other buildings are renovated row houses of Chinese design, some originally dwellings for servants, like the museum building which is part renovation, part new-build, with its origin in the third reign.

Old trees, including a century-old banyan tree, were preserved by being included in the rehabilitation plan. The

main entrance, which is new, leads to the dwellings and a path through them to a plaza with a wooden gazebo, an arbour and a sculptural panel showing community life. Brickwork from old walls is visible, and a 19th-century gate with a pediment. Near the main gate, there is a statue of the Princess Mother seated in the garden. The park is serene, the landscape design and heritage preservation accomplished with sensitivity and attention to detail.

261

Somdet Chaopraya Institute of Psychiatry

112 Somdet Chao Phraya Road

The institute was established in 1889, the first of its type in Siam, named for one of Rama V's officials from whom the property was bought for the hospital. Klong San separates the site from the main road. A bridge leads to the hospital grounds which are leafy with many big trees, and display an unaltered array of 1960s modernist buildings arranged

around courtyards as if on a university campus. The oldest building on the site is a Gothic Revival, slightly Moorish villa in its original garden setting. It was built c.1880 by the Bunnag family. Rama V bought it to accommodate the hospital's director. It was rehabilitated as a museum in the 1980s by the Fine Arts Department.

262
Wanglee Residence
Chiang Mai Road
1881
Chinese merchants dominated rice milling and export in the 19th century, buying crops from farmers up-country from where the commodity was barged on canals and down the Chao Phraya River to Bangkok. The Wanglee business was established by immigrant Tan Chu Huang in 1871 to process and export rice to Hong Kong, eventually from five waterfront rice mills.

The family home, restored in 2009, is a rare example of a Chinese merchant's mansion. The two-storey house is U-shaped in plan, oriented around an inner courtyard, typical of a communal home accommodating more than one generation. Chinese design motifs appear on fretwork, mosaics and stucco, and the gate which is decorated lavishly. The gate faces a garden which extends to the river. Next door to the mansion there is

a steamer dock known as Wanglee Pier, with mill buildings, warehouses and workers' housing. It is one of the most intact and instructive industrial heritage sites on the river.

263
Wat Thong Nophakhun
Soi 17, Somdet Chao Phraya Road
Gilded windows shaped like monks' fans distinguish the ubosot at this late Ayutthaya-era temple, designated a royal wat in 1851. Fans indicate the holder's knowledge on the steps to enlightenment; they are also said to ward off evil or prevent sight of worldly temptations.

The windows are unique, found nowhere else in the kingdom. They are thought to date from the fourth reign when the structure was rebuilt in Rattanakosin style. There is a Sukhothai-style Buddha image, a painted wood ceiling and intriguing murals.

Rama III refashioned the wat with an overlay of chinoiserie evident in the ceramics, peacocks and dragons on the gables of the viharn on which the usual cho fa and bai raka are absent. Inside, there is an Ayutthaya-style brass Buddha image surrounded by over 100 disciple figures. These can be seen only on special occasions, four days a year. The temple was restored by the Fine Arts Department in 2010.

264
The Jam Factory
41 Charoen Nakorn Road, Soi 1
Duangrit Bunnag Architect (DBALP), 2014

A decade or so ago no one would have believed Klong San might become trendy but it is, as this post-industrial rehab shows. The buildings—variously an ice plant, a battery factory and pharmaceutical producer—were abandoned for 30 years or so. No one made jam; that is just the new name inspired by a factory conversion in London.

Workshops were refurbished to contemporary conservation standards by DBALP which was previously located

on the Bangkok side of the river. Existing wood trussed roofs, timber posts and brick walls were incorporated in the makeover. Structural steelwork, inserted where needed to reinforce the old buildings, fits the site's industrial history. The architect's office, an art space and Candide Books define a grass courtyard where a big banyan tree provides shade. The buildings were opened up to create luminous spaces which diffuse the conventional indoor/outdoor relationship. The bookstore, in an old timber building, has a café and a terrace under the big tree; there is also a restaurant by the river.

The compound can be reached from the ferry dock in the shadow of the Millennium Hilton, or the soi across Klong San from a tall flagpole on Lat Yai Road. The pole once flew flags identifying shipping companies when their vessels were in port, and to signal weather to mariners.

265
Siam Commercial Bank
1280 Yo Tha (Soi Wanit 2)
Mario Tamagno, Annibale Rigotti, 1908

SCB is the oldest Thai commercial bank, since 1906. At that time the kingdom's financial system was served by Chinese pawnshops and foreign banks. This headquarters was designed to outshine any of the later, particularly the British-owned Hong Kong and Shanghai Bank.

The Italian architects sought inspiration in the Baroque of their native land for this commercial palazzo festooned with Ionic columns, split pediments, balustrades, scalloped niches for statuary, faux-heraldic crests and high-relief stonework (actually stucco over brick, as are all the exterior surfaces). The bank was oriented to be best seen from the river, from where it impressed foreign visitors who arrived by ship at the time. The original interior is intact with a spa-

cious banking hall still in use as the Talat Noi Branch. The building was restored in 1996 and 2012. A quirky touch is the city's most palatial ATM, in a neo-baroque sentry box by the gate at the soi.

266
Holy Rosary Church
1318 Yo Tha (Soi Wanit 2)
1898

Portuguese descendants of the early missionaries and traders in Ayutthaya who settled in Thonburi crossed the river after a French mission took over Santa Cruz Church. Rama I granted them this site in 1787. Holy Rosary Church took several forms over the years, culminating in Gothic Revival grandeur. The porch is defined with pointed arches and a quatrefoil motif; there is a simulated rose window; the side wall balustrades bristle with pinnacles; the bell tower rises to a slender steeple. The sanctuary is decorated richly in Renaissance and Gothic styles: pilasters alternate with stained glass windows set in pointed arches; there is a wood-carved Gothic pulpit and pews; floors are tiled for decorative and cooling effect; there are statues of Jesus, the Virgin Mary and saints. The painted ceiling is wood, shaped like an upturned boat hull. The church owns a wooden sculpture of Jesus carved in the Ayutthaya period, exhibited only on holy days.

267
River City
Trok Rong Nam Khaeng, Soi 24, Charoen Krung Road
CASA, 1984

When this shopping centre sailed into a

neglected part of the waterfront its architecture was as sleek as an ocean liner, with a façade layered with horizontal white panels alternating with four decks of glass above a waterfront promenade. A circular plaza was created to bring a sense of occasion to the main entrance.

The mall specialises in Asian art and antiques, displayed in over 200 shop units over four floors around an atrium. The top level has a convention and exhibition hall and Riverside Auction House, established in 1985. Interior and exterior makeovers have kept the ship afloat in Bangkok's restless quest for retail novelty. Ferry docks and sail-like canopies on the promenade were added in 2000. These were modest and not out of place. A relaunch in 2011 removed the canopies to make alfresco space for river-view bars and restaurants. The once shipshape modernist façades were re-clad with reflective glass.

268
Royal Orchid Sheraton Hotel
Soi 30 (Captain Bush Lane), Charoen Krung Road
Palmer and Turner, 1982

This resort-style high-rise hotel replaced the Hong Kong and Shanghai Bank's two-storey neoclassical building (1890) which was set in a garden facing the river at Klong Phadung Krung Kasem. It was similar in scale and setting to the Siam Commercial Bank. The building was demolished after HSBC moved its HQ to Siam Centre in 1977. Before the site was cleared for the hotel the old building was a stand-in for a US army hospital in Saigon in the movie *The Deer Hunter*.

The hotel's 700-plus rooms face the river, stacked in a Y-shaped plan which rises from a podium containing public areas and parking. It was one of the first high-rises to intrude on Bang Rak's historic waterfront. It seems more benign now, its functional plan and modernism a counterpoint to subsequent towers of all shapes, sizes and styles.

269

Portuguese Embassy

Soi 30 (Captain Bush Lane), Charoen Krung Road

1875

The Kingdom of Portugal was the first from Europe to establish official contact with Siam, a relationship which began in 1511. Portuguese envoys, explorers and merchants were a common sight in Ayutthaya, which Portuguese mercenaries in Siamese service helped defend against the Burmese. After the city fell in 1767 the Portuguese re-established their community at the new capital created by King Taksin at Thonburi. In 1786 this piece of waterfront land was assigned to them by Rama I, for a trading post with a warehouse (now the Chancery) and a residence for their first consul to Siam.

The Portuguese Embassy is the oldest in Bangkok and one of two (the other is French) still located by the river. It became a permanent diplomatic mission during the fourth reign. The present Residence is a colonial villa begun in 1860. Craftsmen and materials were sent from Goa to help build its three-bay porch, ground floor arcade, trio of fanlight windows framed by pilasters, and wide pediment with the Portuguese coat of arms. It is set in its original garden overlooking the river where there is a parapet for flood protection, which partly obscures the ground floor.

270

CAT Telecommunications Centre

Soi Wat Muang Khae (Soi 34), Charoen Krung Road

Architects 110, 1999

The Communications Authority of Thailand (CAT) was split in 2003 as CAT Telecom and Thailand Post. Thailand Post retained the historic General Post Office building. The CAT Telecommunications Centre was built nearby in response to new technologies and the business boom in the 1990s. It is a vast structure topped with antennae and satellite dishes. The reflective glass cocoon conceals office floors, some rented out, and a parkade. There is a pocket park to one side; on the other there is a ferry dock with a sala in the style of the adjacent Wat Muang Kae.

271

Customs House

Soi Rong Phasi Kao (Soi 36), Charoen Krung Road

Joachim Grassi, 1888

Around 1900 the Customs House shared the waterfront with the Italianate Oriental Hotel, East Asiatic Company office, and Assumption College (its original building long demolished). The ensemble gave European travellers arriving by ship the impression that Bangkok really was the Venice of the East. The Customs

House was their gateway to Siam. Its architect had moved from the Italian region of the Austro-Hungarian Empire to Siam in 1870 when the kingdom was being opened to Western trade and technology. He founded Grassi Brothers and Company with his brothers Giacomo, an engineer, and Antonio, a sculptor.

The building is Palladian in style, symmetrical in elevation with a pediment at the centre and two wings (in this instance detached from the main structure, to which they were connected by covered walkways above the ground). It was one of the most graceful works of Western architecture on the waterfront.

The Customs Department moved to Klong Toei in 1949. The Treasury Department retained control of the site which has been used by the Marine Police and the fire service. It has been Bang Rak Fire Station since 1959. Firefighters and their families inhabit its dilapidated splendour. Much of its fabric is intact but decrepit and deteriorating with water ingress and neglect. The structure is brick coated with lime cement, the common method at the time. It was bedecked with banners to welcome Rama V on his return from Europe in 1897. The king would recognise it today—the façade retains its fanlight windows, and pediment with the original clock and a filigree, regal coat of arms—but be appalled by the landmark's present condition. Proposals to rehabilitate the Customs House as a hotel or by some other adaptive reuse have ebbed and flowed like the tide.

272

French Embassy

Soi Rong Phasi Kao (Soi 36), Charoen Krung Road

The Ambassador's Residence (c. 1875), part colonial chalet, part neoclassical palace, is set in one of the few 19th-century riverside green spaces left.
The embassy is the second-oldest in Thailand, after the Portuguese mission. Contact between Siam and France began in the 17th century when a Siamese delegation was received by King Louis XIV at the Palace of Versailles in 1684 and a French emissary, Chevalier de Chaumont, visited the Court of King Narai in 1685. Rama V made state visits to France during his two visits to Europe. The embassy, then a legation, was the centre of a diplomatic dispute over territory on Siam's frontier with Indochina, which provoked the Paknam crisis in 1893 when two French warships engaged the fort near Phra Samut Chedi and a gunboat anchored upstream and threatened the Grand Palace. French influence is still evident in Bangkok, from Catholic schools,

convents and hospitals to patisserie outlets in malls. History is as much a part of the embassy's fabric as its gingerbread trim and peaceful garden. An origami-shaped addition clad with brilliant white panels, and a new gate and courtyard, are under construction (ADPI architects, 2014).

273
East Asiatic Company
53–55 Soi Oriental (Soi 40, Charoen Krung Road)
c. 1900

Next door to the Oriental Hotel (see entry 226) is this commercial palazzo built by Hans Niels Andersen, a ship's carpenter from Denmark who arrived in Bangkok in 1879. He skippered a tall ship owned by Rama V and sailed it to Europe in 1883. The cargo was teakwood, the profit from which was invested in a start-up, Andersen and Company. He opened a general store, bought and rebuilt the Oriental Hotel and branched out into marine supplies, logging and sawmills. He founded the East Asiatic Company in Copenhagen in 1897 and opened this office on the waterfront in Bangkok.

The façade is Venetian, a style popular with Western merchants in the 19th century for its association with the Venetian Republic's trading empire. There is a

palatial stairway at the entrance. A Dutch gable displays a caduceus (symbol of commerce and trade) and the EAC flag. On Soi Oriental there is a second building (1919) with a bridge across an alley to the first. Their Venetian elevations have arcades on the ground floor and form a memorable streetscape.

The EAC's ships carried passengers and freight between Copenhagen and Bangkok and other ports in Asia. It became the biggest company in Denmark but foundered in the 1980s, was re-floated, moved out of the original Bangkok office in 1995 and left Thailand in 2010. Its warehouses and dock on the Chao Phraya River were redeveloped recently as Asiatique the Riverfront market and mall. Ideas to rehabilitate the offices as a retail centre or hotel surface periodically. Next door is the Venetian Renaissance-style Banque d'Indochine (1908), now occupied by the Catholic Archdiocese.

274
The River
Soi 13, Charoen Nakhon Road
HB Design, SL+A Bangkok, Meinhardt engineers, Tierra landscape design, 2012

This neo-modernist 'icon of river living' was billed as 'cutting edge and environmentally friendly, the greenest condominium in Thailand'. The scale is epic: 650 dwellings in a north and south tower, 42 and 72 storeys respectively, rising from a five-storey podium with a parkade and resort-style facilities. Pilings plunge to 65 meters below grade; reinforced concrete was used throughout; giant tower cranes rose as each floor was poured during three years of construction. The site bloomed with the colourful hard hats of a 1,500-strong team of workers. Most were housed in a labour camp in Thonburi. Many were from up-country—the people who are the pulse at the heart of Bangkok's relentless construction.

Developer Raimon Land and its Dutch-Thai lead architect, Hans Brouwer, adopted sustainable design practices increasingly common elsewhere but fresh to Thailand. An onsite plant produced concrete from aggregate delivered by river barges to reduce emissions and the carbon footprint. There is high-performance double glazing to reduce solar heat gain and the cost of air conditioning; fittings and fixtures are from eco-rated sources; waste water is recycled to irrigate the landscaping. The development responded with clarity to a long deep site typical of Thonburi's waterfront. The orientation, massing and articulation of both towers were the result of a 'view plane' study (of views to and from the towers). The shorter tower is set back to avoid crowding the waterfront where there is a boardwalk. The curving aluminum and glass curtain walls add grace to the structures' vertical slabs. Solar panels power the lighting of the taller tower's steel and glass crown which glows at night like a lantern.

275
Asiatique the Riverfront
2194 Charoen Krung Road, between sois 74 and 76
Urban Architect, 2012

This night bazaar and open-air mall occupies a historic waterfront location and a group of heritage warehouses which were rehabilitated for it. The site was developed originally in the 1890s by the

East Asiatic Company for the export of teak lumber on its ships from Siam to Europe and for goods imported on the return voyage. There was a holding area for rafts of teak logs which were floated down river from the northern forests. The infrastructure—godowns, a sawmill, a wooden office building, a water tower and cranes—was left intact after the EAC vacated the site, which was acquired 30 years ago by developer TCC Land.

A 10-year master plan focussed on adaptive reuse of the steel-truss, brick and concrete godowns as a 'colonial-style mall, festival marketplace and living museum'. Redundant industrial buildings in cities worldwide have been recycled in this way since the concept was first launched in 1964 at Ghiradelli Square in San Francisco. These projects required the disposable income of tourists and an indigenous middle class, which Bangkok's recent growth has produced.

The site's grid of sois and alleys and the relationship of the warehouses to their wharf and the river were retained. New construction fits the scale and style of the old. A romantic waterfront boardwalk was laid after the old teak wharf was rebuilt in concrete. Warehouse walls were opened up selectively for access and ventilation; clerestory windows were fitted on some elevations to bring daylight to the interior spaces. The framework of one warehouse was retained with its travelling crane. On others, the sliding doors and brick-filled gables with original lettering were restored. There is a Bangkok tram, interpretative panels and public art. A neon sign features the EAC ship's anchor motif. A real anchor decorates the boardwalk.

276

First Presbyterian Church

Soi 59, Charoen Nakhon Road

The American Presbyterian Mission was started by missionaries who arrived in Siam in 1840. Their first church was built here in 1860. The present Samray Church opened in 1910, to which the bell tower was added in 1912. These dates appear on the elevations whose style is picture-book Italianate. Missionaries were not architects—the church has a do-it-yourself personality and that is its charm.

Downriver is Krung Thep Bridge (1959), the second road bridge to cross the Chao Phraya River. The engineering is similar to the first, Memorial Bridge. Unlike it, Krung Thep Bridge is still raised for ships to pass. More road traffic required the parallel Rama III Bridge, completed in 1999.

277

Rama IX Bridge

Peter Fraenkel and Partners engineers, 1987

This graceful high-level crossing was

commissioned by the Expressway and Rapid Transit Authority of Thailand after the engineers' study showed a tunnel option would be more expensive. A primary condition was that the six-lane bridge not obstruct navigation. The bridge piers had to be on land and the box girder deck high enough to allow ships to pass below. The solution was a cable-stayed structure with cables strung on a single axis. It was the longest bridge of its type in the world at the time and remains one of the most elegant. It was named to salute the 60th birthday of Rama IX. Originally the cables were coloured black, strung from white pylons, all changed to yellow in 2006 for the 60th anniversary of his enthronement.

It dominated the skyline until 1995 when a corporate HQ was erected for Thai Farmers Bank (now Kasikornbank) on the Thonburi side of the river. The facetted tower (Design 103 International, Arun Chaiseri engineers) complements the angles of the pylons and cables on the bridge.

Hua Lamphong Station

8

Hua Lamphong to Bang Sue

Bangkok's MRT Blue Line metro runs from Hua Lamphong, the city's oldest mainline railway station, to Bang Sue, where the newest station, a huge interchange for existing and new lines, will be constructed. Bang Sue is to be the hub for mainline and commuter trains, metro and skytrain lines, and an extended airport rail link. Hua Lamphong will likely be reduced to one commuter line or closed and its rail yards, which are on prime land downtown, redeveloped. Preservation of the historic station and other railway heritage buildings nearby, like the State Railway's headquarters building, will be an issue. Hua Lamphong station would make a superb railway and transport museum on the most appropriate site in the city for one.

The kingdom's first train line, the privately operated Paknam Railway, started here in a wooden shed on Rama IV Road in 1893 and ran to the mouth of the Chao Phraya River, to serve passengers on ships too large to enter the port upstream. The first state railway line was inaugurated by Rama V at Hua Lamphong in 1896. Klong Phadung Krung Kasem, once clogged with sampans and barges, is parallel to the train tracks. Rama IV Road, a major artery built on Klong Hua Lamphong which was filled to widen the road in 1955, had tramline until the 1960s. The first overpass in the city, the Thai-Belgian Bridge, was built in 1988 at the intersection of Rama IV and Sathorn roads. There is a multi-lane expressway east of the station and the metro is underground. The exhibit about transport history displayed along the main corridor at the MRT station at Hua Lamphong gives a sense of what a museum in the old SRT station could achieve on a grand scale.

When Rama V opened the first state railway line, land to the east of the station was undeveloped, apart from orchards and vegetable gardens which supplied Chinatown. There were royal estates. Chulalongkorn University, established by Rama VI in 1917, was built on one. The architectural legacy from Chula's foundation is a superb group of Modern Thai-style buildings on an axial plan, one of the few examples of formal planning in Bangkok. The Blue Line passes close to the university campus and the central business district before turning north. It crosses Sukhumvit Road at Asok BTS Station and has an interchange with the Airport Rail Link at Makkasan. It runs below Ratchadapisek Road, an American-style boulevard lined with billboards, filling stations, malls, big-box stores and, increasingly, condominiums near the metro stops.

This pattern of development following transit is also evident on Sukhumvit Road where the BTS has been a catalyst since it opened in 1999. In 1932, when the Siam Society moved to a new building 'near the new road to Paknam' (referring to Sukhumvit), the area was undeveloped. It became residential and fashionable in the 1950s with mid-century modern houses built on large leafy lots. Some look Californian. All represented an aspirational automobile-owning North American lifestyle of air conditioning and fridge freezers. A few survive, some rehabilitated as restaurants. Most have been torn down since the Vietnam War when Bangkok was floating on US cash and investment by foreign companies. The Condominium Act of 1979 allowed 40 percent foreign ownership of any condo building, 100 percent since the 1997 crash. Sukhumvit became a dense, up-market high-rise zone. It is notorious for traffic snarl-ups caused by the number of cul-de-sacs created by land owners' desire for privacy and their ability to influence city hall to get it. The main drag is Thonglor, a latte-lifestyle hipster hangout originally named for gold shops and later called Wedding Shop Soi because it had a strip of stores selling bridal dresses. It was where one of the first so-called community malls, a semi-outdoor lifestyle concept, sprang up in 2002.

Makkasan is sprawling site owned by the State Railway of Thailand. It was first developed around 1910 as the railway's primary maintenance depot and retains several brick and concrete, trussed-roofed workshops. Some of those buildings have heritage value as industrial archaeology and have big interior spaces suitable for adaptive reuse. But their preservation will be a hard sell. The depot will be relocated to Bang Sue and the SRT has plans for a massive commercial project bigger than the present central business district on Sathorn Road. This conventional thinking was challenged in 2013 by environmental campaigners who see Makkasan as a future 'central park'. Nature has reclaimed much of the site. The SRT assures everyone that green space will be part of the plan, maybe even heritage preservation. The site is well connected, with public transport links in place at Makkasan Station and City Air Terminal and the MRT Petchaburi Station, and expressways are nearby.

In north Bangkok and the city's outer suburbs there is good contemporary architecture and weird stuff, along with cookie-cutter housing estates and golf courses. There is an 'elephant building' and a Disney knock-off, fairytale castle. Much of the serious work is the result of the dispersal of agencies to the enormous Government Complex at Chaeng Wattana and university campuses at Rangsit. The metropolitan area's first satellite city, Muang Thong Thani, was conceived as a high-density Utopia during the 1980s boom. It stalled after the 1997 crash but its ranks of tower blocks were visionary. They are being revived ahead of the latest City Plan which encourages suburban centres. These are beyond the scope of this book but significant developments within range of the Blue Line's northern stations and the present north end of the BTS skytrain are included.

Readers should note that some Blue Line station names are misleading. There is no direct pedestrian link to the Thailand Cultural Centre from the eponymous station; for Lumpini Park, ignore Lumphini Station and exit at Si Lom; for Central Lat Phrao, ignore Lat Phrao Station and exit at Phahonyothin; for Chatuchak Weekend Market it is better to pass Chatuchak Station and use Kamphaeng Phet.

TICKETS

278

Hua Lamphong Station

Rama IV at Rong Mueang Road

Mario Tamagno, Alfredo Rigazzi, 1910–1916

At the north end of platform 11 a monument commemorates the first rail line built by the Royal Railway Department, founded in 1890. The line went to Ayutthaya. The monument's bas-relief shows Rama V with the director of the department and its British engineer at the opening ceremony at Hua Lamphong—*Stazione Terminus di Bangkok* as the Italian architects wrote on the blueprints for this grand station built later. It is one of the most impressive historic railway termini in Asia. The design was inspired by the train stations of Europe which Rama V had seen, notably Porta Nova in Turin.

There are two distinct parts: a porte cochère and loggia in an extended neoclassical façade, and a spacious concourse leading to 14 platforms. The space is covered by a steel-arched train shed. A postmodern arch with a life-size portrait of Rama V, information screens and ticket counters were added in the 1990s. They were part of an improvement scheme following a train wreck in 1986, when a runaway locomotive crashed through the buffers and overturned on the concourse.

The train shed is functional, the façade flamboyant. The shed's front elevation, flanked by two pavilions, was designed to be integrated visually with the façade, as at Porta Nova. Turin-born architect Tamagno simplified it because the cast-iron ornament to have been made in Milan was unavailable during the First World War. The shed has coloured glass inserts at the platform end; it is open on the west side for ventilation; the east side adjoins the old ticket hall and offices.

To the north of the station are rail yards and the State Railway of Thailand headquarters. Rama V's westernisation, of which railways were a key part, did not change superstitious habits: the bas-relief at the end of platform 11 is patched with gold leaf applied by supplicant railway employees.

279

SRT Headquarters

Soi 1, Rama I Road

Vodhyakarn Varavarn

In 1917 the Northern, Northeastern and Southern lines were amalgamated as the Royal State Railways of Siam (RSR), which became the State Railway of Thailand (SRT) in 1951. The SRT HQ, known as Tuek Daeng (Red Building), was the high point of the RSR chief architect's 20 years of service, before he left in 1949 to teach at Chula. The central block has a château-style steep roof and is flanked by matching wings which embrace a courtyard where there is a statue of Prince Purachatra, the first director of the Royal Railway Department. Two heritage locomotives are displayed and there is a children's park with more old rolling stock next door.

North of the HQ is a three-storey wood and brick administrative building, designed in the RSR's colonial style most fully realised at the famous Railway Hotel (Alfredo Rigazzi, 1922) at Hua Hin. Across Rama I Road is the Ministry of Energy compound where a Tuscan-style villa (Ercole Manfredi, c. 1912) can be glimpsed.

280

Wat Boromniwat

Soi 15, Rama VI Road

The city is silent inside this beautiful temple, originally called Wat Nok, meaning outside the city walls. There is a century-old teakwood assembly hall, traditional monks' quarters, trees and many cats. The oldest part, a separate compound, was established as a forest temple by Rama IV in 1834 when he was a monk at Wat Bowonniwet.

Rama V renovated the temple and renamed it Wat Boromniwat. The historic compound is compact. There are no bai sema stones; the walls are the boundary. Every element within them is in harmony and every decorative feature exquisitely crafted. There is a chedi with mother-of-pearl doors to its reliquary chamber. Chinese tile-roofed cloisters frame three sides of the compound; the walls are lined with 80 golden figures in bas-relief, posed in the 'wai' gesture of prayer. The viharn is small, delicate. Chinese statues here and there are smaller than usually found, and more refined. The chapel gables glitter with glass mosaic tiles, gilded bai raka and cho fa; shutters and doors are inlaid decoratively, not merely painted. Inside, there is a Sukhothai-era Buddha image and murals by Khrua In Khong. They can only be viewed on special religious occasions. A conservation programme was started by the Fine Arts Department in 2012.

281

Thepsirin School

1466 Krung Kasem Road

The school was established by Prince Damrong in 1885 as part of Rama V's educational reforms. It was one of Siam's first royal schools for commoners. Classes were held in the adjacent Wat Thepsirin, founded in 1876 by Rama V and dedicated to his mother, Queen Thepsirinda. The compound is a pleasant green space dominated by a lavish Rattanakosin-style ubosot. Thepsirin School's first permanent building, Maen Naruemit, was begun in 1895, followed by the Choduek Laohasetthi Building, the school museum since 2012. The style chosen was Gothic Revival because, reportedly, the whole enterprise was modelled on the Normal College in New York. Rama V had read a magazine feature about it and asked his superintendent of education, a Presbyterian missionary, to write for information which was duly sent. The modern building across the sports field replaced twins of the existing Gothic buildings after the Second World War and replays the style.

282
MRT Hua Lamphong Station
Rama IV at Rong Mueang Road
SMC Consulting Engineers, 2004

A high water table, varied densities of alluvial sediments, congested roads and buildings were an engineering challenge when construction of the MRT (Mass Rapid Transit) started in 1996. The Blue Line from Hua Lamphong to Bang Sue was the first subway, or metro, built in Thailand.

Two tunnels, one for each direction, were bored and stations constructed by cut and cover. The tunnels are parallel, except under Rama IV Road where they are stacked one above the other to avoid adjacent structures. The line is being extended under Chinatown, Rattanakosin Island and the Chao Phraya River to the Thonburi side, from where it will be elevated like the BTS and loop back to Bang Sue. There are 18 stations on the initial 20-kilometre route, most with high tech

steel and glass pods curving up from the ground. The pods sit on podiums with emergency gates to resist high water. They passed the test during the flood of 2011.

Hua Lamphong is unique to the system. It is the main downtown station and connects to the SRT. There is a pod on the south side of Rama IV Road. The north side has a more elaborate entrance with a pocket plaza and an umbrella-shaped, glazed canopy above escalators which plunge underground. A pyramid was placed on the plaza to show where the MRT's foundation stone was laid. Rama IX and Queen Sirikit presided at the opening ceremony in 2004, an event celebrated inside the station where the royal chairs and the foundation stone are displayed as if in an art gallery, and the story of public transport in Bangkok is told in illustrated panels lining the corridor to the trains.

283
DOB Building
318 Rama IV Road
Keit Jiwakul, 1971

'A building less ordinary, where art meets design' is how this recent rehabilitation of Bangkok Bank's former Hua Lamphong branch is billed. The architecture is certainly unconventional, from the period when brutalism was fashionable. Its chunky concrete composition dominates the street corner with a sculptural flourish reminiscent of Le Corbusier, from whom the convex and concave shapes were borrowed. The intervention includes a café on the ground floor and workshops and seminar rooms on the upper levels. The rehab retained the original volume and visible structural integrity of the double-height banking hall, and the flow of its space upstairs where there is open-plan area for art exhibitions.

284
Samyan Market
Sois 32 and 34, Chulalongkorn 5 and 9 roads
Sarawth Sabsuk, 2007

Sam Yan's shophouses are two- to four-storey concrete structures with solar fins and canopies dating from the 1960s. These modest modernist buildings on a rigid street grid created a townscape of unusual coherence in Bangkok. This was Chulalongkorn University's first commercial property development. Units were leased as shops, offices, restaurants and auto supply dealers who are still here recycling car parts. Not for long. Whole blocks are being razed by Chula's development machine which is rumbling west of the campus.

Samyan Market has been a fixture in the community since 1965. The decision by Chula's Property Management Office to close it and build a replacement a few blocks away was controversial. The old single-storey market was crowded and cramped but integrated with the neighbourhood's street vendor and

shophouse economy. The new market is oriented economically to the university's students and staff.

Gentrification in old neighbourhoods is a global phenomenon but recent in Bangkok. The new market at least tries to be friendly. The new building fits the scale of the area and creates an instant sense of place. It makes much of natural ventilation, is clean, spacious and utilitarian, constructed with concrete, steel and glass. The entrance on Chula 5 Road is double-height, recessed below an expressive horizontal roof. The main floor contains dozens of stalls arranged for vendors to display and sell fresh produce, like a traditional wet market. A pedestrian bridge across Chula 9 connects the clerestory-lit food court on the upper floor to the campus.

285

Chulapat 13, Central Classroom Building, Chulalongkorn University

Chulalongkorn 5 at Chula 12 Road

Pirast Patcharaswate, Sayanee Virochrut and Mark Issarangkul na Ayudhya, 2012

This aggressive monster looks ready to rampage across the low-rise rooftops of Sam Yan. The nine-storey structure with plug-in body parts and a gigantic sloping piloti recalls the fantasies of Archigram, the British futurists of the 1960s who proposed machine-like buildings, some moveable on stilts. Chulapat 13's materials—steel, concrete, glass, wood and ceramic tiles—were mixed not matched in a DIY design which is energetic and experimental. There are contrasting forms in a juxtaposition of voids and functional spaces oriented to maximise natural ventilation and light. There is a library and auditorium, expressed externally by the angle of the sloping floor. External canopies slide to a south-facing loggia. Classrooms and a café are on the upper levels. Huge solar shades dominate the bizarre superstructure. The building was intended as a case study by the architects, members of Chula's architecture faculty.

286

Parotracha House, Chulalongkorn University

Phayathai Road

c. 1925

Restored in the 1990s and named for a former director of the university this colonial-style house has an open ground floor, a verandah, fretwork and a roof with wide eaves. It was successively an administration building, a guest house for visiting professors and, in 1932, a temporary classroom for the school of architecture. Its leafy grounds preserve part of Chula's original park-like campus, noted for its rain trees whose seasonal cycle corresponds to the university's semesters and inspired the official song.

287

Faculty of Architecture, Chulalongkorn University

Phayathai Road

Chiang Koppe and Siwawong Kunchon na Ayudhya, 1940

An architecture department was established in 1930 at Poh Chang College of Arts and Crafts. In 1932 it was relocated to Chula where it was absorbed in the Faculty of Engineering. Faculty status was granted in 1939. A purpose-built facility was completed in 1940 on the north side of the sports field, but not opened until after the Second World War because the Japanese commandeered the campus.

The building is modernist, movie theatre Art Deco at the entrance. The emphasis is horizontal but the entrance bay is vertical, with doors and staircase windows recessed behind two giant columns fronting a massive cube which contains the foyer. A bust of the faculty's founder, Nart Bhodhiprasat, was unveiled inside in 1982.

To cope with increasing numbers of students a multi-storey addition was built in 1990, separated from the original building by courtyards. Directly east is the modernist former Chemistry Building (Ercole Manfredi, 1937) which was given makeover in 2011 as an arts space.

288

Faculty of Arts and Main Auditorium, Chulalongkorn University

Henri Dunant Road

Rama VI granted land in 1917 to establish Chulalongkorn University which he named after his father, King Chula-

longkorn (Rama V), who reformed the kingdom's education system. The university was a culmination of Rama V's quest to create opportunities for his people to acquire modern technical and scientific skills while remaining true to their own culture.

Chula's early buildings—the Faculty of Arts group—express this duality. Their style is Modern Thai, the fusion of Western techniques and Siamese decoration. They were laid out on a Beaux-Arts plan with the axis running west from Henri Dunant Road, where the entrance is flanked by the original gatehouses. The Maha Chulalongkorn Building (1915, south side of the axis) and the Maha Vajiravudh Building (1919, north side) face each other across a lawn divided by a covered walkway linking the two structures. They were designed by Edward Healey, architect of Vajiravudh College Assembly Hall of the same period and in similar style.

The south building predates the university, having been built as the administrative offices of the Royal Civil Service College from which the university grew. The structures are concrete with loggias, ogee openings and Siamese tiered roofs. Gables are inlaid with Sukhothai-style motifs by Italian artist Rodolfo Nolli who also sculpted the nagas which flank steps to loggias and the walkway.

The Beaux-Arts symmetry continues to the Main Auditorium (U Laphanon and Sarot Sukkayang, 1939) which faces the university flagpole. Tiers of Siamese gables are overlaid with Sukhothai-style stucco decoration inspired by the chapel at Wat Rachathiwat whose designer, Prince Naris, was a tutor to the auditorium's architects.

West of this is a monument (Khaimook Chudoo, 1990) with statues of Rama V and Rama IV. The axis crosses the sports

field and an ornamental lake to Phayathai Road which bisects the campus. Across the road, expansion to the west started around 1925 with the neoclassical-style Chamchuri Administration Building. The historic entrance to the campus (where it should be entered to appreciate the plan) is on Henri Dunant Road, opposite the Royal Bangkok Sports Club.

289
Sala Phra Kieo, Chulalongkorn University
Phayathai Road
Vodhyakarn Varavarn, Lert Urasayananda, 1966

The sala was intended to evoke that elusive quality of 'Thainess', but the building could be an Elvis-era resort in Hawaii. No matter, it would be enjoyably eccentric anywhere. It was designed as a multi-purpose hall with an auditorium as big as a convention centre running the full length of the structure. There are identical outward-leaning gables at each end and along both sides, each luminous with a grid of glass shaded with brise-soleil. In the auditorium, structural concrete splays out like tree branches to hold up the roof. The name, Phra Kieo, alludes to a small crown worn by princes and princesses which became Chula's emblem, bestowed by Rama VI.

290

Wat Hua Lamphong

Rama IV Road

Vendors crowd the sidewalk outside Sam Yan metro station whose construction expanded the public space in front of the temple's main gate. The ubosot, viharn and chedi rise on a marble-clad podium. They were renovated for the 50th anniversary of Rama IX's enthronement. The two-elephant seal of the Golden Jubilee is prominent on the gables of the ubosot whose interior is decorated with neo-traditional murals. The chedi glitters with golden mosaic tiles. The viharn, top-heavy, proportioned precipitously, is plain inside. The exterior is unrestrained by stylistic moderation, as if the abbot saw a catalogue of temple decor and picked it all.

This is a working wat. It is neither ancient nor mellow, not a tourist site. There is a pen for cattle rescued from the slaughterhouse; merit-making donations of cash help relocate the animals to villages up-country. There are living quarters for monks and a temple school whose high-achieving students are praised on a wall mural in the soi outside. There is a shrine to Rama V whose statue is patched with gold leaf for luck. At a Chinese temple next door (corner of Rama IV and Si Phraya roads), coffins for the poor can be bought, to take donors' misfortunes away.

291

Queen Saovabha Memorial Institute

1871 Rama IV Road

1922

The Thai Red Cross Society was formed with the support of Rama V during a territorial dispute with France in 1893 which caused casualties. Rama VI donated land for the society's King Chulalongkorn Memorial Hospital (1914) and officially opened this research institute in 1922. The building was set in spacious grounds, now a large complex which includes the National Blood Service Centre and the long-established snake farm which produces anti-venom and other vaccines. A lake still reflects the Memorial Institute whose style is Beaux-Arts, with classical columns and a glazed arch at the entrance and a façade stretched horizontally with Italianate loggias.

292
Alliance Française
179 Witthayu Road
ADPI architects, 2013
Alliance Française promotes French language and culture. In Bangkok, where a branch opened in 1912, it is the oldest European institution of its type. Space was needed for a médiathèque (multi-purpose cultural facility) so it relocated from Sathorn Road in 2013 to this empty zone which extends to Rama IV Road. The area was previously Suan Lum Night Bazaar, an outdoor market which closed in 2011. The site was cleared by Crown Properties for redevelopment, controversially because the bazaar was a popular, pop-up enterprise and an alternative to malls.

The new Alliance Française is a six-storey box with a ripple of stone around three sides which catches the light, like water reflected from a klong. South-facing windows are thin and vertical to keep the climate out. A pattern of horizontal strip windows punctuates the north-facing elevation where the ground floor is glazed, and a square portico leads to an atrium. There is a bookstore, a bistro, exhibition space, classrooms, a media library and a 240-seat auditorium.

The garden terrace doubles as a deck for the bistro, like a sidewalk café. Landscape design is minimalist, elegant. Architects ADPI designed another idiosyncratic building, at the French Embassy in Bang Rak.

293
Queen Sirikit National Convention Centre
60 New Ratchadaphisek Road
Design 103 International, 1991
The centre was the first in Thailand to be purpose-built for international conventions and exhibitions and was equipped accordingly. National heritage was expressed confidently. The structure's vast

halls, essentially horizontal boxes, are concealed by a Thai-style roofscape. The entrance—a monumental glazed space frame in three triangular sections—evokes tradition without pastiche, reminiscent of tiered temple gables but contemporary and secular. Delegates are welcomed with a golden sculpture shaped like a 'wai'. Benjakati Park (2004) directly north is an added attraction.

294
S31 Sukhumvit
545 Sukhumvit Road, Soi 31
Sumet Jumsai, 2010
Architect and artist Sumet Jumsai was enticed out of retirement for this project, commissioned as the last wish of a contractor who had worked with him in the 1970s. The vibrant colours are from the palette of postmodernism, now classic or very dated depending on taste for the style. Coloured columns rise from the street entrance to reappear halfway up and on the roof. There is a retail podium and a boutique hotel (S31 Sukhumvit Hotel). The dual purpose is defined in contrasting shapes and textures: curved edges and punched metal screens soften the retail podium's profile to the street corners; the hotel is a curvaceous sweep of glass with a big 'S31' sign. Postmodern playfulness takes flight on the roof where there is a bird sculpture (hence the 'Bird Building' nickname). The birds are a memory of annual migrations before urbanisation.

295
Emporium
622 Sukhumvit Road, Soi 24
J + H Boiffils, 1994
A plaza, a curved postmodern façade and a giant 'E' logo in a stylised plant stem introduce this upscale shopping centre and mixed-use development. Its high-rise component is Emporium Suites Tower (Palmer and Turner, 1994). Marketing was aimed initially at Sukhumvit's Thai and foreign condo-dwellers but the catchment area is wider thanks to the BTS. Emporium was the first mall to have a skywalk connection to skytrain (sceptical property owners along the route ignored the offer of free connections, but when the line proved popular most realised they are a must-have).

The mall was the first in the city by the Paris-based design combo. Shops, restaurants, a department store and cineplex are distributed around and off a seven-level atrium, with escalators to all floors and an unconventional trapezoid plan. The atrium has a vertical garden by French botanist Patrick Blanc who pioneered soil-free indoor and outdoor 'living walls' after a visit in 1972 to Thailand, where he saw how plants grow on rain-forest trees and in rock fissures on waterfalls in Khao Yai National Park. Bangkok could use more vertical gardens, aesthetic delights which improve air quality. The city has few parks for its size. A panorama of one of them, Benjasiri Park (1992), can be seen from a restaurant in the food court of the department store. Emporium's Mall Group went on to develop an even more luxurious complex, Siam Paragon, and built EMQuartier (J + H Boiffils, 2014) across the BTS from this original centre.

296

Thailand Creative and Design Centre

622 Sukhumvit Road, Soi 24

Duangrit Bunnag Architect (DBALP), 2005

Emporium got a trendy cultural overlay when this multimedia design centre opened on the 6th floor next to the mall's cineplex. It started as a government initiative in 2004 to promote a knowledge-based creative economy and has become a national resource. It includes a 130-seat auditorium, an exhibition gallery, online data, a design library, shop and café. The spaces are open-plan, minimalist and flexible like a factory but as refined as a chic loft in New York. The transition from the glitzy cineplex foyer is abrupt. The centre's floors are hardwood, the shop is a glass box, signage is sans serif, lighting throughout is tracked, suspended from exposed ceilings. The only decoration is the reception desk's floral-painted fascia which greets MacBook-toting worshipers at this cool temple of design. A follow-up designed by the same architect opened in Chiang Mai in 2013.

297

Architects 49 Office

Soi 26, Sukhumvit Road

Architects 49, 1989

The firm was founded in 1983 by Nithi Sthapitanonda, a graduate of Chulalongkorn University and the University of Illinois. Architects 49 evolved into a multi-disciplinary firm, 49 Group, one of the largest architectural practices in South-East Asia. Most of its staff are based in this modest head office which recalls the low-rise urbanism of old Bangkok. The entrance courtyard is welcoming, unpre-

tentious with structural clarity. The firm has produced high quality buildings of which this is one, with its luminosity and spatial arrangement designed to encourage collaboration and creativity.

298
The 49 Terrace
Soi 49, Sukhumvit Road
Architects 49, 2005
Sukhumvit's condoland is mix of high-rise apartments, upmarket eateries, interior design stores and walkable mini malls like this, one of the first. The typology is typically layered with concrete, wooden decks, modernist angles or curves, and intriguing corners to turn. The pedestrian experience is primary. Indoor and outdoor spaces dissolve. There is natural ventilation and existing trees are preserved. Here the plan was sketched around them. There is clear

reference to the spatial layers found in old-style Siamese residential compounds where houses are raised on stilts and connected by walkways. The 49 Terrace replicates their low-rise courtyard idiom to project an image of relaxed urbanity.

299

Samitivej Hospital

Soi 49, Sukhumvit Road

Rangsan Architecture, 1979

Samitivej fits the one-stop healthcare and wellness policy of the Public Health Ministry which promotes Bangkok as a medical hub of Asia. Big hospitals like Siriraj and Bumrungrad (also in Sukhumvit) aspire to that, and many local clinics do one-stop service in functional concrete buildings.

Samitivej was unveiled as 'the first 1980s luxury private hospital concept'. It is a centre for local care and of medical tourism. The interiors were designed to be soothing, with the main circulation floor built around a garden atrium. Medical buildings are essentially utilitarian but here, as everywhere now, Samitivej introduced fast food and shops. The architectural style, fashionable at the time, was inspired by the brutalist concrete of Le Corbusier, rendered here in a terraced composition supported at the drive-in ramp on tree-like columns. The neo-Gothic rose windows were the architect's whim and trademark.

300

All Zone Studios

Soi 49, Sukhumvit Road

all(zone) with Stefano Mirti, 2011

Even the most generous appraisal would dismiss most of Bangkok's built fabric, which is not to denigrate the rows of four-storey concrete shophouses where many people live and work. These mid 20th-century buildings are utilitarian and are adaptable, as this rehabilitation shows.

The inspiration was the lightweight, low-tech, low-cost claddings which shophouse owners apply as solar screens and advertising, an urban vernacular so commonplace it has been ignored. It is being reinvented by young architects not just for a new look but also for sustainability (better to keep the building you have than tear it down and replace it). Here, two abutting empty shophouses were repurposed with live/work units on each floor. A steel frame was

attached to the old elevation creating a new façade which was filled with a pattern of cheap and durable precast concrete bricks. These screen the inner spaces but allow some daylight in. The void between the old and new elevation is open-air, with steel mesh walkways.

301
J Avenue
Soi 15, Thonglor (Soi 55, Sukhumvit Road)
Contour, 2004

Community malls have sprouted in metro Bangkok since Siam Future Development experimented in the mid 1990s with neighbourhood shopping centres. The concept was refined at Market Place Thonglor (2002) and J Avenue. The idea is simple: make the mall human scale, partly open air; commission an eye-catching, contemporary tropical design and make it pedestrian-friendly; provide covered sidewalk retail and parking; plant shade trees, have water features, build modular units, lease them to a mix of stores, restaurants and at least one coffee shop. Anchor all with a supermarket, preferably not a big one. J Avenue has Villa, an independent retailer which started on Sukhumvit in 1973.

302
Pridi Banomyong Institute
Thonglor (Soi 55, Sukhumvit Road)
Plan Architect, 1995

La Marseillaise plays on a loop in an exhibition on the top level of this building dedicated to Pridi Banomyong. He was the intellectual behind the coup d'état which overthrew the absolute monarchy in 1932. He came from a rice producing family in Ayutthaya province, studied law in Bangkok and gained a scholarship

to Paris where he was inspired by ideals of liberté, égalité and fraternité. During the Second World War he led the Free Thai resistance against the pro-Japanese dictatorship of his former co-conspirator, Phibun Songkhram. Pridi was prime minister briefly after the war but his left-bank radicalism provoked a coup in 1947 and he became an exile in China and France, where he died in 1983.

The institute promotes social studies and culture. Its building is postmodern, in brick, concrete and glass block. The street elevation is monumental, almost sculptural with a curved bay. Steps at the entrance and a bridge to a deck above the ground floor parking area lead to an elevated inner courtyard which feels Mediterranean, classical, a forum perhaps . . . architecture with a serious purpose.

303
SJA+3D Office
106 Soi 53, Sukhumvit Road
Sumet Jumsai, 1973

This 18-unit apartment building was designed to accommodate Sumet Jumsai's office and studio on the ground level and penthouse with roof garden. The architect used the same prefabricated concrete components and Le Corbusier's modular manner for the Bangkok School for the Blind. Columns were cast on site. The exposed posts and I-beams express the building's structural simplicity and clarity. It is 'a machine for living in', to quote Le Corbusier, an influence acknowledged by Sumet, one of the few architects to actually live in a building he designed. At the entrance to the property is the Triangular Building (1975), a library on two levels elongated with interlocking triangular forms, which the architect designed for his father.

304
Science Centre for Education
928 Sukhumvit Road
Sumet Jumsai, 1977
Originally the Science Museum and Plan-

etarium, this building was commissioned by the government as the centrepiece of a science park, especially for children and schools around the nation. Part of the structure was built out onto a reflecting pool edged with trees. The entrance is a spectacular cantilevered concrete canopy. It leads to a four-storey exhibition hall which looks industrial with visible columns, catwalks and space-frame roof trusses. The main stair is a vertical concrete slab. Circulation is informal rather than institutional.

The spatial arrangement was planned to be see-through, with the whole interior and its mezzanines visible at a glance. There are workshops, studios, a library, classrooms and an auditorium. The auditorium's volume is suggested by the wedge shape of the entrance canopy, where a vent-like extrusion on its underside shows the position of the projection room. The library is a plug-in pod, also wedge-shaped but inverted above an outside terrace. The poolside corner is glazed. At night the building glows like a space station just landed.

305
Admission and Information Centre, Bangkok University, City Campus

Kluai Nam Thai Road

Office AT, 2007

The centre facilitates the shift from the outside world to academia. Its reception and information area and a lounge

are on the upper level. Floating steps above a reflecting pool suggest an easy physical and psychological approach to the facilities, expressed as a glazed linear strip with an extruded frame and no-nonsense typography at the entrance. Interiors are bright and spacious. The lounge is cantilevered over the door to a restaurant and has a perforated aluminium solar screen. The building plan was angled to be sensitive to the existing landscape and to make the centre's front better seen from the street.

To the north is BU International College and Art Gallery (also by Office AT, 2006). The transition here is the passage from a new street entrance, across a plaza, and through a hole in the building to a promenade, the main axis on campus to which the building is a smart response. BU commissions striking contemporary work, notably the diamond-shaped Landmark Complex (2010) and Southeast Asian Ceramics Museum (2006), both by Architects 49, and cool designs in hot colours by Supermachine Studio, all at its Rangsit Campus.

306

Siam Society

131 Soi 21 (Asoke), Sukhumvit Road

The Kamthieng House, a Lanna dwelling built in 1844 in Chiang Mai province, is the society's showpiece. It was gifted in 1962 by a descendant of the first owner, relocated to Bangkok and rehabilitated as an ethnological museum, the first in Thailand, which opened in 1966. A Lanna rice barn was acquired later. A permanent exhibition of Lanna arts and crafts was designed and installed in 2001.

The society publishes a scholarly journal. Its centenary issue was titled *Protecting Siam's Heritage*, for which it has been an advocate since 1904 when it gained royal support. The first meeting was at the Oriental Hotel and subsequently in members' homes until 1932 when a permanent meeting place was completed, designed by Edward Healey, a member. The building is an extended sala with an Arts and Crafts gable and neoclassical porte cochère. Behind it is the Chalerm Phrakiat Building (Habita Architects, 1997), a library and research centre.

307
Makkasan Station and City Air Terminal

Kamphaeng Phet 7 at Asoke Road

Design Concept Architects, Asian Engineering and Wisit Engineering consultants, 2010

Suvarnabhumi Airport Rail Link is part of Bangkok's expanding urban rail network. There are eight stations, all elevated above the existing SRT eastern right of way, except the one below the airport. Their design is modern transit mode. Materials are concrete, steel and glass. The spaces are functional and their look high tech, suggesting efficiency and speed.

Makkasan Station was designed to accommodate crowds and check-in facilities. It has a vast, luminous concourse roofed with curving, clerestory-lit vaulting parallel to four elevated platforms. A skywalk connection to the MRT Phetchaburi Station was completed in 2013. The line continues west to Phaya Thai where there is an interchange with the BTS. An extension to the city's former and now secondary international airport, Don Muang, is planned. The terminal at Suvarnabhumi (Murphy/Jahn Architects, 2006), an impressive high-tech structure and one of Asia's biggest and busiest, is worth the train ride to see.

308
Makkasan Station and Maintenance Depot

Nikom Makkasan Road

SRT Makkasan Station, now by-passed by the Airport Rail Link overhead, is a survivor of old Bangkok. The architecture is modest, functional, mid-century modern. The transition from the street to the ticket hall and platform is a model of clarity. The front elevation is arcaded and feels Italian, as does the wide-eaved ticket hall. This dignified space is illuminated by high light from glass block windows and retains wooden bench seats and a terrazzo floor. A brass station master's bell is suspended from the platform canopy which is supported on concrete columns.

Across the Eastern Line tracks is the SRT Maintenance Depot, a sprawling site. It dates from around 1910 and some of its impressive if dilapidated workshops

are visible from the station platform. The depot expanded after the creation of the Royal State Railways of Siam in 1917. Makkasan became the kingdom's biggest railway depot. It was a target for Allied air raids during the Second World War and some of its buildings show traces of camouflage paint. The SRT plans to relocate maintenance to Bang Sue and proposed a massive commercial redevelopment of the Makkasan site. An online campaign for it to be a 'central park' gained popular support. Whatever the outcome, the oldest buildings here deserve to be preserved for their heritage value and potential for adaptive reuse.

309

Thailand Cultural Centre

Thiam Ruammit Road

Kume Sekkei architects, 1987

This was a gift by the Japanese government. A condition was that it had to be designed by a Japanese, since their public money was being spent. It was opened by Rama IX and has been managed locally since then. The design was controversial. Critics said it was not sufficiently 'Thai'. The TCC is instructive because it advanced the Modern Thai concept with simplified but traditional massing to house contemporary functions. Tiered roof forms are rendered without fussiness or decoration on the centre's two halls. The larger is a 2,000-seat theatre and concert hall; the smaller a 500-seat multi-purpose auditorium with an open-air amphitheatre at the back. The landscape design includes a plaza and an outdoor event area between the two halls, which are linked by a colonnade. There are two pavilions in the garden, each in a traditional style, one Thai and the other Japanese.

310
China Cultural Centre
Watthana Tham Road
Plan Architect, XSiTE Design Studio landscape design, 2012

The complex cannot be seen from the street but two lions flanking a gateway suggest something might be happening. The approach, along a bamboo-lined, concrete-walled driveway opens suddenly onto a landscaped plaza where there are two striking structures.

On the west side is a classroom and library block; to the east an exhibition and auditorium building. Both have big wide roofs evoking wooden post and beam, multi-tiered Chinese heritage buildings. The effect is achieved not in wood but with painted steel components. These form layers above hollow, square columns. Steelwork, fixtures and fittings were imported from China.

The 300-seat auditorium above the ground floor exhibition space was designed for Chinese opera. It spans the width of the structure at the horizontal point where the tiered roof meets the inward-stepping counter shape. The result is a dramatic interior space with side walls arrowhead in section. Ranks of strip windows can let in daylight or have blinds drawn. The two buildings are linked by a modernist, glazed foyer which has real wood cladding the I-beams above a spider-clamped curtain wall. There is a large reflecting pool and a solar-screened building which accommodates Chinese staff at the centre, which is the Chinese government's first in South-East Asia.

311
Cyber World Tower
90 Ratchadapisek Road
Robert G. Boughey and Associates, Meinhardt engineers, 2008

Begun in the 1990s as Ratchada Towers (Forum Architect), this is a gigantic example of Bangkok's ubiquitous tower on podium typology. It was designed to have a shopping centre in the podium, whose gaping entrance was said to have

introduced negative feng shui. A department store opened briefly, then closed after the 1997 economic crash which left the two towers incomplete. Their structural frames became a landmark, like the many other skeletons of projects abandoned across town.

TCC Land took over the complex. It was redesigned inside and out and marketed with a slick new name to attract IT tenants. A spectacular but superficial fire in 2008 delayed the reboot. The orientation of the towers at an angle to the street was the original plan but the cutaways on each roof were part of the redesign. The podium, with over 1,500 parking spaces and a food court is still a big box but has shed its original postmodernist cladding and with it the feng shui problem. A steel and aluminium pedestrian access bridge (Meinhardt engineers, 2010), elliptical in section, spans Ratchadapisek Road. At 200 metres the bridge is the city's longest street crossing.

312

MRT Lat Phrao

Ratchadapisek at Ladprao Road

2004

This is not a soft drink bottling plant but Lat Phrao Park and Ride, a nine-storey parkade with 2,200 spaces attached to the MRT station. The advertising banner covering the building's glass curtain wall is part of a drive to increase revenue.

This does not happen underground. All the metro's 18 stations have concourse and platform levels, and 11 have retail, but they are generally free of commercial clutter—unlike the overground BTS where there are many vendors at stations and the trains are plastered with ads. With a daily ridership of several hundred thousand people, the train operator has to comply with strict safety regulations for evacuation of the stations if there are accidents, fires or floods.

Lat Phrao Station is entered and exited on the ground floor at the Ladprao Road end of the park and ride. The only point at which the trains surface is at the MRT's Huai-Khwang maintenance depot and control centre (Space Architects, 2003) which occupies a large site east of the Thailand Cultural Centre Station.

313

Issara Ladprao

Ladprao Road, between sois 12 and 14

Duangrit Bunnag Architect (DBALP), 2011

Transit stations attract development and density, which is efficient and eco-friendly because car use and urban sprawl can be reduced. This high-rise was marketed for its convenient location between MRT Lat Phrao and Phahon Yothin stations. Its grounds were landscaped and existing trees kept. The structure consists of two connected slabs, offset to reduce the apparent bulk. It reads as two towers, one taller than the other, with elevations patterned, a play on the usual squared-up grid. There is a variety of flats, from one bedroom to duplex. A parking podium with a pool on its roof was built in the space where the slab's floor plates perform a lateral shift.

314

Sun One

181 Soi 1, Ladprao Road

Department of Architecture, 2009

The design brief for this box of high-tech activity was workspace for 50 staff of software company Sun Systems. The elevation to the soi is severe, relieved only by a deep-cut entrance, a run of top floor windows and a logo. The returns are glazed and carry aluminium solar screens. Daylight filtered through the screens casts patterns into the workspace which is open-plan to promote informality and team spirit. Daylight also enters from a skylight above an atrium which is the main circulation space, over four floors. Materials are steel and concrete. Vertical strips of PVC divide but not hide flexible spaces. Efficient air conditioning cut energy costs below those in company's previous office, which was smaller. Mechanical systems are exposed as in a live/work loft. The focus is internal, with the suburban clutter screened out.

315

Central Plaza Ladprao

Phahonyothin Road

Interdesign, 1982

This massive mixed-use complex developed by Central Group included the first mega mall in Thailand. It is significant not only for its size (it was the largest shopping centre in Asia) but also for its location in a then relatively undeveloped suburb north of Saphan Khwai, the nearest shopping and entertainment zone.

The site, at the intersection of Phahonyothin, Ladprao and Vibhavadi Rangsit roads, was on Bangkok's expanding highway network. This was crucial to the success of the project which followed

the North American pattern of out-of-town shopping. The middle class in Bangkok was growing and its disposable income and car ownership were increasing; tourism and business travel were about to boom and the location was convenient for Don Muang airport.

One-third of the site's ground plan was developed with a multi-storey parkade; another third was assigned to an office block, convention hall, cineplex and the mall, anchored by Central Department Store; the remaining portion was developed with a high-rise hotel, the Hyatt (now the Centara). The buildings were big, in brutalist style. The effect was stunning. No longer: this mall does not even make the top 20 list of the biggest by leasable area in metro Bangkok (Central World is number one), and the brutalist concrete elevations were re-clad during a 2011 makeover.

316
Magic Land
Phahonyothin Road
1976

Magic Land was Bangkok's first amusement park. It had Ferris wheels, roller coasters, animated dinosaurs, a haunted house and this fantasy castle among its attractions, inspired by Disney theme parks in America. It closed a few years before its 30-year lease expired. Everything was removed except for the concrete and fake stone castle copied from the Sleeping Beauty Castle at Disneyland in California. Magic Land's operators updated their take on Disney theme parks at Dream World, north of Don Muang. As for their legacy, a developer prince with a sense of humour and taste for kitsch is required to save this sleeping beauty from the wrecker's ball.

317
Elephant Tower
3300 Phahonyothin Road
Ong-Ard Architects, Arun Chaiseri engineer, 1997

Three towers, also known as the Chang Building, were arranged to look like a white elephant, a symbol of status and good fortune. The effect on the cityscape is debatable but the building's curiosity rating is high. It is mixed use, with commercial and residential space. The overall structure, raised on a parking podium, is reinforced concrete except where bridges connect the towers at level 25. The connections are made with steel truss space frames, each two floors high, an impressive engineering feat. The building's location and unique look attracted investment in 2012 when a boutique hotel opened.

318
Major Avenue Ratchayothin
Ratchayothin intersection (Ratchadaphisek at Phahonyothin Road)
Contour, 2009

Major Avenue, a community mall bigger than most, has the usual elements—curvy architecture with festive canopies, walkable outdoor spaces, landscaping, Villa Market, eateries and stores. Its indoor-outdoor ambience contrasts with the adjacent Major Cineplex (1998) in a conventional enclosed shopping arcade.

A northern extension of the BTS along Phahonyothin Road is planned, which should reduce car use and will certainly boost development and density. The intersection here will have a station which, along with Major Avenue, is already attracting developers. Recent projects include Supalai Park, an 800-unit slab block on Ratchadaphisek (2012), a 322-unit slimline high-rise, The Vantage (Ratchadaphisek at Vibhavadi Rangsit; Architects 49, 2013), and the Wind Ratchayothin (Palmer and Turner, 2010) by

SF, the developer of the mall. The Wind has 390 units in a wafer-thin, 37-storey sandwich. Spatial planning and operable windows allow breezes to flow through every room, potentially reducing energy costs from excessive air conditioning. A simple idea indicating the shift from the sealed high-rise typology imported since the 1960s to a sustainable response to the climate.

319
SCB Park Plaza
9 Ratchadapisek Road
Robert G. Boughey and Associates, 1996

SCB Park Plaza was acclaimed as 'a new world-class complex . . . one of the best facilities of its kind in Thailand'. The design was by an American architect and longtime resident of Bangkok. The intent was to create 'an integrated city environment' with a landmark financial services building at its core. The concept and its typology rank SCB with similar global capitalist projects of the time, like Canary Wharf in London. There are four office towers and a retail plaza set back in landscaped grounds. The master plan on which the individual buildings, colonnades which connect them and the landscape design were composed mandated 40 percent of the site be designated green space, and it remains so.

SCB's tower is the landmark, with an aluminium and reflective glass curtain wall. The cone-shaped roof was said to have been inspired by classical Thai buildings, but elsewhere it would be thought retro Art Deco. The ground floor is defined by the entrance atrium, a sloping triangle of glass. A mural, 'Cosmology of the Thai Universe', painted in situ by Panya Vijinthanasarn and studio assistants, decorates the space between the lobby and the banking hall. A reflecting pool with fountains animates the plaza where there are statues of SCB's founders, Rama V and Prince Mahisorn.

320
Museum of Contemporary Art (MOCA)
Kamphaeng Phet 6 Road (Vibhavadi Rangsit Road)
PLA (PLandscape), PIA Interior, Withlight design, 2012

This five-floor box of treasures was built

by telecom tycoon Boonchai Bencharongkul to house his art collection. It covers over half a century of recent Thai work, mostly paintings, many by leading artists and much of it a response to tradition besieged by the modern world. A salon-style room displays some 19th-century European paintings.

The *Bangkok Post* likened their collector to a modern Medici, and the gallery's granite-clad walls express a Medici-like power. The building had to be big, not only to house around 800 artworks, some very large, but also to compete visually with the hinterland of malls, billboards, and the elevated Don Muang Tollway directly outside. These distractions disappear in MOCA's courtyard, a transition from urban noise to serenity. There is a reflecting pool with a jasmine sculpture scaled to fit the building. The walls are perforated with an Arabesque repeat pattern with a jasmine motif, through which some light penetrates inside. The effect is dramatic in the cathedral-like main hall which has a statue of Silpa Bhirasri, and the Latin aphorism 'Ars longa vita brevis' (Art is long, life short) inscribed on one wall. There is humour too—an installation of Salvador Dali wearing a Thai hat. The lighting design adds to the contemporary feel of the interior spaces which are of international quality—functional, unobtrusive and a perfect backdrop for the art.

321
Laksi Monument
Laksi Circle
Narumitr Lekhakan, 1936

The traffic circle into which Ram Intra, Chaeng Wattana and Phahonyothin roads flow was meant to dignify this monument, known originally as the Constitutional Protection Monument. It was erected by the People's Party as a memorial to 17 police and army officers killed by counter-revolutionary troops led by Prince Bovoradej in 1933. The fighting took place near Wat Thewasunthorn, north of where the Museum of Contemporary Art now stands.

The chedi-like octagon is topped with a bronze replica of the constitution. The pedestal has a bas-relief of the Buddhist wheel of enlightenment, a poem by Rama VI ('Siamanusti' or 'Harmony in Siam'), an idealised image in bas-relief of a family and a list of the martyrs. The style is Art Deco. The monument was sidelined for road widening and an overpass but cleaned for the 80th anniversary of the battle.

322
Wat Phra Si Mahathat
Phahonyothin Road
Ou Laphanon, 1941

Christened the Temple of Democracy, this was a People's Party project to commemorate the political changes introduced after the coup of 1932. Buddha relics, soil and clippings of a bodhi tree were sourced from India. The ubosot and cloisters are conventional, set in park-like grounds. The landmark structure is a white chedi whose outer layer encloses a gold-coloured sibling which contains the relics. An internal circular corridor separates the two. There are four doors on the outer layer. Its inside walls are lined with reliquary niches containing bones or ashes of citizens. Above these is a circular fringe of decoration, then a lofty space with high windows. The bell-shaped form and spire are traditional, with some Art Deco applied.

323
Faculty of Economics Building, Kasetsart University
50 Ngam Wong Wan Road
Tonsilp Studio, 2007

Potential energy-savings drove the design process here, which reduced the use of air conditioning. Social and circulation space is an atrium with trees in a sunken garden and on roof-level loggias. Galleries are draped with hanging plants. The foliage creates a relaxing atmosphere under a trussed and glazed canopy, like being in a botanical garden or a forest.

The space is cooled with natural ventilation using the stack effect. The ground floor is partly open to force the rise of hot air, which is released through openings at the corners on the top level. The structure is concrete with some wooden decking. Fin-like solar shades outside recall those on modernist shophouses of the 1960s. Seminar rooms are climate-controlled but the atrium delivers a lesson in fundamentals of bioclimatic architecture.

Kasetsart University has several green initiatives. They include eco-responsible design taught at the Faculty of Architec-

ture where there is a rooftop urban farm and a 'scrap shop' with products made from recycled materials for sale. The university was established in 1943 within the Ministry of Agriculture. This is the original campus. One of its oldest buildings, which faces Ngam Wong Wan Road is the colonial-style former Animal Husbandry and Chemistry Building, now the Hall of History museum and archive.

324
Toshiba Building
Vibhavadi Rangsit Road
Ong-Ard Architects, 1986

This is architecture as a billboard to be seen from the Don Muang Tollway, like a roadside look-at-me attraction in America. The design is postmodern, clad in brick, Renaissance style. The façade, its arched entrance and pediment look like they were shipped from Bologna. Being in Bangkok this office and warehouse combo has a spirit house, in brick with arches an echo the Italianate style of the building it protects.

325
The Energy Complex
555 Vibhavadi Rangsit Road
Architects 49, Design Concept Architects, 2010

The PTT Exploration and Production Public Company is the national energy enterprise. This new headquarters was designed to fit corporate facilities in one place by relocating staff from offices scattered around town. It expresses a corporate outlook that is progressive, and it achieved LEED Platinum status accredited by the US Green Building Council, the first project in South-East Asia to receive the accolade.

The structure reads like two-towers in a close embrace like dancers, one taller than the other (a separate high-rise was built for the Ministry of Energy). The footprints are shaped like oil drops and the curtain walls curved. The curves are in step with the semi-circular colonnade that is part of the old PTT development whose postmodern tower (Architects 49, Plan Architect, Design Develop, 1989) is nearby. The main lobby of the new building opened with a display of drilling gear and rock samples, a reminder that

the energy business is fundamentally exploitative of nature. The industry's global giants now portray themselves green. PTT focused on an achievable local effort with a building programme for 'a creative workplace for a sustainable future' and systems integrated for maximum efficiency.

Eco-friendly features include energy-efficient glass, a heat exchange system to regulate air temperatures, and sensors which respond to daylight and dim fluorescent light accordingly. The open-plan interiors look futuristic, high tech. Horizontal and vertical integration over many floors promotes staff interaction and teamwork. Navigation is assisted by graphic design with pictograms and transit-style typography. A blue and orange colour scheme was inspired, like the PTT logo, by the gas flame fuelled by oil exploration and production.

326

Buddhadasa Indapanno Archives

Wachira Benchathat Park, Nikhom Rotfai Road

Ashram of Community and Environmental Architect, Plan Studio, Plan Associates, Plan Architect, XSiTE Design Studio landscape design, 2010

Also known as Suan Mokkh Bangkok, this three-level concrete structure steps lightly on pilotis onto the lake at Wachira Benchathat Park, also called Suan Rotfai (Railway Park), laid out in 1999 on the SRT employee's golf course.

Buddhadasa Bhikkhu was a reformist monk of the forest and 20th-century philosopher. The building, a charity project by the architects, contains a comprehensive collection of his texts and other works. The architecture is suitably austere, with rectilinear massing and crisp-edges all finished in polished and unpolished concrete, softened by the wood decking and paneling. There is a bookstore and public space on the main level where the deck is open to natural ventilation and views of the water. The second floor has meditation rooms and exhibit space, with shutters which open to the lake; the third floor has reading and meeting rooms, and the archives in a climate-controlled environment.

The emphasis of the building programme was accessibility, both physical and philosophical. The spatial interplay is stimulating and serene, as is the lakeside setting. The landscape design is sympathetic to the architecture and its purpose. There is a paved and pebbled amphitheatre inspired by the courtyard at Suan Mokkh Chaiya, a retreat founded

by Buddhadasa Bhikkhu in Surathani province. All very Zen, one of the branches of Buddhism which he embraced.

327
Thai Airways International
89 Vibhavadi Rangsit Road
CASA, 1988

This was one of the first tall buildings on the Vibhavadi Rangsit arterial which has become an alternative to Sathorn as a corporate hotspot. The high-rise is the zone's most elegant tower, with concrete and glass elevations composed with reductive purity rising from a wide plaza and reflecting pool. The curtain wall reflects the sky. The logo is the only decorative element.

Thai Airways was established by the government as the national carrier in 1951. The HQ was built around the time the international airline merged with Thai Airways Company (TAC), the domestic airline from which THAI had evolved. The tower rises above the elevated Don Muang Tollway, begun in the mid 1980s to alleviate traffic congestion en route to Don Muang airport.

328
Thai Rath Clubhouse
1 Vibhavadi Rangsit Road
Ongsa Architects, 2004

The clubhouse and cafeteria share the newspaper's compound which has a variety of structures from different periods. The composition and style are neo-modernist, a glass box overlapped with a flat roof which is supported outside on thin columns. *Thai Rath* is the nation's best-selling newspaper with a daily circulation of around one million copies, most printed in a multi-storey, high tech printing and office building (also by

Ongsa Architects, 1992). It has a vertical, automated production line. Newsprint is delivered to the ground floor, then to the press room between floors 3 and 5, printed digitally on six German presses

and collated. The finished product is sent by spiral chutes to a ground floor loading bay where trucks wait. That function determined the building's form which is transparent and symbolic of the free press. Glazed curtain walls are protected by brise-soleil. The printing process and the spiral chutes are visible. As at the clubhouse, the architects sought 'the utmost simplification of building form'.

329
Mo Chit BTS Station
Phahonyothin Road
Halcrow Asia, 1999

The Bangkok Transit System (BTS) dual track elevated railway opened with 24 stations along two lines, Silom and Sukhumvit, since extended on Sukhumvit and across the Chao Phraya River. Mo Chit is the system's north terminus. The architecture and train guideway design were commissioned by the project consortium, Siemens and Italian-Thai Development.

The stations were built to a uniform design, except for Siam interchange which is multilevel. The concrete structures are double deck with the lower level a concourse with ticket machines, information kiosks and vendors. The upper deck carries the train tracks and platforms which are cantilevered out from the guideway's supporting columns. Steel canopies

shade the platforms which are open at the sides for cross ventilation. The guideway at Mo Chit runs on for a short distance, then switches back to let trains enter the maintenance depot on the east side of Phahonyothin Road, on which the line will be extended to the northern suburbs. The depot was built here after the original plan to have it under Lumpini Park drew a barrage of protest.

330

Chatuchak Weekend Market

Kamphaeng Phet Road

A clock tower with the crest of Rama IX is a landmark for shoppers lost in Chatuchak's labyrinth of covered alleys. The weekend market, whose attractions are antiques, bric-a-brac, handicrafts and much more, is the largest and busiest in the kingdom. It dates from the 1930s when Field Marshal Phibun established a weekend farmers' market on Sanam Luang to give rural growers somewhere central to sell their produce. That character and purpose had begun to erode by the time the market was relocated to Chatuchak, to clear Sanam Luang for the Bangkok and Chakri dynasty's bicentennial in 1982. The market was run by the BMA until 2012 when the SRT took over. Not all vendors are outdoors. Some rent space in JJ Mall and InSquare, air conditioned multilevel bazaars on Kamphaeng Phet 2 Road.

331

Or Tor Kor Market

Kamphaeng Phet Road

'Or Tor Kor' is the Thai abbreviation of the Marketing Organisation for Farmers which was founded by the government in 1974 and leased land here from the SRT. There are several buildings, the most striking being the boat-shaped Siam Orchid Centre (2011), designed to help promote exports. It is a permanent addition to the sidewalk plant market at Chatuchak. Traders are moored around its hull and in units on the upper deck.

Or Tor Kor wet market is clean, modern and known for quality produce. Its lightweight steel structure is a recent rebuilding of the original market (1977). It is a model of functionality, being spacious and easy to navigate. Vendors' stands line the aisles according to the produce and products for sale. The building recalls the classic 19th-century iron and glass covered markets in Europe. That influence is indirect but can be traced to Nang Loeng Market which was part the modernisation of Bangkok by Rama V following his first visit to Europe in 1897.

Or Tor Kor is linked to the MRT at Kamphaeng Phet station where one of metro's surface pods is outside on Kamphaeng Phet Road. There are seven roads so named, after a son of Rama V who was a supremo of the SRT which owns the land through which they run. This one was constructed in 1978.

332

Siam Cement Group Head Office

1 Siam Cement Road

Design 103 International, 1983–1987

Siam Cement was established by Rama VI in 1913 to make concrete for buildings and infrastructure, to continue the modernisation of the previous reign. Raw materials (limestone, sand and gravel) were sourced in Siam and water for the mix pumped from klongs. Concrete was the building material of choice, and is still throughout the kingdom.

The contract to build and manage the first cement plant was won by a Danish company, F. L. Smidth. Machinery was imported from Copenhagen on East Asiatic Company ships. The plant's kilns, silos and smokestacks were an astonishing sight rising from a landscape worked by peasants and water buffalo. Three houses were built for the plant manager and staff. The style of the present house (Emilio Giovanni Gollo, 1914) is similar to them. It was rehabilitated recently as a meeting centre and guest house.

The site at Bang Sue was chosen because it could be serviced by canals and railway lines. The plant was hit and damaged during the Second World War when the SRT rail yards were bombed. Siam Cement was restructured in 1972 as Siam Cement Group, with a white elephant logo. The plant here was closed in 1981 (Siam Cement has others) and the site redeveloped as the corporate

HQ. There are two 11-storey office blocks connected by a 5-storey atrium, with floors expressed as horizontal strips typical of the modernism of the time. Recently the grounds were re-landscaped and the entrance to them re-orientated because the MRT Blue Line extension emerges from below ground right outside the original gate. A shiny 22-storey tower (Design 103 International) with rippling glazed elevations was completed in 2014.

333

Bang Sue Grand Station

Design Concept Architects

Bang Sue has been a mainline rail junction since 1927 when the Royal State Railways Southern Line by-passed its original terminus at Thonburi, crossed the Chao Phraya River on Rama VI Bridge and reached Hua Lamphong. Bang Sue is set to become even more significant. Its suburban station and rail yards are the future location of this new project. The idea was first proposed by the government after the creation of the State Railway of Thailand in 1951, but the popular Hua Lamphong was retained.

Bang Sue Grand Station will be the terminus for the SRT Northern, North-eastern and Southern lines, and connect with urban rapid transit—the SRT Red Line, the Airport Rail Link and the MRT Blue Line. These are part of the Mass Rapid Transit System for the Bangkok metropolitan region announced in 2004. The BTS and MRT will be expanded from less than 50 to nearly 250 kilometres with several new lines. The MRT Blue and Purple lines will intersect at Tao Poon elevated interchange station (Design Concept Architects) west of the present Blue Line station at Bang Sue.

In 2013 the SRT signed a multi-billion baht contract for Bang Sue Grand Station. Site preparation has started. It is a spectacular scheme. The building will be the size of an airport terminal. Twenty-four platforms, double-decked, are planned for commuter and long distance routes and, perhaps, high-speed trains. The architecture looks sleek and high tech, structurally similar to the Airport Rail Link station at Makkasan. There will be an airy concourse accessed through a graceful arch, a homage to the great train shed at Hua Lamphong where Thailand's railway history started.

Glossary

Arcade: a row of arches on columns or set in a wall; a covered passageway with arches (or shops) on one or both sides.

Art Deco: a decorative style of zigzag and geometric shapes popularised by the Exposition Internationale des Arts Decoratifs et Industriels Modernes, held in Paris in 1925.

Art Nouveau: a European art and architectural style c. 1900, characterised by decorative motifs inspired by nature.

Arts and Crafts: a decorative arts movement, begun in England in the late 19th century to re-establish craftsmanship threatened by industrialisation and mass production.

Aspara: a female spirit of the waters and clouds in Hindu and Buddhist mythology.

Atrium: originally an open-roofed courtyard or entrance hall in a Roman house; in modern architecture a central space usually glass-roofed, often with multilevel galleries.

Ayutthaya: capital of Siam, 1350–1767, and the name of its historical era; it is a Unesco World Heritage Site.

Bai raka: fin-like projections on a temple roof bargeboard, styled as fins of naga and/or feathers of garuda.

Bai sema: the eight boundary stones around an ubosot marking sacred space for monks' ceremonies.

Baldachin: a ceremonial canopy over a throne, altar or doorway.

Bargeboard: wooden boards, usually decorated, attached to a gable.

Baroque: a 17th-century European style of architecture, animated by bold massing of classical elements and elaborate decoration.

Bas-relief: French for 'low relief'; a sculptural or cast panel on which decoration is raised slightly from the surface.

Bay: a vertical division on an elevation, sometimes with bay (three-sided) windows or to emphasise an entrance.

Beaux-Arts: a style characterised by monumental classicism and formal planning, named after the École des Beaux-Arts, the architecture school in Paris.

Belle Époque: the era of gracious living and lavish decoration in Europe c. 1900.

Bodhi tree: the tree under which the Buddha meditated and found enlightenment; a sacred tree in temples.

Brise-soleil: a solar shade, commonly concrete and horizontal.

Brutalism: from the French *béton brut* meaning raw concrete, and the architectural style of roughly finished concrete derived from it.

Cantilever: a beam fixed only at one end, where it is anchored to a wall or other support.

Capital: the top part of a column or pilaster, usually decorated.

Chedi, also stupa: a memorial with a spire, typically bell-shaped around the base which enshrines relics of the Buddha or his disciples, or the ashes of the dead.

Cho fa: a graceful guardian finial on the apex of a roof in temple architecture.

Classical, classicism: the architecture of ancient Greece and Rome and its many revivals; the classical 'orders'—Tuscan, Doric, Ionic, Corinthian— identified by the decorative details of their columns and capitals.

Clerestory: a strip of windows at the top of a wall or within a roof providing high light to the interior.

Colonnade: a row of columns, in classical architecture carrying arches or an entablature.

Crenellations: openings at the top of a

parapet, also called battlements, originally in forts from which defenders could shoot safely.
Cruciform plan: shaped like a cross
Cupola: a dome-like feature at the top of a roof or larger dome.
Curtain wall: an exterior cladding, commonly glass panels fixed to a building's structural frame.

Elevation: the wall of a building, also called the façade if facing forward.
Entablature: the continuous horizontal lintel in classical architecture supported by columns or a wall.
Erawan: the divine white elephant on which Indra rides; in Thai architecture it is usually shown with three heads.

Fanlight: a semi-circular window with radiating glass panels above a door.
Farang: a westerner; thought to be a phonetic rendering of *française*, from French missionaries in Ayutthaya.
Ferroconcrete: reinforced concrete; originally with iron rods in France where the technique was invented, now with steel 'rebar'.
Festoon: an ornament, usually stone or plaster, carved or moulded as a garland of flowers, leaves or ribbons.
Fretwork: lacy ornament in wood, sometimes cast iron, usually on gables and porches; also called 'gingerbread' trim.

Gable: a triangular section of wall at the end of a pitched roof; in temple architecture it is usually decorated and expressed as part of the roof; also a feature on top of a bay.
Garuda: the Hindu god, king of birds; serves as the mount of Vishnu; lesser garudas also live in the celestial realm.
Gothic Revival: a revival of the Gothic style of medieval Europe, typically for churches.

Hang hong: goose tail; the finial, commonly a naga head, on the low end of a temple bargeboard.
High tech: modernism that pushes technological boundaries, often flamboyantly, expressed in visible structural components and systems.
Ho trai: a temple scripture pavilion for [illegible]
Hongsa: a mythical swan-like bird.

Indra: the ruler of the Hindu gods and Mount Meru; originally the god of war; his weapon is a thunderbolt and his mount is Erawan.
Italianate: architecture inspired by Renaissance forms and details.

Jataka: morally instructive tales of the Buddha's past lives, and the subject of murals in temples.

Kuti: monks' dwellings.

Loggia: the open side of an arcade or colonnade, or of a room leading to a garden; a partly enclosed balcony.

Mansard: a roof that has a double slope, with lower one steeper and higher than the upper, typical of the French Second Empire style.
Massing: the arrangement of a building's volumes expressed externally on elevations.
Mid-century modern: modernist architecture and design from the mid 1930s to the mid 1960s.
Modern Thai: a hybrid style introduced by Rama VI for official buildings; common from the 1920s to the 1960s; characterised by concrete construction and a central gabled entrance, usually with columns, often with loggias either side, all covered with a traditional roof.
Modernism, modernist: the cult of the new in architecture and other arts which rejected historical styles and forms, influenced by the Bauhaus design school in Germany (1919-1933).
Mondop: a structure with a square plan

and tiered roof with a spire.
Mount Meru: the mythical mountain at the centre of the universe in Hindu and Buddhist cosmology.
Mullion: a vertical unit dividing glazed areas in a window.

Naga: king of serpents, enemy of Garuda; often a guardian figure prominent on eave brackets and roof finials in temples.
Narai: the Thai incarnation of Vishnu, one of three gods of the main Hindu trinity, usually shown on his mount Garuda.
Neoclassical: a revival style of classicism in Europe c. 1800 and later; the architecture is formal and was favoured by aristocrats, government institutions and banks.

Ogee arch: a flat arch with two curved sides turned up at the apex.

Palazzo: a palatial building; especially a Renaissance palace in Italy.
Palladian: from Andrea Palladio, the 16th-century Italian architect; the revival of his style in the 18th century and later examples of it.
Pediment: a triangular feature at the top of a portico in classical architecture or above a window, often filled with sculptural groups.
Pilaster: a low-profile rectangular column set in a wall.
Pilotis: structural, stilt-like columns, usually concrete, which support a building and create open space at ground level; they are a feature of modernist architecture.
Porte cochère: a covered entrance for vehicles.
Portico: a roofed entrance porch open or enclosed at each side; in classical architecture with a pediment supported by columns.
Postmodernism: in architecture a reaction to modernism since the 1970s; its sources range from classical architecture to Art Deco and other quotations from the past, or from pop culture.
Prang: a Khmer or Khmer-style Buddhist monument shaped like a rocket.

Rama: an avatar of Vishnu, regarded as the perfect being and symbol of the perfect king.
Ramakien: the Thai version of the Ramayana, the Hindu saga of Rama's adventures.
Rattanakosin: the era of Thai history which started when King Rama I founded the Chakri dynasty and Bangkok as the capital of Siam in 1782; the style of architecture and arts from that time to the present.
Renaissance: the 15th- and 16th-century revival, begun in Italy, of art and architecture from classical times.
Romanesque: architecture in medieval Europe, revived in the 19th-century.
Rose window: a circular window with radiating glass panels conventionally on the front elevation of a church.

Sala: a pavilion, typically with open sides and a gabled roof.
Stile Liberty: the Italian offshoot of Art Nouveau, often a decorative overlay on classical forms.

Ubosot or bot: the assembly or ordination hall where Buddhist monks are ordained; houses a wat's most important Buddha image and is decorated with murals; conventionally it stands on sacred ground marked by eight bai sema.

Vaulted: a ceiling usually arched in churches and other public buildings.
Viharn: a chapel, smaller and on a lower base than an Ubosot, commonly with less decoration; houses Buddha images; is used for ceremonies involving monks and lay people.
Vishnu: the preserver of the cosmos, considered to have had nine earthly incarnations, including Rama.

Wat: a temple and its compound.

Maps 1–8 and metro map

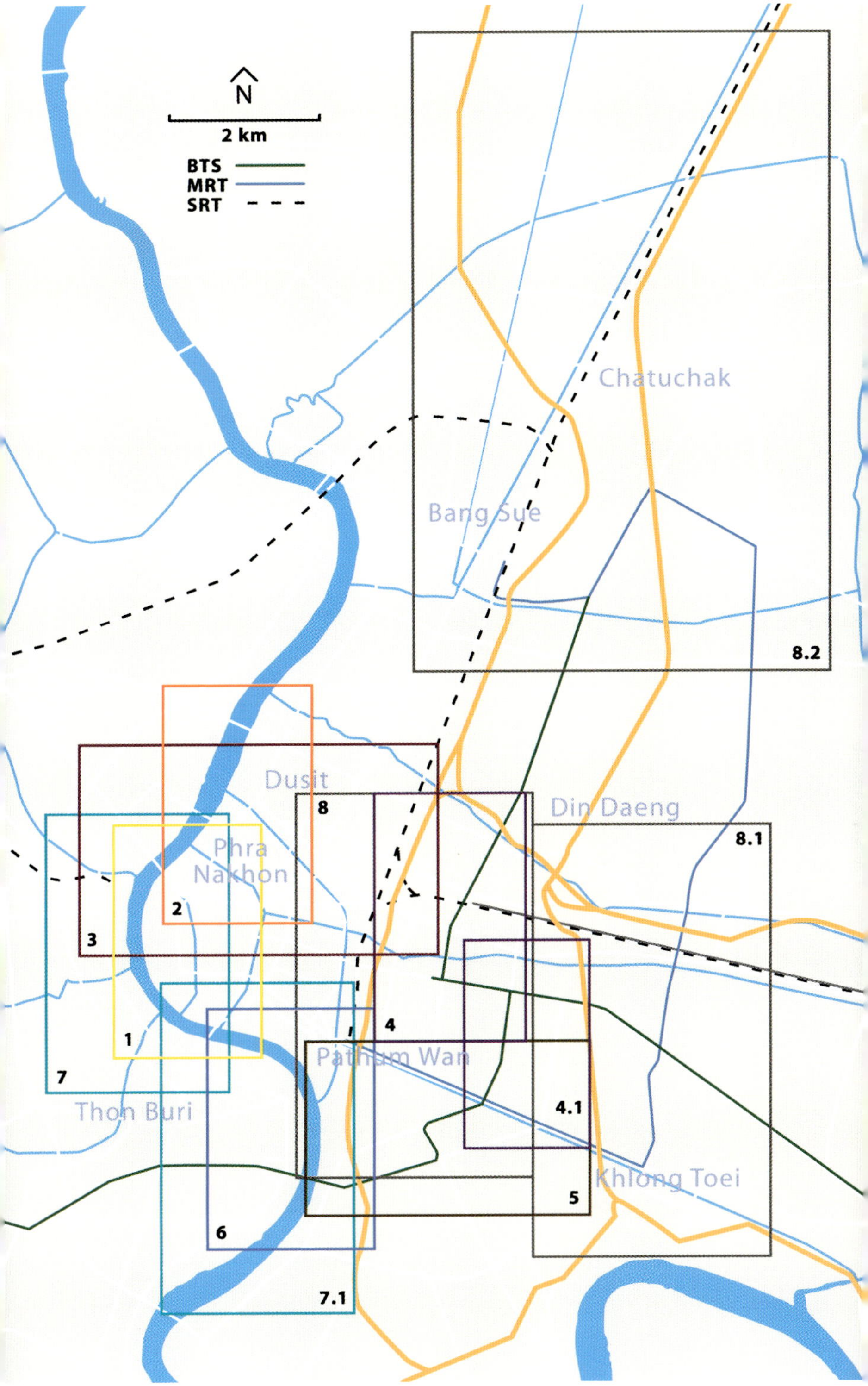
N
2 km
BTS
MRT
SRT
Chatuchak
Bang Sue
8.2
Dusit
8
Din Daeng
8.1
Phra
Nakhon
2
3
1
4
7
Pathum Wan
4.1
Thon Buri
5
Khlong Toei
6
7.1

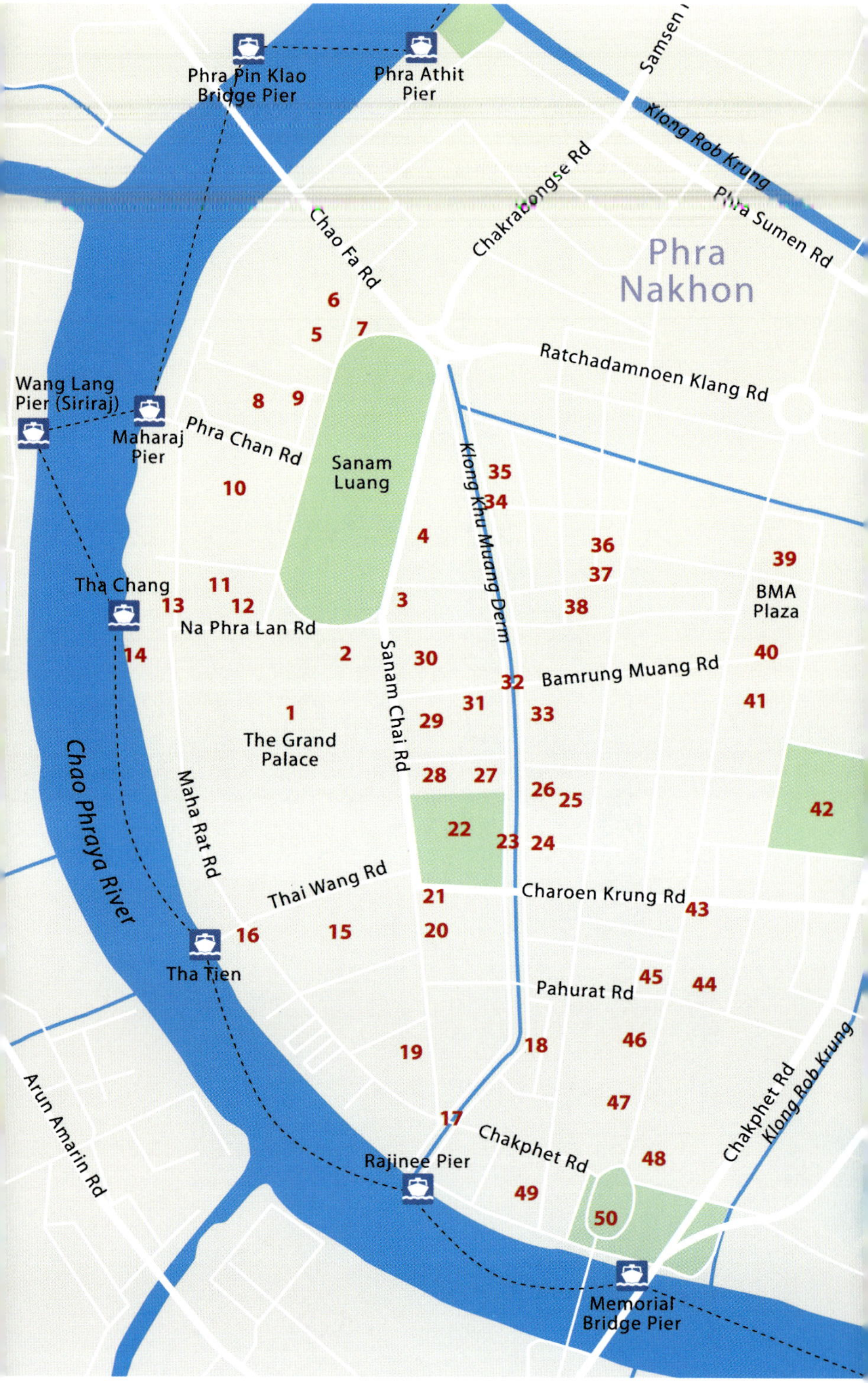
Phra Pin Klao Bridge Pier
Phra Athit Pier
Samsen
Klong Rob Krung
Chakrabongse Rd
Phra Sumen Rd
Chao Fa Rd
Phra Nakhon
Ratchadamnoen Klang Rd
Wang Lang Pier (Siriraj)
Maharaj Pier
Phra Chan Rd
Sanam Luang
Klong Khu Muang Derm
Tha Chang
Na Phra Lan Rd
BMA Plaza
Bamrung Muang Rd
Sanam Chai Rd
The Grand Palace
Chao Phraya River
Maha Rat Rd
Thai Wang Rd
Charoen Krung Rd
Tha Tien
Pahurat Rd
Arun Amarin Rd
Chakphet Rd
Rajinee Pier
Chakphet Rd
Klong Rob Krung
Memorial Bridge Pier
1
2
3
4
5
6
7
8
9
10
11
12
13
14
15
16
17
18
19
20
21
22
23
24
25
26
27
28
29
30
31
32
33
34
35
36
37
38
39
40
41
42
43
44
45
46
47
48
49
50

Bang Phlat
Charan Sanitwong Rd
Irrigation Dept. Pier
Payap Pier
Klong Samsen
Krung Thon Bridge Pier
78
77
Samsen Rd
Ratchawithi Rd
76
74
75
73
Dusit
Dusit Palace
72
Thewej Pier
Rama VIII Rd
70
69
Samsen Rd
71
68
Klong Krung Kasem
Phitsanulok Rd
Rama VIII Bridge Pier
Krung Kasem Rd
Phra Athit Pier
Phra Nakhon
55
54
56
57
52
Phra Arthit Rd
53
58
Phra Sumen Rd
59
Chakrabongse Rd
60
61
64
63
65
66
67
Prachathipatai Rd
Ratchadamnoen Nok Rd
51
62
Khao San Rd
Klong Rob

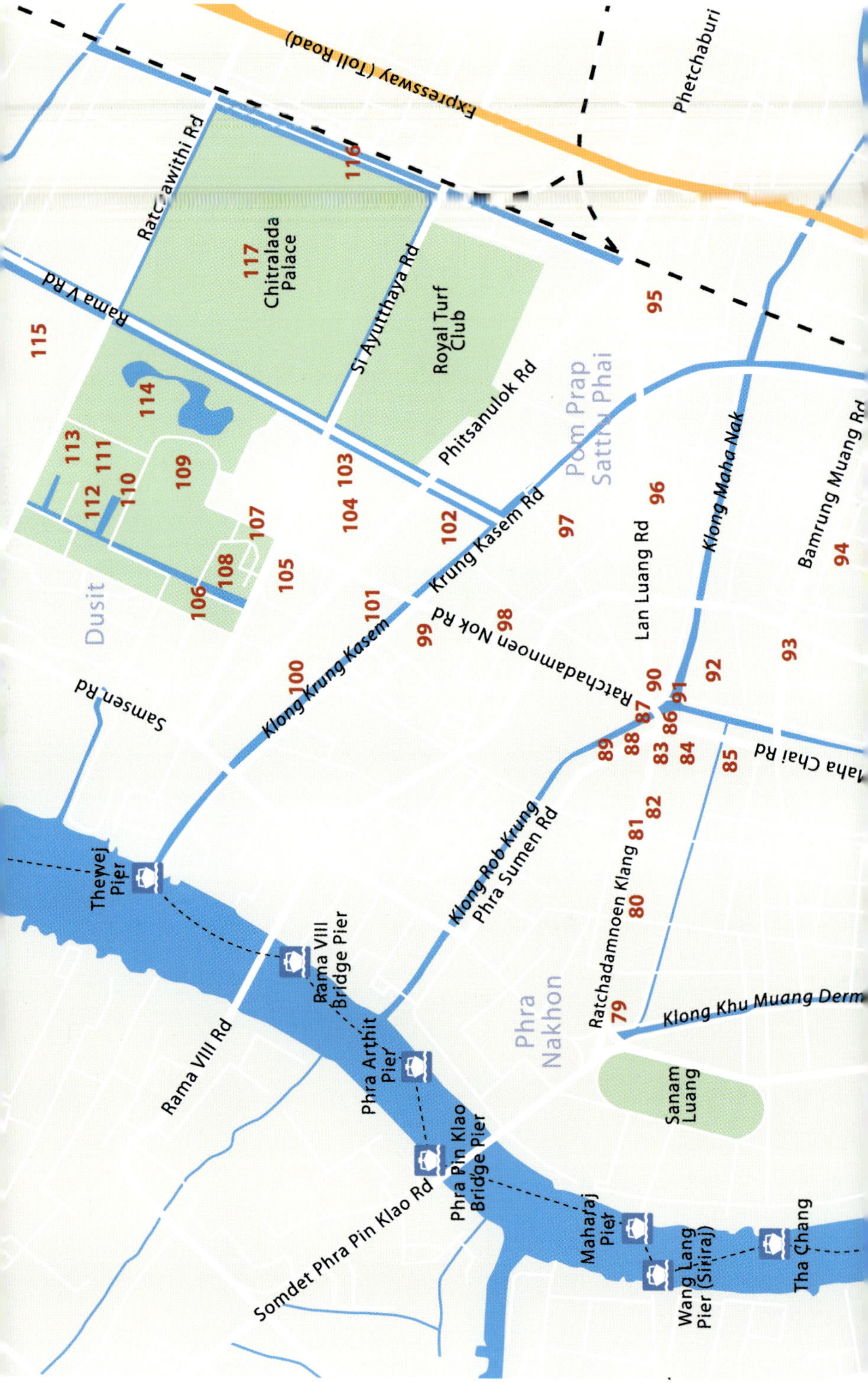
Expressway (Toll Road)
Phetchaburi
Ratchawithi Rd
Chitralada Palace
117
116
115
Rama V Rd
Si Ayutthaya Rd
Royal Turf Club
95
Phitsanulok Rd
Pom Prap Sattru Phai
114
113
111
112
110
109
103
104
102
107
108
106
105
Dusit
Krung Kasem Rd
97
96
Klong Maha Nak
Bamrung Muang Rd
94
Lan Luang Rd
101
99
98
Ratchadamnoen Nok Rd
Klong Krung Kasem
100
Samsen Rd
93
92
90
91
87
86
89
88
83
84
85
Maha Chai Rd
82
81
Klong Rob Krung
Phra Sumen Rd
Ratchadamnoen Klang
80
Thewej Pier
Rama VIII Bridge Pier
Rama VIII Rd
Phra Arthit Pier
79
Klong Khu Muang Derm
Phra Nakhon
Sanam Luang
Phra Pin Klao Bridge Pier
Somdet Phra Pin Klao Rd
Maharaj Pier
Wang Lang Pier (Siriraj)
Tha Chang

121
120
Klong Samsen
Ratchawithi Rd
122
119
123
Victory Monument BTS Station
124
118
Expressway (Toll Road)
Ratchathewi
Santiphap Park
Si Ayutthaya Rd
125
Rang Nam Rd
Phaya Thai BTS Station
126
Airport Link Phaya Thai
Airport Link Ratchaprarop
129
127
Phetchaburi Rd
128
Banthat Thong Rd
Ratchatewi BTS Station
Phaya Thai Rd
Klong Saen Saep
131
132
133
139
National Stadium BTS Station
Rama I Rd
138
Ratchadamri Rd
130
134
Siam BTS Station
140
135
137
136
Pathum Wan
Chulalongkorn University

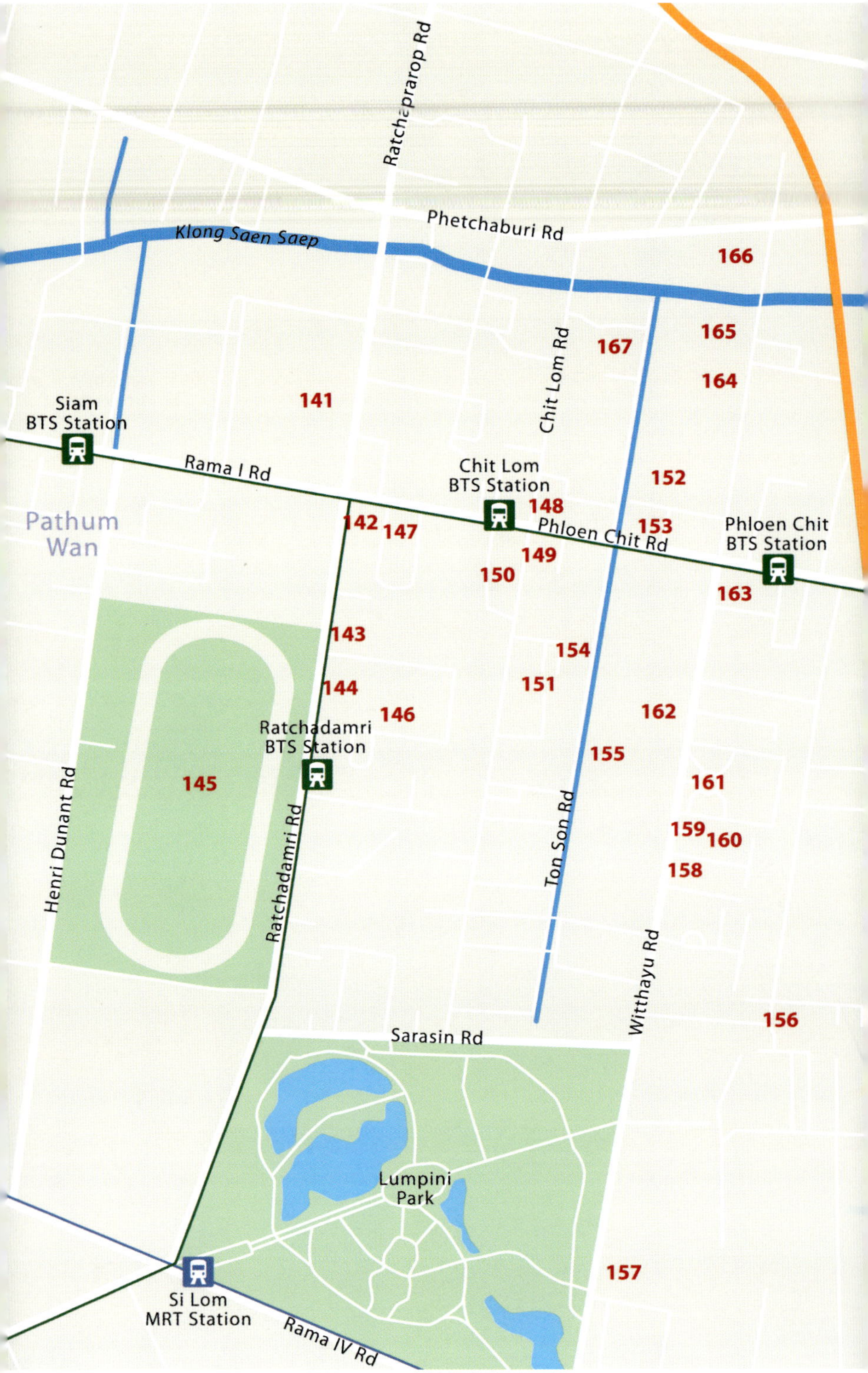
Ratchaprarop Rd
Phetchaburi Rd
Klong Saen Saep
166
165
167
164
141
Chit Lom Rd
Siam
BTS Station
Rama I Rd
Chit Lom
BTS Station
152
Pathum
Wan
148
142
147
Phloen Chit Rd
153
Phloen Chit
BTS Station
149
150
163
143
154
144
151
146
162
Ratchadamri
BTS Station
155
145
161
Henri Dunant Rd
Ratchadamri Rd
Ton Son Rd
159
160
158
Witthayu Rd
156
Sarasin Rd
Lumpini
Park
157
Si Lom
MRT Station
Rama IV Rd

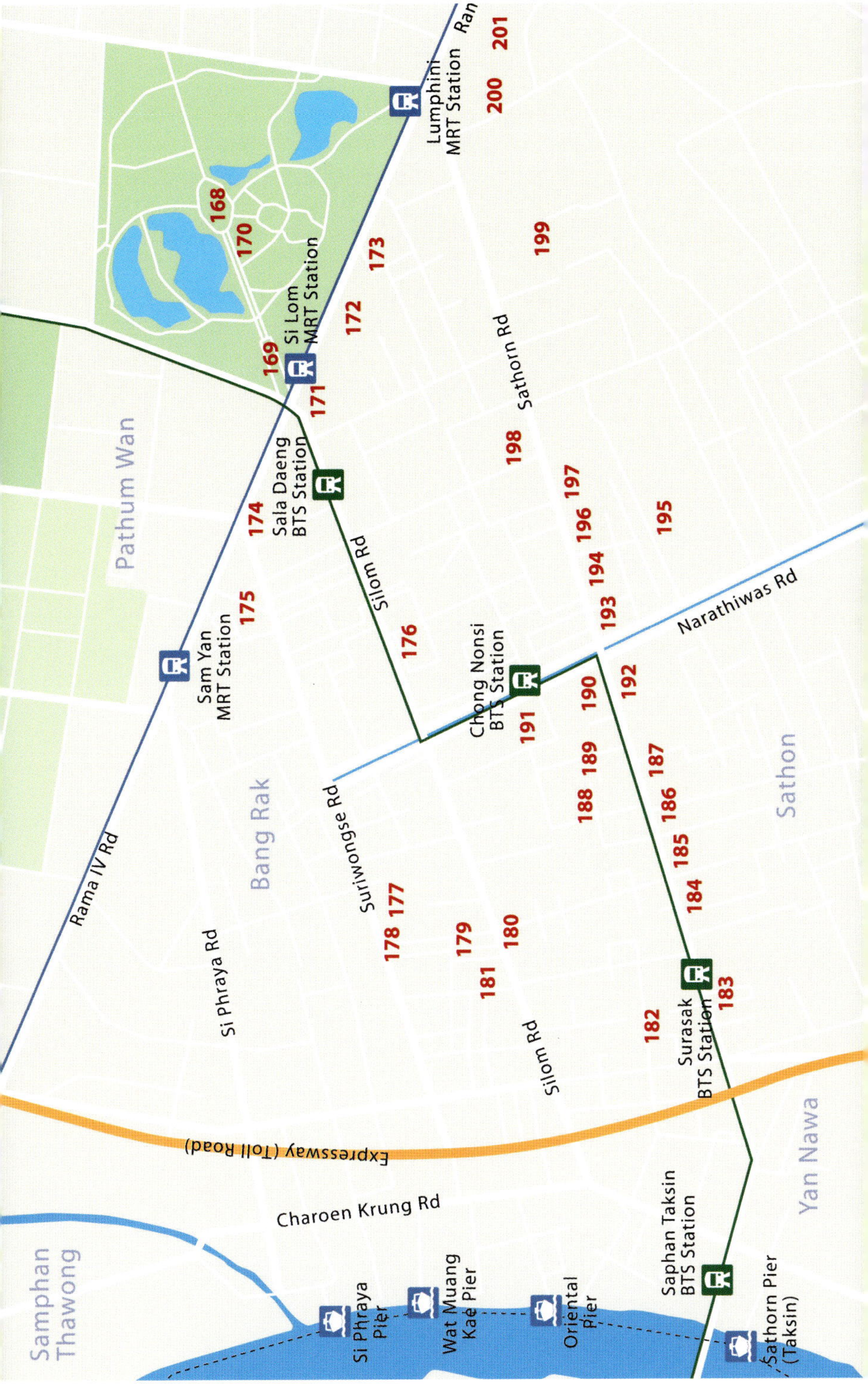
Pathum Wan
Bang Rak
Sathon
Yan Nawa
Samphan Thawong
Rama IV Rd
Si Phraya Rd
Suriwongse Rd
Silom Rd
Sathorn Rd
Narathiwas Rd
Charoen Krung Rd
Expressway (Toll Road)
Lumphini MRT Station
Si Lom MRT Station
Sam Yan MRT Station
Sala Daeng BTS Station
Chong Nonsi BTS Station
Surasak BTS Station
Saphan Taksin BTS Station
Si Phraya Pier
Wat Muang Kae Pier
Oriental Pier
Sathorn Pier (Taksin)
168
169
170
171
172
173
174
175
176
177
178
179
180
181
182
183
184
185
186
187
188
189
190
191
192
193
194
195
196
197
198
199
200
201

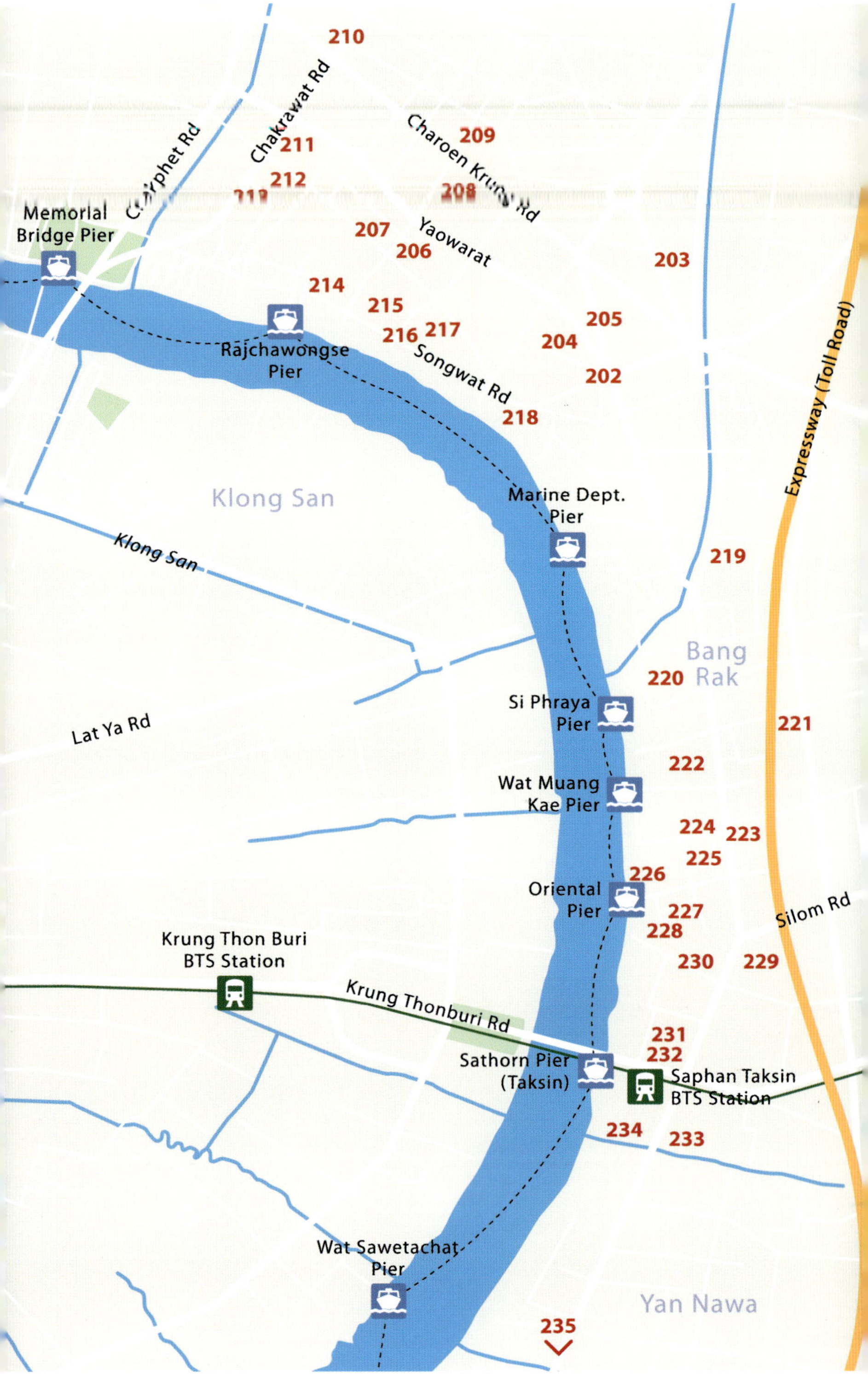
210
Chakrawat Rd
211
212
209
Charoen Krung Rd
208
Memorial Bridge Pier
207
206
Yaowarat
203
214
215
Rajchawongse Pier
216
217
Songwat Rd
204
205
202
218
Expressway (Toll Road)
Klong San
Marine Dept. Pier
Klong San
219
Bang Rak
220
Si Phraya Pier
221
Lat Ya Rd
222
Wat Muang Kae Pier
224
223
225
226
Oriental Pier
227
228
Silom Rd
Krung Thon Buri BTS Station
230
229
Krung Thonburi Rd
231
232
Sathorn Pier (Taksin)
Saphan Taksin BTS Station
234
233
Wat Sawetachat Pier
Yan Nawa
235

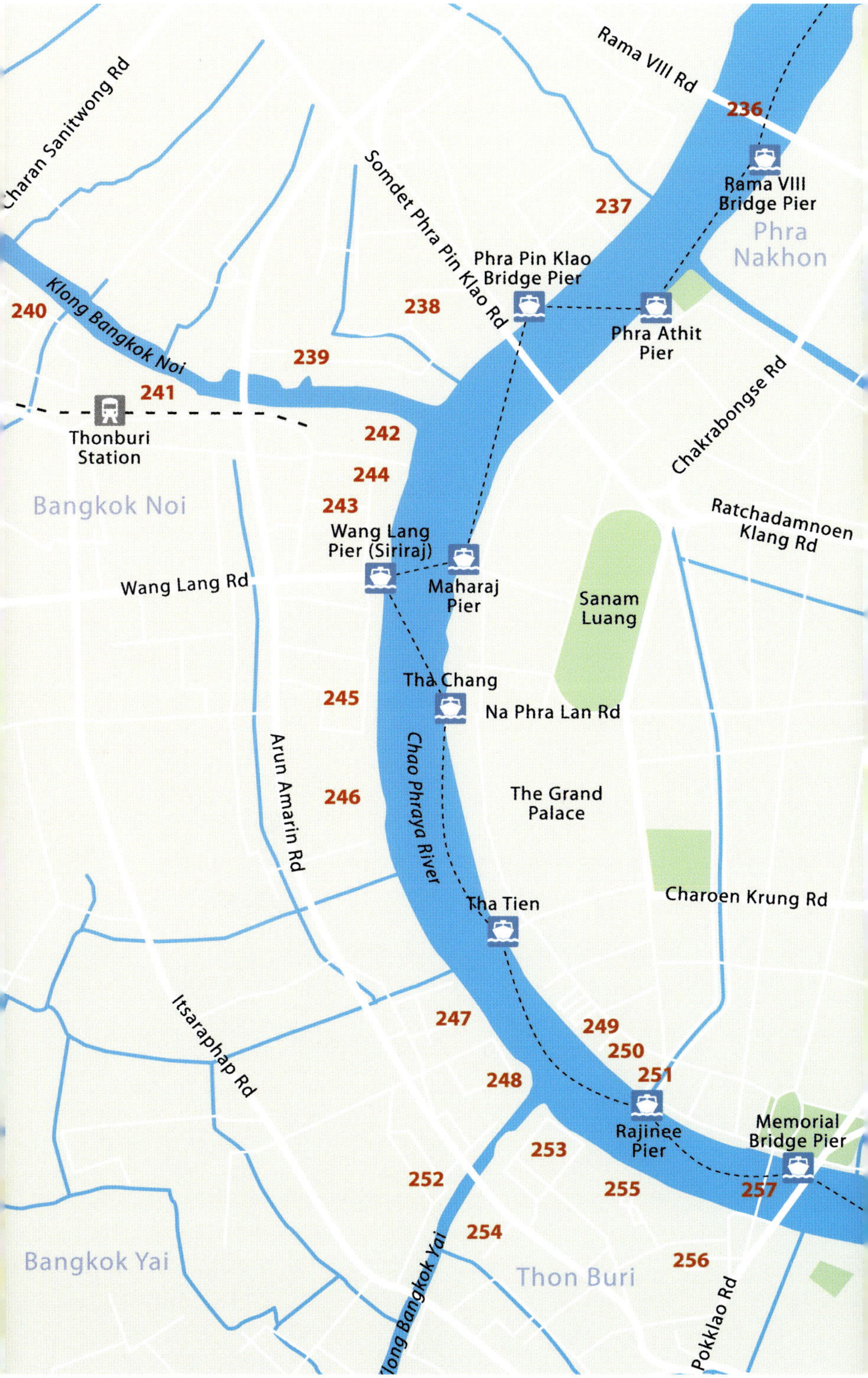

Rama VIII Rd
236
Rama VIII Bridge Pier
Phra Nakhon
Charan Sanitwong Rd
Somdet Phra Pin Klao Rd
237
Phra Pin Klao Bridge Pier
238
Phra Athit Pier
240
Klong Bangkok Noi
239
241
Chakrabongse Rd
Thonburi Station
242
244
Bangkok Noi
243
Ratchadamnoen Klang Rd
Wang Lang Pier (Siriraj)
Maharaj Pier
Wang Lang Rd
Sanam Luang
Tha Chang
245
Na Phra Lan Rd
Arun Amarin Rd
246
Chao Phraya River
The Grand Palace
Tha Tien
Charoen Krung Rd
247
249
250
Itsaraphap Rd
248
251
Rajinee Pier
Memorial Bridge Pier
253
252
255
257
254
Bangkok Yai
Klong Bangkok Yai
Thon Buri
256
Pokklao Rd

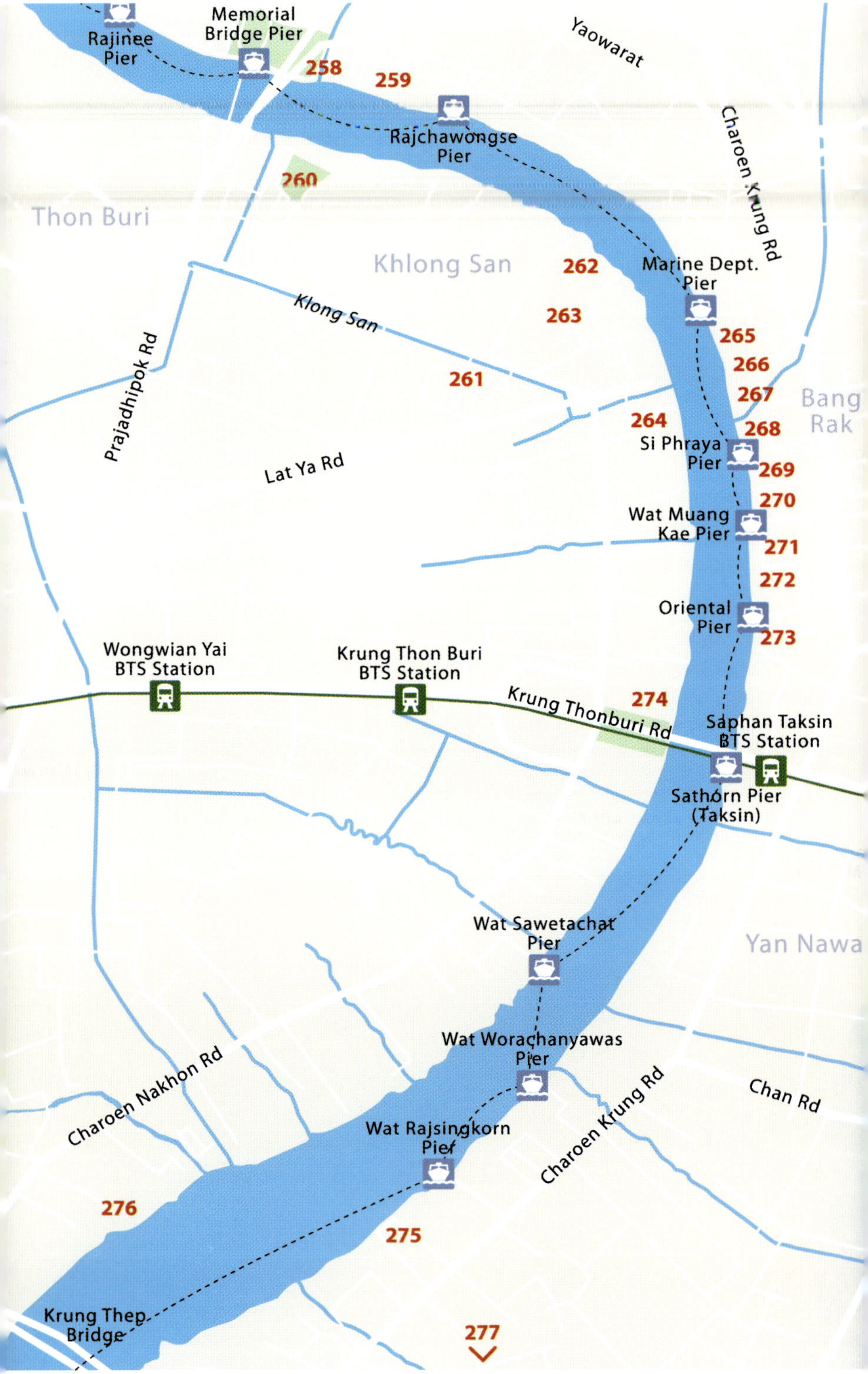
Memorial
Bridge Pier
Rajinee
Pier
Yaowarat
258
259
Rajchawongse
Pier
260
Thon Buri
Charoen Krung Rd
Khlong San
262
Marine Dept.
Pier
Klong San
263
265
266
Prajadhipok Rd
261
267
Bang
Rak
264
268
Si Phraya
Pier
269
Lat Ya Rd
270
Wat Muang
Kae Pier
271
272
Oriental
Pier
273
Wongwian Yai
BTS Station
Krung Thon Buri
BTS Station
274
Krung Thonburi Rd
Saphan Taksin
BTS Station
Sathorn Pier
(Taksin)
Wat Sawetachat
Pier
Yan Nawa
Wat Worachanyawas
Pier
Charoen Nakhon Rd
Charoen Krung Rd
Chan Rd
Wat Rajsingkorn
Pier
276
275
Krung Thep
Bridge
277

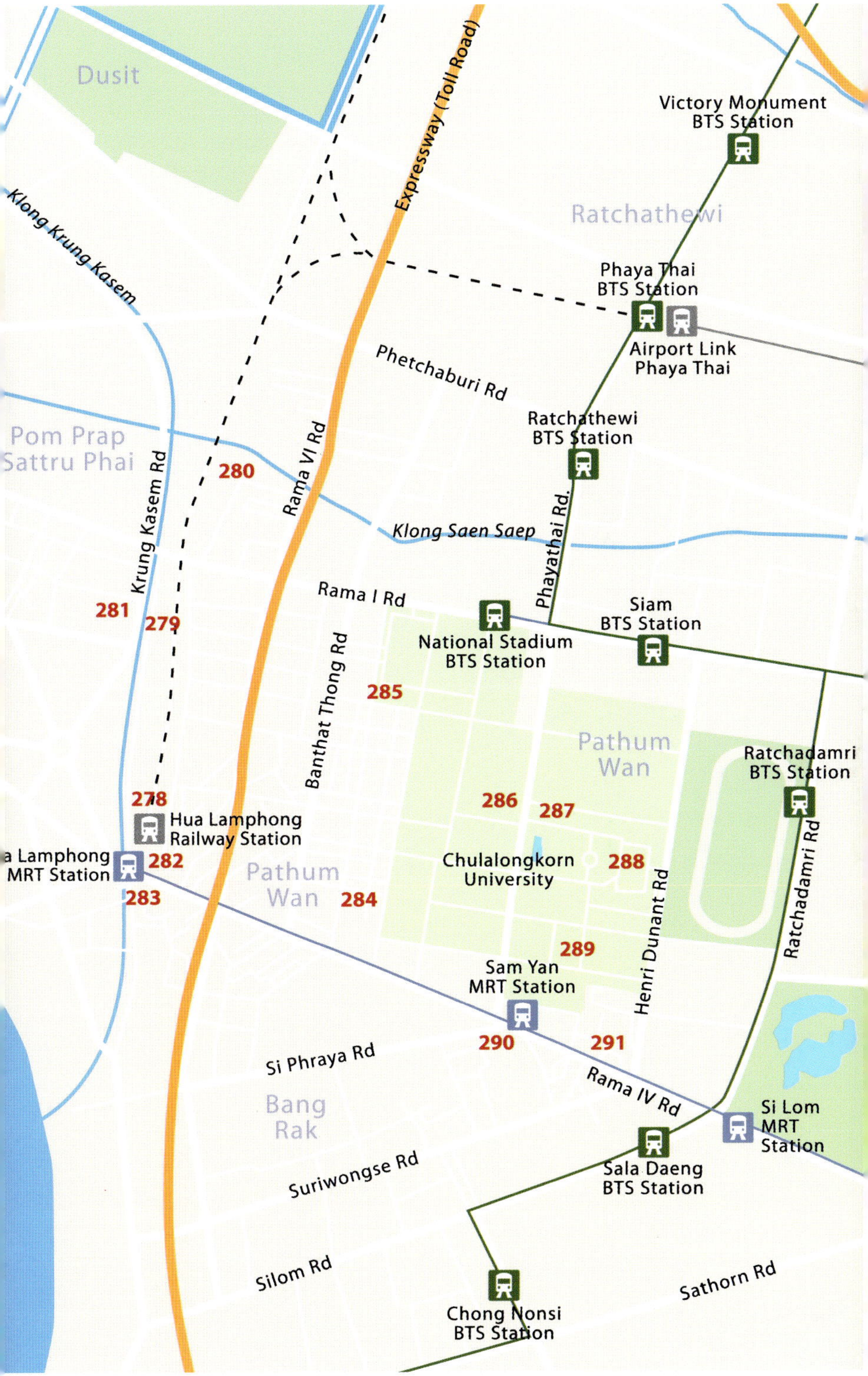

Dusit
Klong Krung Kasem
Expressway (Toll Road)
Victory Monument BTS Station
Ratchathewi
Phaya Thai BTS Station
Airport Link Phaya Thai
Phetchaburi Rd
Ratchathewi BTS Station
Pom Prap Sattru Phai
Krung Kasem Rd
280
Rama VI Rd
Klong Saen Saep
Phayathai Rd.
Rama I Rd
Siam BTS Station
281
279
National Stadium BTS Station
Banthat Thong Rd
285
Pathum Wan
Ratchadamri BTS Station
278
Hua Lamphong Railway Station
286
287
a Lamphong MRT Station
282
Chulalongkorn University
288
283
Pathum Wan
284
Henri Dunant Rd
Ratchadamri Rd
289
Sam Yan MRT Station
290
291
Si Phraya Rd
Rama IV Rd
Bang Rak
Si Lom MRT Station
Sala Daeng BTS Station
Suriwongse Rd
Silom Rd
Sathorn Rd
Chong Nonsi BTS Station

311
Thiam Ruam Mit Rd
309
310
Ratchadapbisek Rd
Thailand Cutural Centre MRT Station
Din Daeng
Huai Khwang
Phra Ram 9 MRT Station
Din Daeng
Rama IX Rd
308
Expressway (Toll Road)
Makkasan Station
307
Airport Link Makkasan
Phetchaburi MRT Station
Phetchaburi Rd
Phloen Chit BTS Station
Watthana
Witthayu Rd
Nana BTS Station
306
Sukhumvit MRT Station
Asok BTS Station
300
299
301
294
298
Phrom Phong BTS Station
Thonglor
Benjasiri Park
295
296
Expressway (Toll Road)
Benjakiti Park
Asok Montri Rd
303
292
Sukhumvit Rd
302
Khlong Toei MRT Station
293
Rama IV Rd
Thong Lo BTS Station
297
Queen Sirikit National Convention Centre MRT Station
304
Rama IV Rd
305

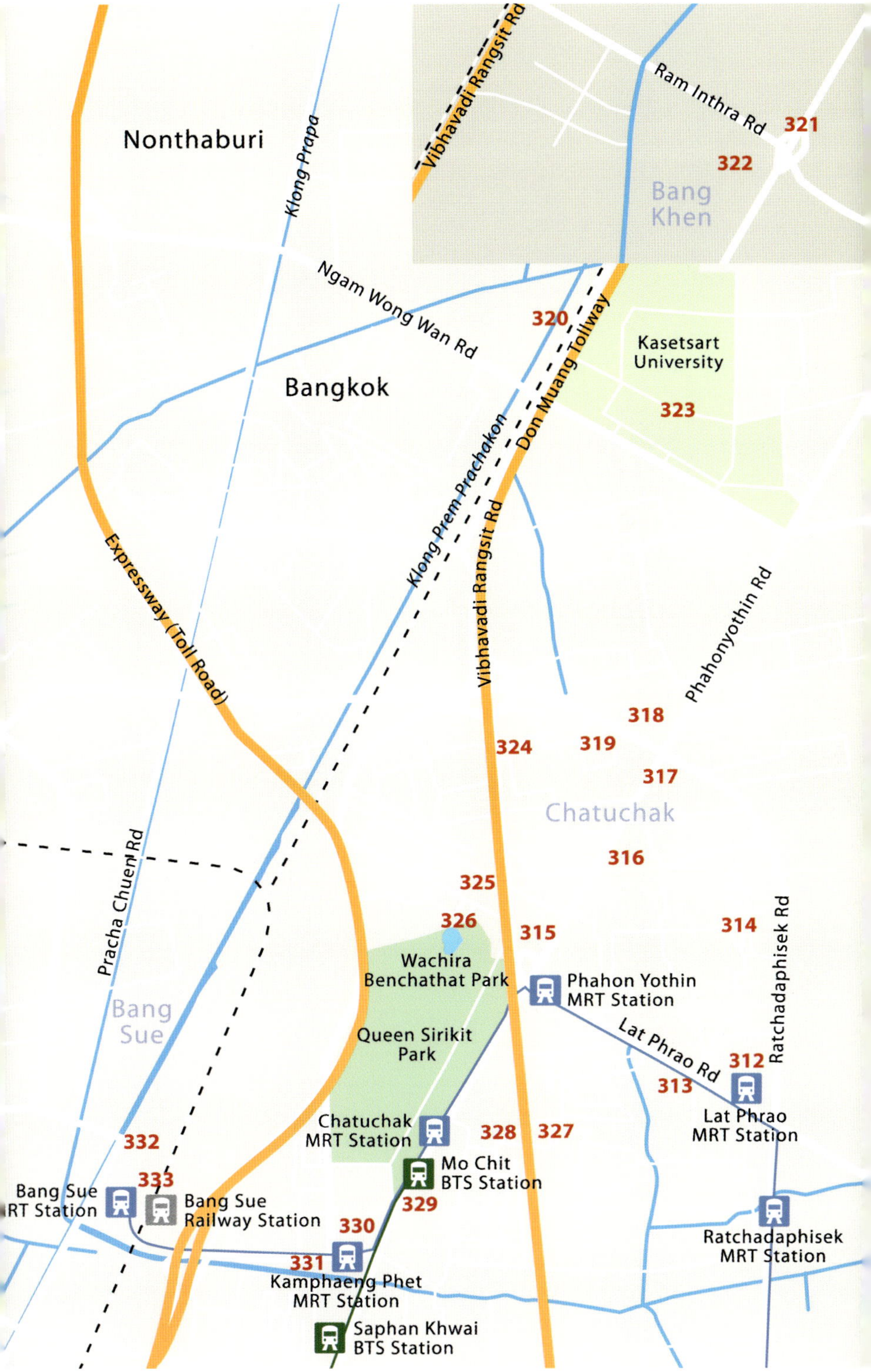
Nonthaburi
Klong Prapa
Vibhavadi Rangsit Rd
Ram Inthra Rd
321
322
Bang Khen
Ngam Wong Wan Rd
320
Don Muang Tollway
Kasetsart University
323
Bangkok
Klong Prem Prachakon
Vibhavadi Rangsit Rd
Expressway (Toll Road)
Phahonyothin Rd
318
319
324
317
Chatuchak
316
Pracha Chuen Rd
325
326
315
314
Ratchadaphisek Rd
Wachira Benchathat Park
Phahon Yothin MRT Station
Bang Sue
Queen Sirikit Park
Lat Phrao Rd
312
313
Lat Phrao MRT Station
Chatuchak MRT Station
328
327
332
Mo Chit BTS Station
333
Bang Sue MRT Station
Bang Sue Railway Station
329
330
Ratchadaphisek MRT Station
331
Kamphaeng Phet MRT Station
Saphan Khwai BTS Station

Index of Buildings and Designers

› ***Index numbers refer to entry numbers***

Chakri Dynasty Kings; Rattanakosin Era

First Reign: **Rama I**, Phra Phutthayotfa ***(1782–1809)***

Second Reign: **Rama II**, Phra Phutthaloetla ***(1809–1824)***

Third Reign: **Rama III**, Phra Nanglao ***(1824–1851)***

Fourth Reign: **Rama IV**, Mongkut ***(1851–1868)***

Fifth Reign: **Rama V**, Chulalongkorn ***(1868–1910)***

Sixth Reign: **Rama VI**, Vajiravudh ***(1910–1925)***

Seventh Reign: **Rama VII**, Prajadhipok ***(1925–1935)***

Eight Reign: **Rama VIII**, Ananda Mahidol ***(1935–1946)***

Ninth Reign: **Rama IX**, Bhumibol Adulyadej ***(1946–)***

The Publisher would like to thank the following companies for their generous support:

Architects 49 Limited
81 Sukhumvit 26, Bangkok 10110 Thailand
T: 66 2260 4370
F: 66 2259 3872
www.a49.com
www.49group.com

Architects 49 House Design Limited
81 Sukhumvit 26, Bangkok 10110 Thailand
T: 66 2260 4370
F: 66 2259 3872
www.a49.com
www.49group.com

August Design Consultant Co., Ltd.
2241/6 Ladprao Rd. (Soi 57/1), Saphan Song, Wangthonglang, Bangkok 10310 Thailand
T: 66 2933 1276-80
F: 66 2933 1275
E: project@august.co.th
www.august.co.th

Habita Architects
408/16 Rama 5 Rd., Dusit, Bangkok 10300 Thailand
T: 66 2668 6934, 66 2668 2706
F: 66 2243 7363
E: contact@habitaarchitects.com
Website: www.habitaarchitects.com

Faculty of Architecture Kasetsart University
50 Ngamwongwan Rd., Jatujak, Bangkok 10900 Thailand
T: 66 2942 8960
F: 66 2940 5413
E: archku.pr@gmail.com
www.arch.ku.ac.th

IA49 49GROUP

Interior Architects 49 Limited
81 Sukhumvit 26, Bangkok 10110 Thailand
T: 66 2259 3533
F: 66 2661 2186
E: ia49@ia49.com
www.ia49.com
www.49group.com

L49 49GROUP

Landscape Architects 49 Limited
81 Sukhumvit 26, Bangkok 10110 Thailand
T : 66 2661 2618, 66 2661 4947
F : 66 2261 1422
www.49group.com

PLAN ARCHITECT

Plan Architect Co., Ltd.
64 Soi Sathon 10, North Sathon Rd., Bangrak, Bangkok 10500 Thailand
T: 66 2237 0080
F: 66 2237 5791
E: plan@planarchitect.com
www.planarchitect.com

PLAN ASSOCIATES CO., LTD.
Architecture / Planning

Plan Associates Co.,Ltd.
114/1 Soi Sathon 10, North Sathon Rd.,
Silom, Bangrak, Bangkok 10500 Thailand
T: 66 2237 0080
F: 66 2237 5498
E: plan@planassociates.co.th
www.planassociates.co.th